797,885 Books
are available to read at

Forgotten Books

www.ForgottenBooks.com

Forgotten Books' App
Available for mobile, tablet & eReader

ISBN 978-1-331-13814-3
PIBN 10149326

This book is a reproduction of an important historical work. Forgotten Books uses state-of-the-art technology to digitally reconstruct the work, preserving the original format whilst repairing imperfections present in the aged copy. In rare cases, an imperfection in the original, such as a blemish or missing page, may be replicated in our edition. We do, however, repair the vast majority of imperfections successfully; any imperfections that remain are intentionally left to preserve the state of such historical works.

Forgotten Books is a registered trademark of FB &c Ltd.
Copyright © 2015 FB &c Ltd.
FB &c Ltd, Dalton House, 60 Windsor Avenue, London, SW19 2RR.
Company number 08720141. Registered in England and Wales.

For support please visit www.forgottenbooks.com

1 MONTH OF FREE READING

at

www.ForgottenBooks.com

By purchasing this book you are eligible for one month membership to ForgottenBooks.com, giving you unlimited access to our entire collection of over 700,000 titles via our web site and mobile apps.

To claim your free month visit:
www.forgottenbooks.com/free149326

* Offer is valid for 45 days from date of purchase. Terms and conditions apply.

Similar Books Are Available from
www.forgottenbooks.com

Beautiful Joe
An Autobiography, by Marshall Saunders

Theodore Roosevelt, an Autobiography
by Theodore Roosevelt

Napoleon
A Biographical Study, by Max Lenz

Up from Slavery
An Autobiography, by Booker T. Washington

Gotama Buddha
A Biography, Based on the Canonical Books of the Theravādin, by Kenneth J. Saunders

Plato's Biography of Socrates
by A. E. Taylor

Cicero
A Biography, by Torsten Petersson

Madam Guyon
An Autobiography, by Jeanne Marie Bouvier De La Motte Guyon

The Writings of Thomas Jefferson
by Thomas Jefferson

Thomas Skinner, M.D.
A Biographical Sketch, by John H. Clarke

Saint Thomas Aquinas of the Order of Preachers (1225-1274)
A Biographical Study of the Angelic Doctor, by Placid Conway

Recollections of the Rev. John Johnson and His Home
An Autobiography, by Susannah Johnson

Biographical Sketches in Cornwall, Vol. 1 of 3
by R. Polwhele

Autobiography of John Francis Hylan, Mayor of New York
by John Francis Hylan

The Autobiography of Benjamin Franklin
The Unmutilated and Correct Version, by Benjamin Franklin

James Mill
A Biography, by Alexander Bain

George Washington
An Historical Biography, by Horace E. Scudder

Florence Nightingale
A Biography, by Irene Cooper Willis

Marse Henry
An Autobiography, by Henry Watterson

Autobiography and Poems
by Charlotte E. Linden

NARRATIVE

of

INCLUDING *a* FULL ACCOUNT *of the*
AUTHOR'S ADVENTURES *and* PERILS
while PERSECUTED *by the* SAN FRANCISCO

𝕍𝕚𝕘𝕚𝕝𝕒𝕟𝕔𝕖 ℂ𝕠𝕞𝕞𝕚𝕥𝕥𝕖𝕖 𝕠𝕗 𝟙𝟠𝟝𝟞

Together with a

REPORT *of* HIS TRIAL, WHICH
RESULTED *in* HIS ACQUITTAL

LINE *for* LINE *and* PAGE *for* PAGE, *from the* ORIGINAL EDITION, PUBLISHED
by the AUTHOR *in* 1857, COMPLETE, *with* REPRODUCTIONS, *in* FACSIMILE, *of*
the ORIGINAL ILLUSTRATIONS, COVER-PAGE TITLE, *and* TITLE-PAGE

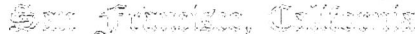

PRINTED *by* THOMAS C. RUSSELL, *at* HIS PRIVATE PRESS
1734 NINETEENTH AVENUE, *Sunset*
1917

Copyright, 1917
By Thomas C. Russell

©Cl.A479783

Printed in the United States of America

To

J. HENRY MEYER

Banker

of

SAN FRANCISCO

THIS REPRINT EDITION *of the* NARRATIVE *of* EDWARD MCGOWAN
IS RESPECTFULLY

Dedicated

by

The PRINTER & PUBLISHER

FOREWORD
TO THE REPRINT EDITION

THE NARRATIVE OF EDWARD McGOWAN needs no introduction, or foreword: it is so well known to collectors of Californiana, and to old Californians, especially San Franciscans, that all that is necessary to be stated in presenting a new edition thereof is, what has been done by the printer and publisher in the reprinting.

No attempt was made to edit the work, nor was there any disposition to do so, or to make any changes from the original. Most of the problems arising during the reprinting, where apparent inaccuracies were met, were solved on the instant, without looking forward for parallel instances, fearful that a Scylla avoided on one page might be succeeded by a Charybdis on another, the line-for-line limitation precluding the correction of many of such typographical errors.

A preference was expressed by several persons interested in the publication of the book, for a reprinting "exactly as McGowan wrote it." This could not be done. Evidence is abundant that McGowan's copy underwent compositorial editing, or that of the proof-reader,— a common practice, and one not always making for betterment, as many a writer has found to his sorrow. On page 69 we find this phraseology: the "sweeper out of Everett's hatter's shop in Clay street." McGowan, of course, did not write this phrase: it is redolent of Bow-bells; its cockneyism is apparent. The work of the compositor guilty of this change can be traced throughout the book. The other "compositors" were of the "woods-and-templed-hills" order, or had gleaned a knowledge of type in some "Tar Flat joint." No indications are there of that "sweeping superficial knowledge" supposed to be possessed by the old-time book-printer. Thus it is that the disposition to make no changes lost its restraining curb as the work progressed, and typographical inaccuracies were corrected in many instances. Hispano-Californian place-names, family names, prænomens, have been corrected; but the "Spanish" of McGowan, in almost all instances, is unchanged, being merely camouflaged in the reprinting by a resort to the unique system of Spanish punctuation. Anglo-Californian names, also, have received some attention. Not all the inaccuracies of the work can be noted here, but merely enough to demonstrate the carelessness, ignorance, and illiteracy displayed, as well as to justify the making of such corrections as were made.*

Misspelling of common English words. turptitude (vi), narative (23), staid [*stayed*] (108), occurence (112), empannelled (200), scurrilious (201), rencountre (223), accessory (234).

Biblical, etc. references. Aaron smiting the rock in the wilderness (126), Dr. Ollipod (50).

Jumbles of Spanish with French etc. pauvrecito (101), pauvre viejo (135), Marie Jesus (134), Donna Rosa (122).

Spanish family names and prænomens. Ortego (61), Ortaga (62), de la Guerra (73), Ignatio (65), Marie Jesus (134), Nicholasa (138).

Spanish place-names. Piscadero (48), San Louis Obispo (104), Las Crusas (62), Arroyo Honde (95), Arroya Honde (145), Cañada Verda (180).

Spanish punctuation. "Paisano! vamos! los Vigilantes!" (101).

Spanish, generally. Cochi Gueri (69), Cochi Guero (145), chapparal (83), pinola (98), pinoli (173), major domo (100), escopet (108), Paisano es bueno Catholico (139), Bastante hombres en el casa (162).

Names of well-known Californians. John [M.] Freeman (26), David Scannel (115), Neely Johnson (116), Don Abel Starnes (148), Arch Bishop Allemany (172).

Punctuation.† 1. "burglary, or arson or any other offense against society . . . was about to be perpetrated" (19); 2. "the man returned from the Refugio bringing only a naked mule with the information" (95); 3. "After leaving the Arroyo Honde, on the morning of the twenty-eighth, I struck out" (121); 4. "a man coming up the cañon leading a horse"; 5. "the bill being prepared on the third day of March, it was placed" (192).

---

* The technicalities of printing, such as punctuation and capitalization, are generally left to the printer, but a change of the diction of a respectable writer is a risky and improper proceeding: the writer may not, in his proof, notice the change, and it may be the source of annoyance afterwards. Even the practice of querying on a proof-sheet, by unskilled proof-readers, often results in disaster. Many writers, authors and business men, express a preference for the orthography of the dictionary they possess, but experienced printers know very well that such expressed preference is not often based on actual knowledge of different spellings. Merriam's Webster is recognized as the standard in the United States, and in this reprint the varying spellings in the original, of both American and English usage, are made to conform thereto.

† Punctuation did not receive the attention it deserved, in the original volume. Thus, in 1, no comma is needed after *burglary*, but one is needed after *arson* and after *society*. In 2, the comma should be used after *Refugio* and *mule:* the man brought the mule and the information; without the commas, the language means (and says) that the Refugio brought the mule, and the mule the information. In 3, the comma should be omitted after *Honde*. In 4, a comma is necessary after *cañon:* the man, not the cañon, led the horse. In 5, the comma after *March* is misplaced: it belongs after *prepared*. The experienced printer, in gauging the quality of printing, can readily come to a decision from even a slight inspection of the punctuation, capitalization, and division of words; these failing, the poor quality is established. Typographical inaccuracies may be found in the best work; even the dictionaries violate their own rules. Thus the inferior printer can say, in Kipling's words," They wink their eyes, the same as us."

NARRATIVE
of
EDWARD McGOWAN

INCLUDING A FULL ACCOUNT OF THE

Author's Adventures and Perils, while persecuted by the
San Francisco Vigilance Committee of 1856.

PUBLISHED BY THE AUTHOR
1857.

NARRATIVE

OF

EDWARD McGOWAN,

INCLUDING A FULL ACCOUNT OF THE

Author's Adventures and Perils

WHILE PERSECUTED BY THE

San Francisco Vigilance Committee of 1856.

VALERE.—I have not merited these names. 'Tis true,
I have committed an offence against you;
But, after all, my fault is pardonable.
HARPAGON.—How! pardonable? what! a wilful murder?
A foul assassination of this kind?
VALERE.—For Heaven's sake, don't put yourself in rage,
When you have heard me you'll perceive the damage
Is not so great as you imagine.—*Old Play.*

SAN FRANCISCO:
PUBLISHED BY THE AUTHOR.
1857.

FACSIMILE OF ORIGINAL TITLE-PAGE

Entered, according to Act of Congress, in the year eighteen hundred and fifty-seven,

BY EDWARD McGOWAN

In the Clerk's Office of the District Court of the United States, for the Northern District of California.

Dedication

This Book is Respectfully Inscribed

to

NICHOLAS A. DEN, M.D.

of

SANTA BÁRBARA COUNTY
CALIFORNIA

WHOSE KINDNESS *to the* AUTHOR MAY BE SAID TO HAVE TRANSCENDED *the* CHARITY *of the*

Good Samaritan

IN THAT HE DID NOT CONFINE HIMSELF *to the* DISCHARGE *of a* MERELY CHRISTIAN DUTY, WHICH BROUGHT WITH IT ITS OWN REWARD, *and* NOUGHT *of* DANGER *to the* DOER, *but*, FEARLESSLY BRAVING *the* INSANE CLAMOR *of the* MULTITUDE, *and* LISTENING ONLY *to the* VOICE *of* UNSELFISH *and* CHIVALROUS COMPASSION *for the* HUNTED *and the* HELPLESS, NOBLY SOUGHT HIM OUT *from the* INHOSPITABLE WILDERNESS, *and* BRAVELY SHELTERED HIM *from the* FURY *of a* CRUEL MOB

THAT LENGTH *of* DAYS, PROSPERITY, *and* HAPPINESS, MAY BE HIS, IS *the* HEARTFELT HOPE *of* HIS EVER GRATEFUL *and* FIRM FRIEND

EDWARD MCGOWAN

INTRODUCTION

THE idea of this work was suggested by the reflection that Providence places no one on this earth without affording him, at some period of his life, an opportunity to be useful to his fellow-creatures, if he will. I thought, then, that perhaps I might turn to some account, in the way of a lesson to unthinking fanatics, the history of the sufferings to which fanaticism has subjected me. Conscious that I did not merit, at the hands of my persecutors, their cruel treatment, and equally conscious that I had, nevertheless, been the recipient of it, I, for the first time in my life, became painfully aware to what extent injustice may be carried, even by men with tolerably good intentions. Here, then, was my opportunity to be of some use to the world, by communicating my experience. The authors of the movement in which my troubles originated are undoubtedly deserving (not particularly on my account) of all the reproaches which the pen of censure, armed with its keenest point, could inscribe upon their records. I have humbly conceived, however, that, although upbraiding's administered in that way may often be judicious, and sometimes beneficial in their effects, nothing can so readily awaken the human understanding to an appreciation of the horrors into which men may be led by fanaticism, and the facility with which badly balanced minds may become victims to that moral disease, than a calm, true, and, as far as may be, dispassionate recital of a great wrong which actually *has* been committed in the name and under the garb of virtue.

Therefore, in submitting the following pages to the reader, I have been prompted less by a desire to gratify the morbid appetite for the wonderful,—so characteristic of Californians,—than by a heartfelt conviction that from this simple and true narrative a lesson may be derived, whose teachings, in future years, will serve as warning beacons to any misguided men who, mistaking the voice of passion for the call of duty, may be tempted to assume the fearful responsibility of setting the laws of the country, and even the Constitution itself, at defiance, enlisting in their unhappy cause a reckless mob, whose responsibility they afterward vainly rely on for support, and whose fury they idly attempt to control. It is my sincere hope that the following summary of my *supposed* crimes, and true history of the cruel sufferings to which I have been subjected,—sufferings so incommensurate with even my *alleged* transgressions,—may induce others hereafter to pause ere they incur the hazard of inflicting like injustice on their fellow-man.

As my conduct as a *politician* has been made a fruitful theme of animadversion by my enemies, it may be as well for me here to state what have been my *political* antecedents. I do not do so for the purpose of vindicating myself from those charges of political misconduct which have been preferred against me, so much as to show how suddenly I must have become unscrupulous and corrupt, if, after enjoying for years the respect and confidence of the first men in my native State, and being honored time and again by the majority of my fellow-citizens with offices of honor and trust, I have suddenly left them, in the decline of life, to set an example of such political turpitude on the shores of the Pacific, that I have been deemed deserving of the persecution, the details of which form the subject of this narrative.

I entered political life in 1837. In the year 1838 I was elected Clerk of the District of Moyamensing, in Philadelphia County, living, at the time of my election, in the District of Southwark, where I was born. I immediately moved into the District to which I had been elected, and was re-elected *five years consecutively* to the same position. During the time I held this office, I was Secretary to the Watering Committee of the District, and was also, one year, Clerk to the County Board, composed of the Senators and Members representing Philadelphia in the State Legislature. I was recommended for this position by the Hon. Charles Brown, then State Senator, afterwards Member of Congress for the First Congressional District of the State, and subsequently Collector of the Port of Philadelphia, under the administration of Mr. Pierce. In the year 1842 I was elected to the Pennsylvania Legislature, and in the fall of 1843, appointed, by Gov. Porter, Superintendent of the State Magazine for the Eastern District of Pennsylvania. I held this post for two years, when a new Governor came into power, and I was removed. I was then elected Superintendent of Police for one of the Districts of Philadelphia, and held this position for several years, during which time I was on terms of the most familiar intimacy with the Hon. Richard Vaux, then Recorder and now Mayor of Philadelphia. While I held this post, the California excitement led me to this country, where I arrived in 1849. Since I have resided in this State, I have held offices of honor in the gift of the people, and have also been intrusted, by appointment and otherwise, with most responsible positions, during my incumbency of which, princely fortunes of the money of the people have passed through my hands, and no murmur of defalcation was ever heard in the State in connection with my name. The records of the State Treasurer and Controller, under all administrations, now show a full and fair accounting for every dollar of public money ever intrusted to me, and to them I fearlessly appeal. Can some of my persecutors say as much? I will only add, that, in my native city, I enjoyed the most intimate social and personal relations with Governor David R. Porter, Hon. Richard Vaux, Hon. James Campbell, United States Postmaster-General, Hons. T. B. Florence and Henry M. Phillips, now Members of Congress from Philadelphia, Harry Connelly, Esq., Hon. John W. Forney, and a host of others, to each and every one of whom I now refer my traducers. So much for my *political* and personal antecedents. The charges of corruption which have been so lavishly heaped upon me by men who never saw me, I despise; and have inserted this brief history of my past life in the Introduction to this book more to gratify my personal friends at home and here, than from any solicitude as to the good or bad opinion of my slanderers.

It is not, of course, to be supposed that he who has been the victim of a popular persecution, which challenges the annals of his country for a parallel, can, by any ordinary human effort, purge his bosom of all feeling of resentment against his oppressors; nor, indeed, is it to be supposed that when Time, the great vindicator, shall have brought men once more back to the paths of duty, and opened their ears to the voice of reason, I shall be at all backward in visiting upon the heads of some of my persecutors the thunderbolts with which they have sought to annihilate me, and though, I trust, with more justice, yet no less vehemence.

The main object of this little work, however, is to lay before the people a true narrative of my adventures, with the circumstances which led to them, leaving with the reader's own heart and judgment the task of deducing the moral from the story.

CHAPTER I

> * * * "his crimes!" — *What* crimes?
> Were it not better to record the facts,
> So that the contemplator might approve,
> Or at the least learn *whence* the crimes arose?
> *Marino Faliero.*

IT will be remembered that, some time in the fall of 1855, JAMES KING OF WM., who for many years had been a banker in San Francisco, and in the latter part of his business career connected with the defunct firm of Adams *&* Co., having by the reverses of fortune been reduced to bankruptcy, commenced the editing of a newspaper called the *Evening Bulletin.* The tenor and style of his editorials are too well remembered by the people of California to be here descanted upon. Suffice it to say, that, while they apparently aimed at the correction of abuses which undoubtedly existed in the San Francisco community, it was thought by hundreds of our best citizens that the example of unbridled license set by this paper to the press was far more dangerous in its tendency than even the evils it sought to eradicate; and it was well known that I, among others, entertained this opinion, having frequently and freely expressed it.

The boldness, arrogance, and not unfrequently reckless mendacity, which characterized this sheet, as might have been expected, awakened, in due season, a feeling of disgust, not unmingled with resentment, in the breasts of many of our citizens. Day after day this self-created censor fulminated his abuse indiscriminately on the innocent and the guilty, making shuttlecocks of the reputations of some of the best and most enterprising men in the state, till, emboldened by impunity, his apparent zeal in the cause of reformation ran into the wildest fanaticism, at whose insane bidding many a proud and honorable hope was forever blighted, and many a happy heart was broken, never to be healed.

It was while the *Bulletin* was in the zenith of its career of slander and detraction, and when all men were in dread lest every day should bring the fearful *ukase* which was to herald them to the world as scoundrels, and place its indelible blight upon their reputations, that some person, doubtless considering that before the people should be expected blindly to believe and obey the teachings of this new monitor it would be well for them fully to understand what claims it had to the public confidence, published a card in relation to the present editor of the *Bulletin*, Thomas S. King, a brother of James King of Wm., and to a certain extent engaged with him in the conduct of that sheet. The communication was signed *Caliban* — a *nom de plume* it was well known I had sometimes adopted, and hence, perhaps, the pretty general suspicion at the time, that I was its author. It so happened that the article in question *was not written by me*, as any one at all conversant with my style may, by a careful perusal, easily perceive.

It was published in the *San Francisco Sunday Times*, a newspaper edited by James P. Casey. As the reader will perceive, it was not very personal, and certainly, under the circumstances, not severe enough to be looked on as requiring a bloody atonement. It appeared on the eleventh day of May, 1856, and was as follows: —

[COMMUNICATION.]

The following communication finds place in our columns because we believe some good may be effected by its publication. "There must be some fire, where there is so much smoke."

EDITOR SUNDAY TIMES: — Although you do not make so much parade of your courage and independence as some others in your profession, yet I, for one, believe that you have as good a share of these qualities as generally falls to the lot of even editors. In my opinion, he who assumes the tripod, and squats in the editorial chair, assumes a responsibility of such magnitude as entitles him to the strictest scrutiny of that public whose opinion he affects to direct. Acting on this assumption, I beg the use of your columns to state briefly my present object.

One of the chief traits in editorial management I take to be consistency, without which the editor loses prestige and becomes a mere object of ridicule; for the higher a man climbs, the more noticeable he becomes. I propose, therefore, to test somewhat the consistency of the editor of the *Bulletin*. In his issue of to-day, Friday, the editor exhibits a most marked favoritism for Mr. Latham, in his editorial remarks recently made by him. The *Bulletin* says: —

> "If, in making his appointments, Mr. Latham, instead of selecting his own personal friends, has appointed indiscriminately from all factions, we doubt very much whether the use he has thus made of his official patronage to harmonize the difficulties in the Democratic party will injure him in the slightest particular with the authorities at Washington. According to our way of thinking, it is wrong for Mr. Latham, or any other public man, to appoint any other than good men to office, and we cannot approve of some of those charged on him by a 'Purifier' in another column to-day."

Contrast this language with the sweeping, persecuting tone of the same paper in reference to the appointment of Mr. Clarkson by the Governor, and Mr. McDuffie by the President, without taking notice of others of a more insignificant character. Day after day, the *Bulletin* has inveighed in no complimentary terms against some of the persons named in the "Purifier's" communication; day after day has that paper held them up to public notice as the worst men in the country; and yet mark its tone now that Mr. Latham has enlisted their services to fight against the honest expression of public opinion through the ballot-box. Now, Mr. Editor, the question arises, Whence this great and monstrous sympathy for Mr. Latham? I will tell you. Mr. King, James King of Wm., has a brother who holds a lucrative position in the Custom House, under Mr. Latham, and this brother is one of the *proprietors* of that consistent, courageous, independent, and immaculate sheet, the *Bulletin:* "*Hine illæ lachrymæ.*" Another point to which I desire to call the attention of your readers is this: the brother I allude to was an applicant for the office of U. S. Marshal for California at the same time with Mr. McDuffie. Is it not possible, aye, even probable, that the bitter, unrelenting, and malicious persecution of that gentleman by the editor of the *Bulletin* was instigated by motives of revenge for the defeat of his brother, who, I say, is a large shareholder in the *Bulletin?*

Yours truly,   CALIBAN.

A personal acquaintance with the writer of the above communication induced us to give it place in our paper; but until we read the article we knew not that Mr. King had a brother in this country. Our readers will judge and comment for themselves. — *Ed. Sunday Times.*

On reading the above, Thomas S. King called at Casey's room, which was at the house of John Burns, a deputy sheriff, and demanded of him the author. Casey replied that the person in question was an old man with a large family, and he would prefer withholding his name, or words to that effect, and King, though apparently not satisfied with the answer, left him.

The next day, he again called upon Casey, at his office, in company with John Walton, a deputy collector of the port, and repeated his demand, though with no better success than he had met with the day before.

Casey then consulted me, and I told him I thought the matter would end there. I knew by the antecedents of Thos. S. King that he *must* be a poltroon, and told Casey that I did not think he ever meant to bring the matter to an issue of arms. Casey, however, differed with me in opinion, and said that he had made up his mind to pretend to be shy of King, to encourage him, if he would, to take further notice of the card. I advised him to let King take his own course in the matter, and to trouble himself no more about it, unless again called upon.

In the mean time, King consulted with a gentleman, and acting, I presume, under his advice, addressed two or three notes to Casey on the subject. He also published a card in the *San Francisco Herald*, asking for a suspension of public opinion on the communication of *Caliban*.

Having received, as I understood, no satisfaction from his correspondence with Casey, Thos. S. King, notoriously connected with a sheet whose every issue teemed with the vilest and most indiscriminate personal abuse, one morning repaired to the pistol-gallery kept by *Natchez*, on Clay Street, and had his derringer pistols cleaned and loaded. He then went in search of Casey, saying to several persons that he was following him, would make him give up the author, etc. He finally met Casey at the corner of Merchant and Montgomery streets, next door to the *Bulletin* office. I happened to be standing near the spot, in a little cigar-store. King approached Casey and told him that he would give him until ten o'clock the next day to give up the real name of *Caliban*. Casey replied that he did not desire another minute; that he was himself the author, and responsible. Upon this, King said that "*he thought the author was a gentleman,*" and walked away. I could not refrain from bursting into a loud laugh when I found how correct had been my opinion as to this man's poltroonery. He favored me with a malignant scowl as he left the spot, and thus I supposed the difficulty between himself and *Caliban* was at an end. But, alas! the cowardice of this man — Thomas S. King — was destined to be the polluted spring from which was to flow the stream of anarchy, treason, and almost civil war. Better, far better, had it been for the community, the country, and the lovers of free institutions all over the world, if, on that morning, King, Casey, and myself had all fallen in a street *mêlée*, and the seeds of internal discord, afterwards sown so broadcast in the land, had been buried in our obscure graves. But it was not to be so. James King of Wm., provoked to retaliate on the cause of his brother's discomfiture and disgrace, published, the next day, in the *Bulletin*, a very severe article, in which he alluded, in terms of the bitterest opprobrium, to Casey's antecedents in New York, and stated facts in connection with his life there, which, being published without any explanation, of which they were to a certain extent susceptible, had a tendency to degrade Casey in the estimation of all good men. The following is an extract from the article: —

"The fact that Casey has been an inmate of Sing-Sing prison, in New York, is no offense against the laws of this state; nor is the fact of his having stuffed himself, through the ballot-box, as elected to the Board of Supervisors, from a district where it is said that he was not even a candidate, any justification for Mr. Bagley to shoot Casey, however richly the latter may deserve to have his neck stretched for such fraud on the people. These are acts against the *public* good, not against Mr. Bagley in particular; and, however much we may detest Casey's former character, or be convinced of the shallowness of his promised reformation, we cannot justify the assumption by Mr. Bagley to take upon himself the redressing of these wrongs."

Casey, upon reading the above, repaired to the editorial room of the *Bulletin*, and told James King of Wm. that he desired he would not rake up the events of his past life in New York. He said that he was perfectly willing his conduct in California should be scrutinized, and that if anything could be proven against his character here, he was willing it should be published; but with reference to past matters he was exceedingly sensitive; that he was young and inexperienced when the offense for which he had been imprisoned was committed, and, as the evidence and the record showed, it was, at worst, but a case of *constructive* larceny. King replied that he would publish whatever he saw fit, and that on the next day he would be still more severe. Casey then told him he must be prepared to defend himself on the street, as he intended to attack him on sight, upon which King ordered him out of his office, and threatened to kick him out if he did not go. Casey left the office, and immediately arranged his private affairs preparatory to attacking Mr. King.*

While all this was going on, I was attending to a cause be fore Justice Ryan of the First Township, for Captain Dodge, of the schooner "Matthew Vassar." About twenty minutes past four o'clock of the day on which Mr. King was shot, seeing that another cause which was being tried was likely to occupy the rest of the afternoon, I asked to have that of Capt. Dodge postponed until the following day. This was granted, and after my client and I had stepped out of court, I saw the *Evening Bulletin* containing the above remarks with reference to Casey. I had not up to this time even heard that Casey had had an interview with King. I went from the courtroom down on to Montgomery Street, and stopped in the neighborhood of the *Bulletin* office. I saw many persons gathered in knots about the streets, and everything indicated to me that a fight was expected. It was now about twenty minutes of five o'clock. While I was standing on the street, a friend informed me that Casey wanted to see me at a barroom kept in the rear of the City Hall by James Godfrey, Esq. I at once went there, and among a great many other persons I saw Casey. He and I immediately stepped into the alley on which the house is situated, and I there learned for the first time what had occurred between him and Mr. King. He was very cool, but apparently very angry. He told me that his determination was to attack Mr. King, and that he had finished the adjustment of his affairs, so that in the event of his fall there would be no difficulty about them. He said that he expected the meeting would result in a des-

---

*The author is indebted for this information to James P. Casey, who detailed it to him before the attack, and afterward in the County Jail.

perate fight, as Mr. King was greatly his superior physically, and, moreover, from the daily tone of the *Bulletin*, as well as from the notice he had given him, he took it for granted that he would be fully armed.* He begged me not to be in the street at the time the fight took place, lest, in the event of Mr. King's death, I should be suspected of complicity, on account of my supposed connection with the *Caliban* matter. He then embraced me, and I left him. I was secretly determined, notwithstanding his injunctions, to see the encounter. Like almost all old Californians, I was accustomed to such sights, and, naturally enough, when I knew that a fight was about to take place, curiosity prompted me to witness it. Accordingly, I returned to Montgomery Street, and, after standing there some minutes, I concluded, as I saw nothing of Casey, that perhaps he had changed his mind about making the attack.[†] I sauntered up Montgomery Street, and entered the Bank Exchange, on the corner of Washington. Here I met an old Philadelphia acquaintance named Peter Whiteman, and invited him to drink with me. While we were standing at the bar, the boy *Butts* (whose name appears in the subse-

---

*The following are among many passages of the kind to be found about that time in the *Bulletin*: —

Bulletin, Dec. 6th. — "Mr. Selover, it is said, carries a knife. We carry a pistol. We hope neither will be required, but if this rencontre cannot be avoided, why will Mr. Selover persist in periling the lives of others? We pass, every afternoon, about half-past four to five o'clock, along Market Street, from Fourth to Fifth Street. The road is wide, and not so much frequented as those streets farther in town. If we are to be shot or cut to pieces, for Heaven's sake let it be done there. Others will not be injured, and in case we fall, our house is but a few hundred yards beyond, and the cemetery not much farther."

Ib., Jan. 7th. — "If these fellows are really determined to attack the editor of the *Bulletin*, *why don't they do it at once and be done with it?* Why keep everybody in suspense? Here we have been carrying a pistol for nearly three months because of the braggadocio bullying of this crowd, until we are heartily tired of it."

[†] I have since been informed that during this time Casey was in a lawyer's office with a friend, arranging the final disposition of his effects in the event of his fall. This office was in Bolton & Barron's building, fronting on Montgomery Street, and commanded a full view of the scene of the meeting.

quent examination of the case before the Grand Jury) entered the room and said something to Whiteman which I did not hear, and Whiteman immediately left the room. I suspected that King and Casey were about meeting, and went into the street myself. I looked down the street and saw many persons standing about the sidewalks, but, seeing nothing of Casey, concluded once more to leave the scene and started up Washington Street, on my way to my rooms on Dupont. As I traveled up Washington Street, I was met by Henry B. Truett and Hamilton Bowie — the latter since dead: peace to his ashes! They were riding in Mr. Truett's buggy. Being intimate with both of them, I informed them of what was going on, when Truett remarked, "If such a fight is coming off, it is no place for me." I told them if it did come off I did not intend to witness it, and they drove away in an opposite direction. I continued up Washington Street, and on reaching Kearny I met James T. Green of the Police, (now Justice Green of El Dorado County,) together with John Nugent and Samuel Stevenson, also of the Police. We all went into a place called the Boomerang, on Kearny Street, to drink. While we were conversing about my applying to Mayor Van Ness to have Nugent, who had been suspended, reinstated on the Police, a man rushed by, on his way, as he said, to see Mrs. King, informing us that her husband had been shot by Casey. Presently I saw the crowd rushing up Washington Street, following Casey, who was in charge of the officers, to the City Hall. From thence he was shortly taken to the jail. I went up to the jail and there found Thomas S. King haranguing the mob in a very excited manner.

I remained there some time, and then went with a friend to my usual place of dining. After dinner, H. H. Byrne, the District Attorney, entered the room, laughing and apparently exulting over the occurrence of the day. He had, I think, been drinking a little. Presently, with a very knowing air, and running his fingers through his locks, he exclaimed, "Judge, this is your pistol," at the same time exhibiting a derringer which he said his brother, Lafayette Byrne, a deputy sheriff, had taken from Casey. After Casey had shot King, Byrne was the first officer who approached him, and it is said that Casey, believing him to be his friend, slipped this pistol into his hand before entering the City Hall, not wishing to compromise the party from whom he had borrowed it.

I replied to District Attorney Byrne, "If it is mine, give it to me." It was not mine; mine were in my pockets, where I habitually carried them. They were gold-mounted, and are well known to hundreds of men in San Francisco. I wished, however, to get possession of the pistol, for I thought I recognized it, and considered it no harm to shield, if possible, the party to whom it belonged from suspicion; the more especially as it will be remembered that Mr. King was not shot by a "derringer," but by a revolver.

Byrne refused to give me the pistol, and I said no more about it, taking care to leave him still under the impression that it was mine, knowing that, if called upon, I could easily clear myself of the suspicion. A few days afterward Mr. King died, and Lafayette Byrne swore at the inquest that his brother, the District Attorney, took the pistol, saying, "*Don't say anything about this, but try to find out the owner. I think some one else is engaged in this, and I want to ferret it out.*" Since my return from southern California, he declares to my friends that he did not in that remark mean me. If he did not mean me, believing, as he said he did, that the pistol was mine, who did he mean? If he *did* mean me, why does he, now that I have, contrary to his expectations, returned, so solemnly asseverate that he did not? The reason *is known to me*, and shall, at the proper time, be made public. I here venture to assert that no man in San Francisco felt more heartfelt exultation in the death of James King of Wm. than this same exemplary and zealous District Attorney. Indeed, a reference to a few back articles of the *Bulletin*, where the editor has had occasion to use his name, will at once convince the reader that the District Attorney had very little cause to love the conductor of that paper.*

[FROM THE S. F. BULLETIN, MARCH 17.]

* "The Ordinance which went into effect on the 15th February, by the joint connivance of the District Attorney, the Mayor, the attorney

It was necessary for him, however, to keep up a fair appearance of devotion to his duty in this matter. *His*

---

of the Recorder's Court, and Col. James, the counsel for Josephine Burr, has been overruled, set aside, and made of no avail! Mr. District Attorney Byrne has falsified his promises of reform.''—[*Bulletin, March 11.*]

* * * * "By the way, what has become of that Bill Lewis case? Hurry up that case, Mr. Byrne, and let's see what you are doing in the way of carrying out your promises."—*Ib.*, *March 13*.

* * * * "The *Chronicle*, as usual, is opposed to any censure being passed on Mr. Byrne. We rather guess we know the secret of this course on the part of the *Chronicle*. The 'editor-in-chief' and Mr. Byrne are old friends, and we have it from undoubted authority that the 'editor-in-chief' himself, from former associations, is averse to any action against the class of houses referred to. This will account for the glee with which that paper announced, the other day, that 'the ordinance was a failure!'"—*Ib.*, *March 14*.

"THE BILL LEWIS CASE. — When will this case come up for trial? We very much fear there is too much ground for the complaints against District Attorney Byrne on the score of leniency to criminals of a certain class. Why does Mr. Byrne show so much reluctance in bringing up Bill Lewis, and so much regard for the latter's welfare, whilst, at the same time, acting so insultingly to Mr. Brown, the witness against Lewis? Is it a part of the District Attorney's business to browbeat *his own* witnesses, and drive them away? A bystander, who was present on one occasion when this brutal attack of Mr. Lewis on Mr. Brown was being talked over in the District Attorney's office, says he heard Mr. Byrne say, '*I'll fix Mr. Brown off, before I get through with him!*' Now, what did Mr. Byrne mean by that speech? The District Attorney says he will 'fix off' his own witness! Does he mean that he will pursue the same course in this Bill Lewis case as he did with the ordinance of the 15th February, give it up in *advance?* Take care, Mr. Byrne; it won't do to try that too often."—*Ib.*, *March 17*.

"'Is the District Attorney the gentleman who was reported to have said in the Mayor's Court recently that "the office did not confer honor on him, but that he conferred honor upon the office"? Judging from the frequency of quashing indictments, the long period elapsing before trials in most of the important criminal cases take place, and the escape of notorious criminals on trial, it seems to me that *he confers quite as little honor on the office* as "the office does" (in his own words) "upon him." JUSTICE.'

"[The District Attorney's estimate of his abilities, we doubt not, is fully as great as they deserve, but, from the frequent faults found with his indictments, we incline to think he either favors his friends, or else don't know so much of 'the lor' as he professes. — ED. BULLETIN.]"—*Ib.*, *May 8*.

own safety demanded it. Once convinced of that fact, no feeling of honor could prevent him from turning the full tide of unjust suspicion against one who had ever been his unselfish friend. But I am digressing. At a future time I shall probably have something to say to the public, not only in reference to this official, but very many others who have shown a remarkable readiness to join in a hue and cry against a former friend and benefactor in order to shield themselves. That matter is, however, for the future; and I here close all further remark upon it so far as this book is concerned.

I have been thus minute in detailing my connection with the circumstances which, as the reader knows, led to the organization of the Vigilance Committee, in order that it may be fully understood how far I have merited the cruel persecution to which I have been subjected at the hands of its myrmidons. I have simply set down *the truth, the whole truth, and nothing but the truth;* every word of which is susceptible of proof by gentlemen now residing in San Francisco; and I ask any candid man to say whether there was anything in my conduct which justified the bitterness of their persecution. It is true that a short time before the attack was made on Mr. King I knew that it was to be made. So did hundreds of others, who had thronged the streets to see it, and probably most of them had, by some means, ascertained it before I did. And what did I know? That a murder was going to be committed? By no means. That burglary or arson, or any other offense against society or any of its members, was about to be perpetrated? Certainly not. Had such been the case, it would have been my clear duty to communicate my knowledge to the authorities, or be content to be regarded as an accomplice. I simply knew that a man whose character had been blackened by an editor was about to seek redress for the injury, in the only way that editor would give it. I knew that that editor had refused to recognize the code by which gentlemen all over the world are guided in the adjustment of their difficulties which cannot otherwise be settled; and I knew that he had repeatedly declared in the most arrogant and bullying manner that the crack of his pistol was the only explanation he had to make to those who felt aggrieved by his articles. I knew that he who sought redress had endeavored peaceably to obtain it, and had been met with scorn and contumely; and that he was now left to the alternative of obtaining it in this way or forever remaining with the mildew of dishonor on his name. I knew that he contemplated no assassination, but that he simply anticipated a desperate conflict, before entering into which he had set his house in order," anticipating death in the attempt to vindicate his reputation. This I knew, and did not inform the authorities. If in this I sinned, then hundreds of others sinned with me, who were "clothed in purple and fine linen, and fared sumptuously every day," while I, knawed by the pangs of hunger and thirst, was forced to hide my houseless head among the forest dens of the wild beasts,—like them, hunted, but not, like them, comforted with the sympathy and companionship of my species. But I digress. I only desire to lay before the world, up to this point, the exact extent of my culpability, and in the succeeding pages the fearful punishment which an unthinking and frenzied mob has inflicted on me.

The excitement caused by the attack on Mr. King, it will be remembered, induced the Sheriff to summon a *posse* of the citizens to protect the jail against any attempt to take Casey therefrom. I, among others, was notified to serve, and did so. On the evening of the sixteenth of May, however, an event occurred, never to be forgotten or sufficiently deplored. On that fatal evening, while there was yet hope that the majesty of the law would be respected, and a popular outbreak prevented by an exhibition of firmness on the part of the Sheriff and his *posse*, the Governor of the state, doubtless actuated by the best of motives, suffered himself to be influenced by weak counsel, and, relying on the bad faith of seditious and designing men, encouraged the Sheriff, by his countenance if not advice, to admit within the walls of the jail a party of men connected with the band of conspirators then organizing under the name of the Vigilance Committee. From that hour I knew that the fate of Casey was sealed, and believed that nothing could avert the storm that seemed about to burst upon the city. Several of us threw down our arms in disgust and left the jail.

I went down Montgomery Street, and into Barry & Patten's saloon.

As my narrative has now brought me to the organization of the Vigilance Committee, before proceeding further it may not be amiss, perhaps, in connection with the current events of which I write, to state one little fact. Not with a view of injuring the gentleman on whom it in some sort reflects (for, I believe, had he been gifted with more natural firmness, his own heart would have made him more consistent), but from the illustration it affords of the hollowness and instability of the foundation on which the so-called "reform movement" was based. The evening *before* the rencounter of King and Casey, I was in Barry & Patten's drinking-saloon, on Montgomery Street, in company with J. C. Cremony, Esq., of the *San Francisco Sun*, and Mr. Casey. While we were drinking at the bar, we were joined by Frank Soulé, Esq., of the *Chronicle*, and another gentleman, also, I think, connected with that press. The subject of conversation, when they joined us, was the braggadocio and threats of the King family, and the "white feather" shown by Tom, in the *Caliban* matter, that morning. Mr. Soulé stated that he had been persecuted by James King of Wm., and had even gone so far *as to procure a double-barreled shot-gun for the purpose of killing him, and that nothing but the entreaties of his partner had prevented him from doing so.**

---

* I need only ask the reader to contrast this declaration with the following extract from the Steamer *Chronicle* of the 21st May:—

"James King of Wm. is no more! Another victim of the bloody code lies still forever. One martyr more for liberty has paid his penalty for speaking what he thought. What threats could not effect, bribes failed to accomplish, the pistol has done, assassination has finished. The bold denouncer of wrong, the fearless antagonist of crime, the brave citizen, who risked life and reputation, happiness and home, in the herculean task of tearing the mask from vice and laying villainy open to the view, lies in his bloody shroud because he felt it his duty to expose evil, and possessed the daring to do it. * * * He brought to the press an intense antipathy to wrong, and unquenchable ardor in opposing it. From the first number of the *Bulletin* till the last one which he edited, his life hung upon a thread; for no man in this city could attack its constantly occurring deeds of darkness

The evening of the shooting of King, Mr. Soulé called upon Casey in the County Jail, and, taking him by both hands, shook them heartily, saying that the people would thank him for what he had done. The day after the shooting of Mr. King, the fifteenth day of May, it will be remembered that the *Chronicle* advocated "Law and Order," but by some mysterious influence best known to the *Chronicle* and its patrons, "a change came over the spirit of its dream" before the setting of the sun, and on the following morning it was among the most rabid of the Vigilance press.* Pursuing the same course, and tacking at the same time, and, doubtless for the same weighty considerations, whatever they were, was also found the *Daily Town Talk*, and in a few days that sheet was enlarged.†

I have not thus digressed for the purpose of gratifying any petty spite entertained toward Mr. Soulé or others; but merely because I think it due to those who have suffered by the acts of that damnable league of hypocrites styling themselves the Vigilance Committee, that the world should know exactly how much of *sincerity* and how much of *self-*

---

and crime without risking his life every time he did so. Mr. King did this, and he felt the risk he ran—yet he swerved not. He had 'set his foot upon the heated plowshare, and he was determined to pass the fiery ordeal.'"

*"What, then, shall we do? Appeal to the courts, and *see* that they do their duty. Let reason and law—nay, *make* reason and law—vindicate the outraged laws and peace of society. * * * * * Our courts *must* protect us, and vindicate at once the character of the community and the violated laws. * * * * * There *must* be henceforth no trifling. Offended law *must* be vindicated—Justice *must* be satisfied—Murder *must* be punished. Homicides *must* cease. Riot and bloodshed *must* be prevented—or society is at an end, and irremediable havoc and ruin will cover us like a pall."—*Chronicle, 15th May.*

†"We do hope and trust that the sober second thought will prevail, and that our city's fair name may be preserved. Though a great wrong has been committed against society, and a lasting injury inflicted upon our city, let the law have its course and punish this offense. It is due to the courts to see the law faithfully administered and justice done. Violence on the person of Casey would neither vindicate the law, restore the lamented King, nor correct the crying evil that exists in our community—the constant use of deadly weapons."—*Town Talk, 15th May.*

interest there was in the professions of purity made by that great engine *the press*, by whose powerful aid the unhealthy fever was so long kept up, and by far the greater part of the treason perpetrated.

But to return to the thread of my narrative. As before stated, I left the jail and went down town, and into Barry & Patten's drinking-saloon. While there, some one told me that the Committee were organizing, and that they intended to send me a notice to leave. I replied that "whoever brought it had better provide himself with a coat of mail," or something to that effect, intending to give the bearer of such a document, whoever he was, good cause to repent his mission. In the course of the evening I returned to the jail, and remained there till nearly daylight. While I was down town I had ascertained that one J. L. Durkee, a member of the police (and afterwards so notorious as Captain Durkee of the Vigilance Committee police, who was tried for piracy in seizing the arms of the state), was a spy upon the Sheriff in the jail, under pretence of being there on duty. I got an opportunity to notify James Herbert, and another person whom I recognized on the top of the jail, of this fact. Going around the jail, I discovered a guard stationed in the rear of the building, and saw Charles Doane, afterwards Marshal of the Vigilance Committee, apparently in command. I remained in the vicinity of the jail till near morning, and then retired to my bed.

I had by this time begun to regard it as prudent to keep out of the way. I had received many intimations from various sources that I was suspected of complicity in the shooting of King, and well knew what I had to expect at the hands of an excited mob in the event of Mr. King's death, whether I was guilty or not. Madame Show, the lady at whose house I had rooms, received that morning a note in a disguised handwriting, stating that my life was in danger. It was supposed to have been written by a German who had joined the Committee. On Sunday, the eighteenth of May, I rose late, and went cautiously and well armed to a different barber's shop from the one where I had been in the habit of getting shaved. On coming out, I observed the housetops in the vicinity of the jail crowded with people, and ascertained that a demonstration was about to be made by the mob. I secured a position where, unobserved, I could witness all that occurred. The events of that black day will never be obliterated from the memories of those who witnessed them. After I had seen them lead poor Casey from the jail and place him in the carriage which was to convey him to his death, I left my place of observation and returned to my rooms. Here I was shortly visited by a few friends, one of whom was the bearer of a message to me from Casey, who desired me to leave town, as he *knew* the Committee intended to take me. I remained within doors the whole of that day and the next, and had my meals brought to me by Mr. Thos. Finlay, formerly one of the police, while my friends were on the *qui vive*, and in constant communication with me. On Monday night I removed to the opposite side of the street. Here I received several secret messages from persons who had friends connected with the Committee, begging me to be on the alert and trust to no one. My whereabouts was known to a German named Schmidt, and a Frenchman whose name I have forgotten,—both members of the Com mittee,—also to a Jew cigar-vender, one of their corporals, named Wasserman. I also received many offers from per sons, who knew where I was, to take me into the country. I listened to all, but accepted none, and kept my own counsel.

On Tuesday, the twentieth of May, the tolling of bells throughout the city announced the death of James King of Wm. I knew that they pealed the death-knell of Casey, and, with the unjust suspicions then aroused against me, perhaps of myself. I changed my room in the house I was in, and sent to a friend, by a sure hand, a note I had received from one of the Vigilance Committee advising me to get out of the way. My friend supplied me with money, and I prepared to leave the city.

Arrangements had been made that, on the evening of the day on which I was supplied with money, some of my friends were to call and go with me to a spot where a pair of horses and buggy were in waiting, in which one of them was to accompany me into the country. There was a woman named Mrs. Eliza Greenwood who had some little things of mine, and before my departure I wished to call and get them, and also to bid her good by. She was a friend of John M. Freeman, Esq., of Freeman's Express, a leading member of the Vigilance Committee, and afterwards a captain in what they called their Light Brigade. Freeman was absent on duty, and about five o'clock in the evening I called at her rooms, which were in the same building with mine. While I was conversing with her, I heard footsteps on the stairs. A friend, who had called with me, immediately escaped from the room by a window opening upon a balcony, and she begged me to do the same. I asked her to see first who it was, and she replied, "It is John." While I was reflecting that it was too late to escape, and he was but one man at any rate, the door opened and he stood before me.

On seeing me he appeared very much surprised, and even startled. He presently recovered himself, however, and said to me, "McGowan, I don't think you are a very bad man." I replied that "I hoped I was not as bad as my enemies would have it appear." He then said, "You are in my house, and hospitality forbids that I should betray you." He told me that I was hunted, and if others knew what he then did with regard to my whereabouts, my life would be of little value, and offered to give me an asylum at his rooms on Montgomery Street. I declined the offer, and apologized for my presence there, telling him that I had only called to say good by, preparatory to my leaving town. The remains of a bottle of champagne which we had been drinking were on the table, and Freeman sent for another, pressing me to remain and drink it with him. All this time the lady of the apartment was signaling me to go out. I heard the sound of footsteps! Freeman told me not to be uneasy; that he would protect me while there. I thanked him, at the same time thinking that a knife, revolver, and pair of derringers, with which I was armed, were a better protection. I took a parting-glass of wine, and got out on the balcony, which overhung the courtyard of the building, and so along it to my own room. My arrangements to leave were all made, and I lay down on the bed, awaiting the arrival of my friends. Presently they came, four in number. I immediately put on a covered California hat, and accompanied them into the street, and high time it was that I did so. The bloodhounds had struck the scent, and were on my track. As I afterward learned, fifteen minutes after I left, the neighborhood was surrounded, and some ten or fifteen *braves* entered and searched the premises. They were armed with sabers and pistols, and ransacked every hole, nook, and corner, making a terrible to-do and clatter among pots, pans, and kettles, but the bird had flown. They were very curious, and the lady before referred to was very furious, and spoke her mind in no measured terms, while Mr. John Freeman sat a mute spectator of the scene.* My friends and I pursued our way through the streets, which seemed to be alive with people, toward the spot where the horses waited; but before we reached there, the heart of the friend who was to drive me out failed him. He dare not risk incurring the displeasure of the Star Chamber, and we bent our steps toward Commercial Street. The rooms of an old friend, Mr. James P. Rynders, were on that street, opposite the "Polka," and forthwith I appropriated them. Mr. R. was himself absent in Sacramento, and knew nothing of the uncemonious manner in which I had taken possession of his lodgings.

The next day, the coroner's inquest was held on the body of James King of Wm., and a few hours afterward I was indicted by the Grand Jury for being accessary before the fact. The news of my indictment spread like fire,—several members of the Grand Jury were sympathizers with the Committee, and afterwards members of it,—and, simultaneously with the finding of the bill against me, the Committee were made acquainted with the fact; ten or fifteen minutes afterward, I was myself notified of it. Then came the "tug of war." The exertions of the Committee to get me, and those of myself and friends to keep out of their bloody fingers.

Thomas Finlay was arrested, and imprisoned in the Vigi-

---

*Some of my friends have thought that Freeman betrayed me. Whatever may have been his intention *after* he found me in the room, I do not believe he *expected* to find me there, and consequently do not attribute to him the descent of the enemy upon the premises. He had no opportunity to give them the cue. Besides, I am very loath to believe, under the circumstances, he could be capable of so dastardly a breach of hospitality, if he *was* Captain of the Light Brigade.

lance rooms, where, I learned, they used entreaties, threats, and bribes to induce him to disclose to them my place of retreat, but in vain. Finding him, at length, utterly impracticable, they discharged him after two days' imprisonment.* William Mulligan, whom they had also arrested, was offered his liberty, I learned, if he would assist them to capture me, but he indignantly spurned the offer, and suffered banishment rather than tell them where he had last seen me. He had called on me only two days before his arrest. I remained ten days in my hiding-place in Commercial Street. As may be supposed, the hunt for me had waxed sufficiently hot, as I had been unable to execute any manœuver by which to delude my pursuers into the belief that I had left town. After the first few days, my friends began to be *afraid* to come near me, and I actually consulted with one of them as to the propriety of giving myself up to the authorities under my indictment; but I have now no doubt that a calm reconsideration of that matter saved my neck from the fingers of the Committee's hangman. I requested my friends not to visit me any more, and indeed the request was almost needless, for there was a ban upon me, and by this time it seemed to them that my very touch was leprosy, and my breath was poison. I bade them have no fears of my being hung, as I never intended to be taken alive. I had no less than ten shots and a good knife always about my person. They embraced me and bid me good by, all but *one*, who still stood by me, and a faithful negro boy who brought me my meals. In a miserable state of mind I remained here several days, eagerly watching for the first chance of escape, and reading the surmises as to my whereabouts in the daily papers.† One day, I feared, from an in-

---

*The following is an extract from an article which appeared in the *Herald* of May 28th:—

We are also informed that one of the police force of this city has received a promise of a large contingent to ferret out McGowan, and that another man, who was supposed to be acquainted with all McGowan's movements, has been kept in close confinement in the rooms of the Vigilance Committee for the last two days, in the hope of compelling him to make some revelations. He was discharged yesterday.

† It is also said Judge Edward McGowan has been arrested in Ne-

cident that occurred, that my hopes and fears were about to be brought to a speedy termination. I heard at the door

---

vada, while some assert he is in possession of the Committee here.—*Herald*, May 25th.

THE SEARCH AFTER MCGOWAN.—The search after this individual was continued yesterday, but, we believe, without result. It is said by some that McGowan is still in this city, while others assert that he left long before his arrest was contemplated. Towards evening a considerable stir was observable among the members of the Vigilance Committee. They were in every portion of the city—some riding—some walking. The object, no doubt, was to keep a sharp eye upon those places which have fallen under suspicion.—*Herald*, May 30th. [May 27th.]

MOVEMENTS OF THE COMMITTEE.—The search after McGowan was continued yesterday, but with the same result. It is said by some that he sailed a few days ago for Mazatlan—by others, that he left this city a few days ago, on horseback, for the southern country, and in support of this theory it is stated that a gentleman in this city, who is the owner of two fleet horses, yesterday received a telegraphic dispatch to the effect that one of his horses was knocked up some distance below San José; while large numbers insist that he is still in this city. The only fact that we have any knowledge of is, that McGowan has not yet been arrested by the Vigilance Committee. —*Herald*, June 20th. [May 30th.]

A DARK SCENE.—On the 18th of June, 1856, a party of armed men might be seen slowly wending (as G. P. R. James would have said) up Clay Street, in the city of San Francisco,—the Queen City of the Pacific,—to Stockton. Having arrived in front of a low shanty on the west side of the street, they halted, and drew up in battle array. The noise occasioned by their movements attracted the attention of those residing in the neighborhood, and window-sashes were thrown up, and nightcaps protruded in every direction. Having formed in front of the dwelling, three individuals, who, by the number and variety of the warlike implements each carried, seemed to occupy a position of command, ascended the rude steps leading to the door of the domicile, and knocked violently. Rap, rap, rap. No answer. The knocking was repeated until the echo reverberated throughout the whole neighborhood. At this stage of the narrative, though we should lay ourselves open to the charge of being literary "Marplots," we would state that the beleaguered shanty was occupied by a colored gentleman, whose only offense against the peace and dignity of the commonwealth was, that he, in the pursuit of a legitimate business, took in the shirts of the ubiquitous McGowan and washed them. Hearing the hubbub, he rushed to the door, and, placing his hands on his hips, with his "eyes in a fine frenzy rolling," roared out at the top of his voice, "Who's dat knocking at de door?"

A gruff voice on the outside ordered him to open it, which he accord-

the usual signal made by my friends when they visited me (three knocks). I opened it, and found a strange Frenchman, who asked me, in his own language, where *Gustave* was. I answered that he was downstairs. From the scrutinizing manner in which he eyed me, I felt sure that he was one of the Committee; and, notwithstanding my disguise, which consisted of a Mexican or California hat, face browned, and hair and mustaches blacked, I feared, if he had ever seen me before, that I was detected. He soon left, without further conversation. He had no sooner gone than I quitted my room, and entered a water-closet which was at the head of the staircase, and commanded it.

Knowing it to be impossible to escape by the street, and fearing that my hiding-place was known, I here determined to make a stand, and if any armed body ascended the stairs to take me, to commence shooting, and sell myself as dearly as possible. I remained here about an hour, when, hoping that I had not been recognized, I left my position and entered the room of my friend, adjoining the one I had been in, taking care to hide the food and other evidence of my having inhabited it. I got under my friend's bed, and remained there till night. When he returned home, I told him what had occurred, and he appeared to be very much alarmed. He informed me that bands of the Committee were hunting me high and low in all parts of the city, and that one H. P. A. Smith* (former member of the

---

ingly with trembling hands did, and the whole band rushed in and ransacked the house from top to bottom, while the poor darky stood inside the door, in rather a ludicrous *déshabillé*, with his teeth chattering and his knees smiting each other. It is said by those who witnessed his sad plight, that he became almost livid with fear. Not having been able to poke anything out of the piles of dirty clothes with which the house was filled, the armed band retired and searched several other houses in the vicinity, making no distinction between white and black. Whether they were searching for McGowan or a dozen of superfine shirts, which he is said to have left behind in his flight, could not be ascertained. [*Herald, June 20th.*]

*DOMICILIARY VISITS.—The detective police of the Inquisition, the amateur "Buckets" of the Vigilance Committee, adopting the maxim that "The early bird catches the worm," were wandering about the city early on Saturday morning, in search of subjects, but we regret to state they finished their labors by sunrise without securing another

legislature from Marin County) was among the most industrious in the search, and loudest in his denunciations of me. It now struck me, for the first time, that, after all, it might be more for a desire to wreak political vengeance in certain quarters that my pursuers were so eager after me, than from any honest belief in my complicity in Mr. King's death. It is not for me, in this relation of my wrongs, to make any specific charges against any one, nor do I now do it; but my reasons for my suspicions were simply these:

victim for a sacrifice and practical illustration of the philosophy of hanging. On Saturday morning, at four and a half o'clock, Mrs. Catherine F. Hewitt, the proprietress of the Washington Saloon, on Washington Street, between Dupont and Kearny streets, was awakened by a loud noise, apparently proceeding from the entry of the house occupied by her. She immediately observed a number of persons in the entry, and, feeling greatly surprised and alarmed, went to the door of her bedroom and asked them what they wanted. Whereupon one of them replied that they had come to search her house. She then ran to the window and screamed, whereupon one of the persons who entered took hold of her and placed his hand over her mouth, so as to prevent her making any outcry. She was so terrified by the conduct and demeanor of the parties so entering her apartment, that she fainted, and became for a time wholly unconscious. Some one of the party then threw a quantity of water over her person; and, after they had remained in her room for some time, they left the house, and stated, previous to their departure, that they had made the visit by authority of the Vigilance Committee, in search of Edward McGowan. [*Herald, May 25th.*]

RUMORS. — We learned, at a late hour last night, that Judge McGowan, whom the Committee are now hunting, left this city on the steamer John L. Stephens, on Wednesday last. He was put aboard some distance outside the Heads, in a complete state of disguise, having shaved off his mustache and darkened his complexion. We give the rumor for what it is worth. — *Herald, May 25th [24th].*

THE VIGILANCE COMMITTEE. — Nothing definite could be ascertained as to the course which the Vigilance Committee intended to pursue. It is said — but we have no authority for it but street rumor — that the agents of the Committee have succeeded in ferreting out Judge McGowan somewhere in the interior, and that he was to be brought down to this city last night; that several persons are to be notified to leave in the next steamer, and that, in the event of the persons refusing to comply with the mandate, forcible means are to be resorted to. The Committee was in session yesterday morning, and also again in the afternoon. They have called into existence a formidable organization. It is, we are informed, extending throughout the interior of the state, and will, we presume, be converted finally into a political movement. — *Herald, May 28th.*

This fellow Smith, it was well known, was a warm advocate of the claims of a certain distinguished gentleman to a high official position, while I was an equally zealous friend of his principal opponent. Perhaps, then, it was the hope that I was in the possession of some political secrets, which, if divulged, would be destructive of my friend's interests, which induced this man, and others of his kidney, to pursue me so diligently, in the expectation that threats of death or banishment would wring them from me. How shrewd my suspicions were, I leave to certain *political* gentlemen to say who appeared most patriotically to sympathize with the so-called reform movement. But a *few days* before, this man Smith had requested my influence to secure his nomination for one of the San Francisco seats in the legislature, pledging himself to support my friend as well as his own for the position above referred to. I courteously declined helping him, for good and sufficient reasons, and now he was at the head of a squad of "Reformers," seeking my life!

It so happened that the information of my friend was verified that very night; for, about two o'clock, A. M., it being very dark outside, I was standing in my friend's room, without a light, and with the window raised, and *actually heard a party of my pursuers talking about me, on the street below!* Among others, I heard Smith, whose voice I recognized, exclaim, "*The d——d old rascal, I'll have him before five days more!*" When I remembered the fawning manner in which he had asked my assistance only a few days before, and the entirely inoffensive way in which I had refused it; when I remembered the confidence with which he had even borrowed from me the poor sum of his passage down the Sacramento, *knowing* that, though a political enemy and almost a stranger, he would not be refused; when I remembered his truckling protestations of good feeling notwithstanding political differences, and then with my own ears heard him speak thus of me to the pack of sleuth-hounds of which he was the leader,—I confess that for a moment there was murder in my heart. Instinctively I grasped my knife to rush down and kill him, even though it were my own last act on earth; and I believe that in the fury of that moment nothing stayed me but the timely reflection that I would bring destruction on an innocent friend, whose roof sheltered me. If his eye falls on these pages, let him not deny the truth of what I have written, for, so sure as he does, his trembling lip will betray to his hearer the lie it utters. He *knows* how truly I have spoken, and his own heart best knows the motives that prompted his conduct.

But let him pass. It may be of some interest now to him to know *all* who composed his audience on that night, and how near he came to meeting with a round of applause to which his modest merit would, of itself, never have aspired. I dismiss him to the guardianship of his own conscience, and the mercy of its reproaches.

While lying under the bed in my friend's room, I had observed a false face or mask, such as is generally used at the fancy balls given by the French *artistes* in San Francisco. I had been out of my retreat once before, disguised as a policeman, and afterward discovered by the papers that I had been recognized.* My object in incurring the risk was to get possession of some private papers I had left in my office, but I was unsuccessful, the Committee having been there before me and taken everything they could find. I was now very anxious to get possession of some correspondence which had passed between a gentleman (one of the foreign consuls) and myself, in reference to a lady, a countrywoman of his; I had left this in a little dressing-bureau in my rooms, and fearing that if it fell into stranger-hands it might injure him, I determined to make a second *sortie*, if possible, to get it. For this purpose, I availed myself of this mask. My foolhardiness may be wondered at, but the gentleman was my friend, and

---

* SEARCH FOR MCGOWAN. — It is now pretty well ascertained, reports to the contrary notwithstanding, that this noted individual has not left the city. It is asserted positively that he was seen as late as Saturday night, and followed by some members of the Vigilance Committee. But he again managed to secrete himself, and elude their most vigilant search. It will be rather a difficult matter for him to escape detection. He has been indicted by the Grand Jury as well as by the Vigilance Committee, for being accessary to the late murder, and he must have more than ordinary good fortune to slip by and escape from the Police and the Committee. — *Bulletin, June 2.*

wrote me the notes for my own protection. I should have destroyed them, but not having done so, my duty, in justice to him, was, if possible, to get them. I cut the nose out of the mask, blacked it, and, putting it on with my California hat, sallied out. I reached my rooms unobserved, and saw the landlady. At first, she did not recognize me until she heard my voice, and then she was very much frightened, the mask gave me such a horrible expression. I took off the nose to convince her that it was I, but she refused me admittance, telling me that the Committee had been there and taken everything, and it was useless for me to incur any further risk in trying to secure any of my papers. Finding it impossible to even get access to my rooms, I returned to my hiding-place, very fortunately attracting no observation.

Since my return from the lower country, the Vigilance Committee have restored to me my papers, but this corre spondence is not among them. I trust if, among the mem bers of the Committee, there are any of that gentleman's countrymen into whose hands these papers have fallen, they will return them to the source from whence they originated.

The time had now come when it was absolutely necessary for me to remove from Commercial Street. I could not hope much longer to escape detection if I remained in the city, and it was far better, if I had to be captured, that it should be done when I might have a remote chance of escape by flight, than to be taken like a bird from a cage. Besides, the friend who fed me had gone to the Atlantic states, and to remain there longer was impossible, as every one else, who knew where I was, were watched night and day. A very kind friend, who had faithfully stood to me through everything, cast about him, day after day, to secure me a place of safety, but in vain. I even agreed to the proposition of a friend to take me to his room on Montgomery Street, *next door to the room of No. 33 Secretary* of the Committee. This, however, was overruled by all my friends who were consulted.

At length a retreat was found for me with a pious old lady, who lived a short distance from the city, on the Mission Dolores road. The difficulty now was, how to get me there. The outlets of the city were surrounded by armed horsemen, continually on patrol, relieving each other at stated hours, night and day, and all on special watch for me. In a word, escape seemed impossible.

Those who were in San Francisco at that time will remember how high and fearfully public opinion ran against me.* There was nothing in it of reason; no deliberate action based upon proven guilt on my part; but the blind and aimless fury with which the death of Mr. King seemed to have fired the bosoms of the masses was, for want of a more available victim, directed in a resistless torrent against me. People had evidently mixed up the Thomas King affair, with which it was known I was connected, with the death of James King of Wm. Every witness summoned before the Committee was greeted with the question, "What do you know of McGowan?" Col. A. J. Gamble, as an instance, was cited to appear before them, and gave in his evidence touching a conversation I had at Mr. Hunt's stables the day before James King of Wm. was shot. Subsequently he was recalled, and his testimony being read over

---

* *Bulletin*, June 2d.—Should Ned McGowan fall into the hands of the Vigilance Committee, and receive the punishment he so justly merits, he would a tale unfold that would make the quills of the porcupine stand erect. We think the porcupine comparison quite applicable. The naturalist tells us it is [one of] the most destructive of all animals, and lives on the bark of trees, and when it has attacked a tree, never leaves until it has completely stripped it of all the bark on trunk and branches. And so with these political leeches, they will hang on and return so long as there is a drop of blood to be drawn from this outraged community. Out upon the heartless hypocrites! In our opinion, these men, Iscariot-like, would sell their best friend for even less than thirty pieces.

CREDITORS OF ADAMS & CO.—Did it ever occur to you that the speediest way to get that $100,000 out of the hands of P., C., & Co. would be to find the whereabouts of Ned McGowan? They would let your, as well as the city and county, money flow like water ere they would run the risk of his disclosures.

GENTLEMEN OF THE VIGILANCE COMMITTEE—Did it ever strike you that the best place to look for the aforesaid Ned would be in the state prison or some county jail? Ned is a "law-and-order man," and, like all villains of his class, would flee to his friends—the ministers of the law—for protection. Such scamps love "law and order," but it is the law of their own making, and after their own order.

to him, he pronounced it correct, except that Thomas S. King should appear throughout where James King of Wm. appeared. The conversation was about the other affair!

Thus a portion of the mob, mistaking one affair for the other, persecuted me perhaps from an honest conviction of my guilt. The other portion, and they the leaders, in default of proof against me, but absolutely knowing my innocence, joined the hue and cry through blind rage at the death of King.* Another portion, and they the politicians opposed to me, threw themselves on the top of the wave, and circulated wonderful stories about ballot-box frauds. McGowan was a politician, boxes had been stuffed, perhaps, at primary elections, consequently McGowan was a ballot-box stuffer, and must die; and, under all this pressure, even the Grand Jury had to yield. When the question of indictment came before them, there was no evidence on which to find the bill. The foreman of the jury, Mr. Thomas J. Poulterer, than whom a more worthy and respectable gentleman does not live in San Francisco, told the District Attorney, Mr. Byrne, that there was no evidence to warrant an indictment, but it was of no avail. On the jury there were many friends of the Committee; one of them (one Jobson) my bitter personal enemy! Add to that the tremendous howl from without, and the weak nerve which, in that hour of peril, induced the District Attorney to tell Mr. Poulterer that if they believed I *knew* anything about the matter prior to the shooting of King, the jury were bound to indict, and it will be seen how even my indictment was found in response to a wild and unreasonable demand of the populace.

Such was the state of the public mind with regard to me,

---

* The day before Casey was hung, a friend was admitted to see him. This gentleman is now holding an honorable position under the Federal government. He was allowed to speak to him in the presence of Captain Aaron Burns, a member of the Executive Committee of Vigilance. It was the last time he was permitted to see a friend (except one other, Mr. Charles Gallagher) in this life. This gentleman questioned him about my connection with the death of James King of Wm., and he stated that I was entirely free from all complicity in it, and if I was present, nothing but curiosity or a *penchant* for such sights prompted me to be there.

and such had been the measures adopted to prevent my escape when the time arrived for me to attempt it. After much time had been spent in consultation among my friends as to the best plan to be pursued, it was at length decided that my own proposition was the best; which was, to disguise myself, and walk boldly forth through my enemies. Accordingly, arrangements were made for me to leave my hiding-place just at lamplight on the evening of the third of June. My friend was to send some one to me, and not come himself, as it was considered dangerous for him to again visit me, he being by this time very narrowly watched.* He applied to at least twenty persons to come and make with me the arrangements, but none of them dare come near me, and he was at last obliged to do it himself. He came, and it was agreed that he should meet me with a carriage on the Mission road. Before he left, I struck a light, and asked him if he would know me. He appeared astonished at my disguise, and said he would not. My face, hair, and mustaches were blacked with pomatum and shoe-blacking, my stomach was drawn in and confined with a pair of French stays, and over my clothes I had an overcoat, with a derringer in each pocket. I also had on my slouched hat, and a pair of derringers in my pantaloons pockets, together with a six-shooter and a knife in my belt. Thus armed and disguised, as soon as my friend had left I sallied forth alone. It was just in the dusk of the evening as I walked up Commercial Street, toward Kearny, on my way to the Mission. I passed several

---

*The following is taken from the *Herald* of May 28th [26th]:—

RUMORS.—Yesterday, Merchant Street was closely watched throughout the entire day. It was thought by the Vigilance Committee that Edward McGowan was somewhere concealed in that neighborhood, and therefore every person that was known to be intimate with him was watched wherever he went.

VIGILANCE COMMITTEE.—Everything was quiet around the Committee rooms yesterday. Matters remain in the same condition today. Late last evening, word was communicated that Ned McGowan was seen to go into the building at the corner of Sutter and Kearny streets, where he had a room. A portion of the Committee, soon after, surrounded the building, and early this morning a thorough search was instituted, but he could not be found.—*Bulletin*, June 2d.

I walked boldly out Kearny Street, an as I went, found many a fearful reminder of my peril, in tramping hoofs and clashing sabers.—*Page 38.*

whom I knew standing in front of Whipple's club-house, and afterward, on the road, I met Mr. Dan Sweeney and Sandy Marshall. None of them, however, recognized me for a moment. I walked boldly out Kearny Street, and, as I went, found many a fearful reminder of my peril, in tramping hoofs and clashing sabers. I could not forget, in a thousand centuries, the feeling of mingled hope and horror with which I walked, that evening, an unjustly outlawed man, through the hosts of my enemies.

It was not the fear of death itself that made these moments terrible; for death I could face, and had faced before. But it was the thought of *such* a death as awaited me in the event of my capture, and the reflection that myriads of tongues would ring into the ears of my children how ignobly their father died, but none would tell them how unjustly. The starlight that glistened back from the sabers of my enemies was not more quick and sudden in its coming and its going than the changes of my thoughts from hope to fear, and back again from fear to hope, as, marking every incident around me, I walked unquestioned and unheeded through the meshes of the net my persecutors had thrown about me. Thanks to a kind Providence, I at length was enabled to draw a long breath, on the Mission road, far beyond the outmost sentinel. I here met my friend with the carriage, who was surprised to see me out so soon. I talked and laughed with him, for it appeared as though a mountain had been lifted from my soul in the last half-hour. He reproved my ill-timed merriment, in his anxiety for my safety, and told me I had been so long an outlaw I must have got used to it. I told him I did not intend to die but once. May he never undergo the agony of mind necessary for him fully to appreciate my happiness at that moment. We turned around and went back toward the city, to the place which was to be my refuge during the rest of my stay in the neighborhood of San Francisco. This, as before stated, was the house of a pious old lady, a member of the Baptist Church. She lived on the Mission road, with no companion but one sweet little daughter, about ten years of age. This child was going to school in the neighborhood, and I was at first fearful that she might betray me. I knew that children of her age generally had some little female friend, or some lad whom they called *sweetheart*, to whom they told all their little secrets. I found she had a sweetheart, and she told me who it was. I asked her if she knew the importance of keeping my secret, and she said she did, and would keep it. I told her that I had four boys, one of them no bigger than herself, and if she were to tell anybody that I was there, men would come with guns and take me and kill me, and then my four little boys would be without anybody to love and protect them, and they would think it was her fault, and would not like her or her mother. In this way I awaked the dear little thing's sympathy, and I felt quite sure from the way she listened to me that she would never tell her sweetheart or any one else of my being in her mother's house. I then asked her what kind of silk dress she would like to have, and she told me she would like to have a pretty plaid silk; so I got the old lady the next day to go out and buy her one, and little "Ariel" and I became sworn friends.

The front part of the house was not inhabited, and the next morning, when the old lady had gone out, I took up two of the planks in the floor of the kitchen, to provide myself with a hiding-place in case of necessity. That day my kind hostess prepared for me quite a sumptuous dinner. I suspected that she was somewhat changing her usual mode of living, and this I objected to for various reasons.

I told the old lady that I wanted plain food, as, in all probability, if the Committee did not disband, I would be compelled to take a long and tedious journey, and wanted, by way of preparation, to accustom myself to rough fare. To this end I also changed my drink, and in the place of brandy and water, to which I had been accustomed, I took gin. There was also danger in the tradespeople remarking an alteration in her style of living, and I reminded her of the story of the French gentleman who, in the "Reign of Terror" in Paris, secreted himself at his washerwoman's house, and she, imprudently enough, so changed her style of living on his account, that her neighbors, who were of the Robespierre faction, remarked it, and searched her house, where her friend was arrested, and subsequently guillotined. Accordingly, she went back to her old style of living, and we got on very comfortably.

I remained with this good old lady about four weeks, during which time nothing worthy of note occurred. My friend, who visited me twice a week, brought me all the papers, and I had the pleasure of reading all the kind and good-natured things that were said of me, and also all the profound surmises as to my whereabouts.* It was while I

---

*NED McGOWAN.— Notwithstanding it has been reported that the individual whose name heads this paragraph left on the Sea Bird last Saturday, he was seen by several parties in the city last evening; a fact which appears strange to us, when it is well known the Vigilance Committee have been diligently searching for him. It will hardly be fair to punish Casey only, for a crime of which others are equally guilty. — *Town Talk*, *May 23*.

NED McGOWAN. — This ubiquitous individual, who appears to have as many hiding-places as a cat has lives, was reported last evening as having been taken at the State Marine Hospital, which, in common with other reports, proved to be without foundation. It has been said that McGowan has been seen on board of a storeship in the harbor; again, that he is stowed away in one of the steamboats off Mission Creek, and a hundred other surmises equally as absurd. We are of the opinion that if the Committee do track the fugitive to his lair, it will be when he is napping, as his cunning and ingenuity are proverbial. We hope, however, that it will not be long before he is safe in the hands of the Committee.—*Ib*.

STILL AFTER McGOWAN. — Quite a number of members of the Vigilance Committee, with perhaps some of the police, were keeping close watch upon and around a block fronting upon Stockton Street, yesterday afternoon. It was finally concluded that they were upon the wrong scent. If Ned be in the city, he has firm and shrewd friends who know how to conceal him. Among so many reports as to his whereabouts, it is impossible to say which is true, or whether any be true.—*Chronicle*, *June 10*.

AQUATIC SPORTS OF THE COMMITTEE.—Towards the close of yesterday, considerable excitement prevailed. The Committee, having received some information that McGowan had been conveyed on board of some vessel which was to put to sea this morning, chartered the steam-tug Martin White, Captain H. A. Cheever, and started in pursuit. At an early hour in the afternoon, the Martin White got up steam and cleared. The chase was anxiously viewed from Telegraph Hill. Two schooners were observed crowding all their sail to make the Gate. The Martin White puffed and labored, and appeared to gain on the schooners steadily. The chase became exciting. The schooners were the Queen of the West and the Francisco. In a short time the Martin White came alongside. The schooners were overhauled, but, as the sequel will show, no discovery was made. By this

was at this house that I received the agreeable, though rather surprising, information that I was in Carson Valley. A kind friend had started the story for the purpose of throwing my pursuers off the scent, and I here beg to tender him my most heartfelt thanks for his good offices.*

---

time the excitement in town became intense. It was rumored that McGowan had been captured, and a rush was accordingly made to the wharves to obtain a glance at the ubiquitous individual, about whose whereabouts so much had been said. At length, the Martin White hove in sight. The people rushed. She came alongside the wharf. A large number of the parcels of the Committee came ashore. They brought with them an ominous-looking box, about six feet in length, wrapped in blankets. The rumor was immediately circulated that the aforesaid box contained the mortal remains of the ubiquitous McGowan. It was generally believed. The box was placed on a cart; it was conveyed to the rooms of the Vigilance Committee; it was carefully brought upstairs; five thousand people witnessed the sight. In concluding this account of the aquatic sports of the Committee, we would state that, from all the inquiries that we have made on the subject, we are of the opinion that the box over which so much parade was made did not contain the remains of McGowan, and that it was filled with tower-muskets, warranted by the maker not to explode.—*San Francisco Herald*, May 27 [29].

*The following appeared in the *Daily Town Talk* of June 25th:—

NED MCGOWAN NEAR CARSON VALLEY.—This notorious individual is said to have been met by a Mr. David J. Barnes, from Missouri, at a place called Silver Creek, just below Carson Valley. Mr. Barnes had been wintering at Bear River, on his way to this state, and on his way across the mountains met a man at Silver Creek, called Judge McGowan, who, in company with five other persons, was spending his time in hunting. From an article in reference to the discovery of this noted character, in the Sacramento *Spirit of the Age* of yesterday, and telegraphed to the *Evening Bulletin*, we glean the following:—

Says Mr. Barnes: "After I camped in the evening, I went down to their camp, some four or five miles off the road. They had lost one of their horses. They (four men) came to my camp next morning. One of them said, 'Judge McGowan, you can send that saddle to Placerville by this emigrant.' The men reported that they were hunting, and sometimes prospecting."

Mr. Barnes brought the saddle with him to Placerville, and endeavored to leave it at a hotel, as directed, but the landlord refused to accept it, or Barnes either. He then brought it to this city, and left it at the store of Heard & Osborn, where it remains, subject to the order of Judge McGowan.

Mr. Barnes reports that when he asked what name he should leave with the saddle, McGowan answered, "No matter what name—just leave it there till called for." McGowan's party were apparently out of provisions.

I knew more of what was going on inside the Committee rooms—except the Executive room—than many who belonged to them. The Law and Order party had their spies in the Vigilance camp, as, doubtless, they had theirs in ours. I used frequently to see the Light Brigade drilling, with John M. Freeman and Frank Baker in command. One day I distinctly heard John give the word of command,—"Trot!" The first day I saw them, although, as I afterward learned, they numbered but a hundred men, they looked very numerous, and I thought they had come to surround the neighborhood. I was about to get into my hiding-place under the floor, but, after looking at them a few moments longer, I saw that they were only exercising. A pretty-looking set they were! charging and slashing around, and mowing down fictitious enemies with the most brilliant gallantry imaginable. I could not help wondering how long some of those heavy-set Dutchmen and tape-selling *Bayards* would have kept their clumsy seats if charged upon by half a dozen well-mounted and determined men. They "were a motley crew." Most of them appeared to have quite as much on their hands as they could well attend to in managing their sabers and bridle-reins and sticking to their saddles, without the additional trouble of attempting to learn cavalry manœuvers. O puissant warriors! had you only have known that one weak old man, whose imaginary sins had awakened your terrible wrath, and marshaled you in that awful battle array, was calmly amusing himself by looking at you at the distance of a few hundred yards, what a gala day would it have been for you! You would have dismounted and given up your ridiculous attempts to ape the soldier, and most incontinently, then and there, proceeded to tie a rope around my old neck and hang me up to the first telegraph-post. And, in good sooth, it were an occupation better befitting your natural gifts and tastes than that of endeavoring to play the part of chivalry, which, in order to be successfully done, requires some modicum of the gentleman.

While I was in this place, I lived in hope, from day to day, that the lawless proceedings of the Vigilance Committee would be put a stop to, either by force of arms or otherwise. I understood that the Law and Order forces were preparing, when they had a sufficient number of arms, to compel the Committee to disband. And although it was generally understood by their best military men that matters had been and were being managed very badly for them, still I shared the hope entertained by many, that something would finally be done. The fatal mistake was that of leaving their forces and arms scattered about in various defenseless armories, where they could at any time be taken in detail by the Committee's superior numbers, instead of going at once into an encampment, and thus concentrating their strength and forming a nucleus around which their friends from the mountains could rally; and to this mistake the Vigilance Committee may attribute their undeserved success. The proper orders, however, did not come from headquarters, and the junior officers had only to lie on their arms and swallow their chagrin. My friend had promised me, that if a fight took place, I should be notified of it in time to participate. When, however, the man Hopkins was stabbed by Judge Terry, and the Committee availed themselves of the occasion to take the arms of the state, my hopes died within me. The effects of the wretched policy that had been pursued were then, as had been predicted, felt, when too late to remedy them, and the supporters of the constitution and the laws were left not only powerless to maintain their cause, but exposed, personally naked and defenseless, to the pitiless storm of treason and fanaticism that swept over the city. I became disgusted and disheartened, and begged my friend to set his wits to work to devise some means by which I could leave the county of San Francisco. It mattered not to me where I went, so that I could but go, and go speedily. I not only was in peril of my life by remaining, but, had I not been, I no longer desired to breathe the polluted air of the Doomed City. At length, matters were arranged and the plan formed for my departure.

CHAPTER II

> If there fled
> One Argive from the slaughter, be it said
> Of old Adrastus he hath learned to fly;
> We count it death to falter, not to die.
> *Trans. Ancient Poem.*

FRIDAY evening, the 27th of June,—the day that Judge Terry's trial before the Vigilance Committee commènced, and while the Executive Committee were busily engaged in that gentleman's case,—was the time fixed for my flight from San Francisco. I was to endeavor to make my way home to Philadelphia, by the southern route, through Mexico. I did not much like to start on a Friday, inasmuch as it was *hangman's* or *Vigilante* day; and I have never been entirely free from superstition. However, as the journey was not properly to commence until the following day, I overcame my scruples, and prepared for the start. My friend called early in the evening to inform me that all was arranged, and the horses, together with a guide who had been provided, (James Dennison,) and a companion, were in waiting at the Mission Dolores, so that all I had to do was to go there, mount, and ride for life.

I bid an affectionate farewell to the good and kind lady who had sheltered me, kissed the faithful little "Ariel," who had kept my secret, and, thoroughly disguised, stepped out into the night, and, accompanied by my friend, bent my steps toward the Mission. Having arrived there, and found everything in readiness, I put on my spurs, embraced my

While he was upbraiding me, I waved my hand to him and Shear, put spurs to my horse, and galloped away.—*Page 46.*

kind friend, who had been more than a brother to mé,—may God reward him,—and mounted the good horse who was to carry me, I trusted, safely from danger.

I felt sad, very sad, not only at parting with my true and faithful friend who had been so constant and so kind throughout my many perils, but also at leaving the city of San Francisco. An hour before, I was all anxiety to turn my back upon it forever, but when the time of parting came, involuntarily my mind recurred to the many happy days I had passed there, and the many friends whose cheerful smile and pleasant laugh I was, as I supposed, on that evening bidding farewell to forever. I kissed my hand to my friend, and, turning my head toward the city, notwithstanding the dreadful plague-spot that marred its beauty, I bid it a sorrowful yet affectionate "good night."

So soon as the form of my friend had vanished in the darkness, I turned to Dennison, and said to him I could not make up my mind to leave until I had said "good by" to my old friend William Shear, the proprietor of the Nightingale. I was near his hospitable threshold, and I felt as though I was acting meanly to depart without saying farewell to an old and tried friend. Dennison at once rode up and called Shear out. He came and shook me warmly by the hand, telling me for God's sake to take care of myself; that the Committee, unless I was very cautious, would certainly hang me. "That is," said I, "if they catch me." He brought me out two bottles of his best old brandy, to comfort me, as he said, on the journey. All this while my friend, who I supposed had gone back to town, was within a few yards of me, and, seeing me talking to some one, came back, and was perfectly furious at my temerity in taking so many chances. While he was upbraiding me, I waved my hand to him and Shear, put spurs to my horse, and galloped away.

That night we were only to ride to Dennison's rancho at Halfmoon Bay, a distance of about twenty-five miles from the Mission, in what is now the county of San Mateo. We had to traverse a rugged mountain road, bad enough in the daytime, but at night, except on the surest-footed beasts, almost impassable. Our object was to keep off the main roads as much as possible, both night and day. However, we got on pretty well till within about three miles of our stopping-place, when my horse, who was quite a colt, and full of spirit, knowing that he was approaching home, started to run, and threw me. I fell very heavily, and was badly hurt. Indeed, I thought for a time that my back must be broken. He did not run far, however, before the Californian who accompanied us caught him. I could scarcely walk, my back pained me so dreadfully. I knew, though, what I had to go through in the journey before me, and thinking it too soon to begin to complain, I again mounted with great difficulty, assisted by my companions, and rode on to the house. It was daylight when we reached the end of our ride, and right glad I was to have an opportunity to rest. I went to bed and slept until eleven o'clock, A. M., when I arose, and while I took breakfast Dennison and the Californian — who, by the way, was his brother-in-law — caught the horses that we were to take with us for the journey. This Californian, whose name will figure considerably in this narrative, I may as well here describe. His name is Ramon Valencia. He is very dark-complexioned, though his skin is as soft and polished as a woman's. He is of medium stature, very well formed, and has most expressive features, a fine bright and intelligent eye, a great deal of vivacity, and much good sense. He had married the sister of my friend Dennison, but had lost her under most unhappy circumstances. He was very kind-hearted, and many a weary mile he beguiled by his agreeable chat in broken English. I can never forget his kindness to me during my weary pilgrimage, and beg now to offer him my thanks and good wishes for his future. Would that it were in my power to return him even one of his many disinterested and generous acts of friendship to me.

Dennison selected six of his finest California horses, and in another hour we were in the saddle and had commenced our journey. I felt very sore from my fall of the preceding night, but said nothing about it, determined to bear up until I had placed many leagues between myself and danger. Nothing in the way of incident occurred to us during that day's travel. We followed the Coast Range, always keeping, as far as possible, the trails, and avoiding the main road.

After crossing the Santa Cruz line, I was struck with the

splendor of the scenery. Living so long pent up among the brick-and-mortar walls of San Francisco, I was prepared to enjoy with a peculiar zest the loveliness of nature. It was midsummer, and the plains and hillsides were decked in their gayest robes. Flowers of every odor and every hue were showered lavishly over the landscape; and the sweet breeze that came to our nostrils, laden with their perfume, also brought to our ears the songs of a thousand birds, who, in the recklessness of their joy, seemed to mock my sorrows; and I confess, as I bounded along on my active little horse, drinking to the fill of nature's fresh, delicious charms, I forgot that I was a fugitive, and that my path of flight from death lay through all that made life most lovely.

The termination of that day's ride was a little Spanish settlement near the coast, called the *Pescadero*, where we found only a few Californians and two or three Americans. It is some twenty-five or thirty miles south of the ranch of my friend Dennison, which we had left in the morning. We arrived there just before dusk, and found quarters with a California widow lady. She was, like all her countrywomen, a most kind-hearted and estimable soul. There were several houses in the place, but none near hers, and this was our reason for selecting our quarters with her.

Dennison and I thought that, in the event of our being pursued, it was as well to cover up our tracks as well as possible, and give rise to as little surmise as we could as to who we were. Accordingly, he told the widow that I was an American priest traveling through southern California for the purpose of visiting the various Missions, and obtaining material for a book I was writing concerning their history. At the same time, to guard against accidents, he informed her at once that I could speak no Spanish. Of course the Californian, Ramon, was in the secret. This introduction was sufficient to insure *Padre Don Eduardo* —as Dennison called me—a good supper, the best bed in the house, and the attention and respect of everybody, great and small, about the premises. I was born and educated in the Roman Catholic Church, and when the old lady and her daughter, who spoke a little English, were making my bed, I made the sign of the cross,—not in derision,—far from it. I thanked God for my safe deliverance from my enemies so far, and repeated the prayers of the Church.

In the morning, I found a very nice breakfast prepared for me, and, having finished it, we got ready to resume our journey. I asked the widow for my bill, but she replied, *Nada, nada, Padre,* and seemed astonished that I should suppose any charge would be made to a priest in her house. I managed, however, after a good deal of persuasion, to get her to accept a five-dollar piece. All being in readiness, I bid the old lady good by, and we mounted and commenced our second day's journey.

We were to travel, that day, as far as the city of Santa Cruz, distant forty miles from the Pescadero. We attempted, in pursuance of our invariable plan, to avoid the main road, and started along the sea-beach, but soon found that the road was impracticable. We came to a point rendered impassable by the high tide, and were compelled to turn back and follow the public road. We met no one, however, except a nephew of ex-Governor McDougal, who was going to a sheep-ranch near Santa Cruz. He looked very hard at me, and asked me if my name was not Johnstone, and if I did not live at Halfmoon Bay. I knew the gentleman he took me for, and answered "Yes." Thus I passed myself on him for James Johnstone, Esq., an old friend of mine, and owner of a large tract of land at Halfmoon Bay. He was a mere lad, not over sixteen years of age, and had been on the road, alone, for three days. He asked me if I knew his uncle, Governor John McDougal; I replied that I did, and that his uncle George was an old friend of mine. I also told him that I was slightly acquainted with his father, Colonel William McDougal, when he was a member of the state legislature. Poor little fellow! he little dreamed that the man who knew his people so well was a fugitive for his life. He traveled with us until we had crossed a small river a few miles this side of Santa Cruz, which we had to swim, and then left us, having arrived at the place of his destination. We continued on toward the city. The ride was, of course, the more tedious to me on account of the soreness which I still felt from my fall.

On arriving within about half a mile of the town, Dennison proposed that I should wait outside while he and Ramon went in to reconnoiter. It was desirable, if possible, to pass Santa Cruz without going through it, the more especially as it was Sunday, and almost everybody from the country was in town. Besides, we had no means of knowing what reports might have reached there with regard to my flight, nor how the people stood affected as to the Vigilance Committee. Accordingly, Ramon furnished me with a fresh horse, and, while he and Dennison rode into town, I fastened him to a fence in a lane near the city, and hid myself in a ditch hard by until they should return. The heat and fatigue of the day had thrown me into a burning fever. There was very little water in the ditch, and a great many cattle about it. Nevertheless, I had to drink every few minutes, notwithstanding I discovered, from the singular taste of the water, that, in the language of Dr. Ollapod, "the cows had been here." Ramon and Dennison did not return for three hours. At last they came, having ascertained the only feasible route without having to inquire while I was with them. They informed me that it was necessary we should travel some fifteen miles farther, in order to get to a suitable stopping-place. Accordingly, all sick and sore as I was, I again mounted, and we galloped straight through the town without let or hindrance.

On the outskirts on the other side, we fell in with one of the brothers Castro,—a family well known in that section of the state. He was a relative of Ramon, and appeared delighted to see him. Dennison told him the old story about my being an American priest unable to speak Spanish, which was, of course, enough to insure me his good will and respect.

This Castro sympathized with the Vigilance Committee. His reason for it was that he thought it was a demonstration against the judges and lawyers. He had been subjected to many vexatious land suits, as he said, and, besides, disliked "los Yankees," as he called the Americans. One of them had married one of his daughters, and inveigled him into a speculation of building a grist and saw mill, by which he had lost several thousand dollars. It stood upon the opposite side of the town; indeed, the ditch above mentioned, in which I was hid, was the mill-race of the establishment. There was not enough water in it to swim a toy boat, much less to turn a wheel for a mill.

We soon parted company with this gentleman, and rode on until we reached the hacienda of his brother, distant some fifteen miles from the city of Santa Cruz, where we stopped for the night. This hacienda was, in itself, quite a little village. The mansion, although built of adobes, was unlike the generality of California houses. It has been built since the acquisition of the country by the Americans. It is a large, well-finished two-story house. What particularly struck me about it was the ceiling of the upper rooms, which was composed of most beautiful colored wood. There were, in all, some fifty persons about the premises.

These were the daughters, sons-in-law, and other relatives of the master, together with his dependents, servants, etc. As soon as we entered the house, our host embraced his relative Ramon, and welcomed us very kindly. Our horses were cared for, and after we had partaken of a fine repast, the old gentleman invited us upstairs into a sort of drawing-room or parlor.

Here we found a large number of persons of both sexes, who seemed to be gathered there as at a sort of evening party. Our host directed some of his people to play for us, which they did delightfully. It is seldom that one fails to observe about these large haciendas some four or five musicians who play upon instruments for the amusement of the household. It being Sunday night, after nine o'clock the dancing commenced. My friend Dennison, who is a very fine-looking fellow, and perfectly posted in the customs of the country, had brought with him a suitable dress for the occasion, and, being a good dancer, figured very gayly in the revels. He spoke the language of the country very fluently, was quite a beau, and apparently a great favorite with the dark-eyed *señoritas*. Ramon also took an active part in the festivities, while a son-in-law of my host, who spoke English, and myself entertained each other in conversation. Thus the evening passed off very pleasantly. Long before the dancers had begun to flag, I retired for the night to a good bed and sound sleep.

While at breakfast the next morning, the old gentleman, through Dennison, who interpreted, asked me a great many questions. We had dropped the character of the priest, and I found that the title of Judge gained for me the respect of all. He asked me, among other things, how old I was. I told him forty-three. He replied that I must be at least sixty. "Why," said he, "I look younger than you, and I am fifty-five." I should suppose, from his appearance, that that was about his age. He was very large, probably weighing from two hundred to two hundred and twenty-five pounds. I must have looked much older than forty-three, for my beard was quite white, and I had not shaved for six weeks. As there was no necessity, however, for deceiving him with regard to my age, I told him the truth,— that I was forty-three. He said that he had observed the Americans to be like women in this respect,— that they never told their real age.

We remained at the hospitable mansion of the old gentleman nearly all that day, waiting for one of his sons to get ready, who was to accompany us as far as San Luis Obispo, a distance of two hundred miles. He was going in search of a younger brother, who had wandered away from home in company with some Sonorans. He was the youngest child, and they were anxious to get him back. Mr. Castro's family are as fine specimens of the old Californians as one would wish to see. The old gentleman himself, hale, hearty, and robust, with a frank, manly countenance, bespeaking the kindness and benevolence of his heart; his sons, tall, active, and graceful, and withal very intelligent. His wife, a good-natured, amiable, and lively old lady, still retaining the traces of her youthful beauty; while her daughters are possessed of all the bewitching little graces of mind and body which make the Spanish beauty so irresistible. Long shall I remember the happy hours of respite from sorrow and anxiety which I enjoyed under that hospitable roof, and I here again and again thank them from the bottom of my heart for their kindness to me.

At length, young Castro being ready, and having caught four fine horses for his journey, we bade adieu to our kind host and hostess, and in the cool of the afternoon again departed on our way. We rode, that evening, some twenty miles, leisurely cantering along the road, driving before us our spare horses, now numbering ten in all. A little after night we stopped at the house of —— ——, a Mexican, whose name I have forgotten. Here we found tolerable quarters, and were amused by the story of our host's adventures during the war with Mexico. He had been a lieutenant in Santa Anna's army, and, in one of the engagements with General Scott's forces, was taken prisoner. His strong resemblance to an Irishman, who had deserted from the American ranks, nearly proved fatal to him. Indeed, he was about to be ordered to be shot, but managed at the last moment to convince the Americans that he was really a Mexican. He lived here on a little ranch of his own, and stated that before the war he had been acting in the capacity of private secretary to one of the governors of California. He was an important witness in many of the land cases then and now pending.

We retired for the night, intending to make an early start in the morning, and, if possible, spend our Fourth of July in Santa Bárbara, distant three hundred miles. I slept very well and enjoyed my rest, and, after breakfast on the following morning, the first day of July, we left Santa Cruz County and entered Monterey. We considered that, after passing through San Juan,—a little town in Monterey County,—we should be fairly on our journey, and I out of danger; for from that point we would bid adieu to the "white settlements" and enter the hospitable land of the Spaniard. I now began to get accustomed to riding, which at first fatigued me dreadfully. When I started, I was very fat, weighing one hundred and eighty-two pounds, and entirely unused to exercise. Add to this the entire novelty, to me, of our mode of traveling, and it may be imagined that I suffered not a little. I was getting the better of it, however, by this time, notwithstanding I was still very sore from my fall. We started away at a slashing pace. It was a lovely morning; our horses felt fresh, and we were in good spirits. There are many beauties in the scenery of Monterey, but I saw nothing that struck me as agreeably as the flowery carpet of Santa Cruz. It was just twenty-seven miles from our point of departure to the Mission of Soledad. This distance we rode at a full gallop, Ramon and young Castro driving the extra horses ahead of us. When we arrived there, some of the people about the place seemed to be very anxious to know who I was; and to their inquiries Dennison replied with the story of the priest. They were just taking their coffee as we rode up, and invited us to partake, but we declined, and rode on without making any stay, thus affording me but a poor opportunity to observe the place. From the hasty view I had of it, however, it appeared like most of the old Missions in the lower country, — considerably gone to decay, yet bearing evidences of former wealth, taste, and industry. Some miles farther on, we came to the Mission of San Antonio. There is nothing remarkable about this Mission. The usual amount of dirt was to be seen, and the usual number of lazy *peones* and Indians lying listlessly about. Here we stopped about two hours, in order to feed and water our horses, and give them time to rest. After taking some refreshment ourselves, and washing it down with one or two bottles of bad claret, we again mounted, and continued our journey. We rode until dark, and then, for the first time prepared to *camp out*. We had ridden, in all, that day, ninety miles.

We pitched our camp near an Indian's hut, and, having purchased of him a rabbit and a piece of mutton, we cooked and ate our supper, and laid down to sleep. It was a beautiful summer night, and I slept as quietly under the stars as ever I did under the canopy of a luxurious bed. Nothing disturbed my rest, except a curious dream I had toward morning, — that the Indians had robbed me, and thrown me down a well. At daylight we were astir, and, having eaten our breakfast and saddled the horses, we started at a gallop for San Luis Obispo.

After we had ridden by the most unfrequented roads several miles, just as the trail we were following turned around the foot of a low hill, we suddenly came upon a band of Sonorans, twenty-five or thirty in number. Apparently, they were returning from the mines, and having found water, encamped, and were in the act of cooking part of a beef they had just killed when we came upon them. This was in a very wild and lonely place. I had about my person a large sum of money, and my companions appeared somewhat alarmed. Nevertheless, the best policy was to show no fear; so we rode boldly up and asked them where we could get some water. They pointed to a clump of flags or rushes a short distance from their camp. They were all well armed, and he who was apparently their leader was a very fine-looking and well-dressed man. Their horses, which were also very fine, were grazing about them unsaddled. We went to the water, and, while there, Dennison cautioned me not to speak, and, above all, not to dismount, saying that they were probably banditti, and, at any rate, had a great aversion to Americans, who sometimes drove their people from the mines.

We found the water very bad. It was as white as milk, being strongly impregnated with sulphur; nevertheless, being very thirsty, we dipped some of it up in a tin cup and drank it. As we rode off, my companions bid the Sonorans good day, and Ramon, to prevent appearance of alarm on our part, carelessly asked them for a piece of their meat, which they gave him, and as soon as we had got a few yards from their camp, we put spurs to our horses and galloped away, very glad to get out of such dubious company.

We rode but a few miles before we stopped to feed, water, and change our horses at the Mission of San Miguel. While here, the young horse that Castro was riding was stampeded by some Indians, and three hours were lost in endeavoring to recapture him, but without success. We secured the saddle, which he had thrown off in his flight, and went on without him. Without anything of note occurring, we shortly arrived at a large plain or desert, in which was a hot spring. Here we dismounted and took a most refreshing bath. We likewise met here some of Castro's friends, and he, after conversing with them a little while, determined to go back and again attempt to recover his lost horse, and so parted with us. After two or three hours of brisk riding, we came to the Rancho Santa Margarita, where we again stopped to rest and change. This rancho was once a Mission, but is sadly gone to decay. The old Mission building is inhabited by a California woman, who keeps therein a kind of restaurant and liquor-store. The place, however, in point of stock and extent of land, is said to be one of the most valuable in the state.

After resting sufficiently, we again started, and soon completed the remaining twelve miles of our journey, which brought us to the town of San Luis Obispo, making a day's ride, in all, of eighty miles. I remained outside of the town, while Dennison and Ramon went in to reconnoiter and find a place for the horses, taking mine with them, but leaving the saddle with me to avert suspicion. About dark they returned, and, reporting that all was right, we went together into the town, and ordered supper at a sort of hostelry near the old Mission building. While we were seated at the table, a party of Americans entered the room and eyed me very closely. I joined immediately in the conversation of my companions, and, from certain indications, feared that one of the newcomers knew me. After supper, Ramon and I followed him out to see if he would make a demonstration, or if any attempt was on foot to arrest me. He entered a place where a number of Spaniards were playing at billiards, and sat down. I seated myself at once beside him, determined to ascertain whether he really knew me. I now became convinced, though he looked at me very hard, that, if he had ever known me at all, he did not now recognize me, and felt greatly relieved. We applied to a blacksmith to get our horses shod, but on being informed that it would require half of the next day to get it done, we were compelled to postpone it until we should reach Santa Bárbara. I did not see much worthy of note in the town, except the old church. There are no fine buildings there, and, after wandering about an hour or two, I became sleepy, when, instead of going to the tavern, I entered the *corral* where the horses were feeding, and, making a bed of the sweat-blankets and my overcoat, with plenty of hay, I laid down and slept soundly. This, the second night of my "camping out," was, like the first, marked by a singular dream. I dreamed that I was in Sacramento, and that a party of *Vigilantes*, headed by Richard N. Berry, were pursuing me, and succeeded in capturing me, but that I subsequently escaped. What put Berry's name into my head I cannot imagine, for he never was, that I know of, a member of the Committee.

At daylight, we started from San Luis Obispo, determined, if possible, to reach Santa Bárbara that night. Just outside the city, we found a man lying on the road with a bottle of brandy beside him and his horse quietly standing near. As we approached, he mounted and joined our company. He informed us that he was a blacksmith, and was then building a shop about five miles from town. He said that, the preceding evening, he had been to town on some business, but that while there he had drunk too much, and his bottle proving too heavy for him on his way home, he had fallen asleep on the roadside, while his horse quietly stayed by him all night. After looking intently at me for some time, he told me he thought, he knew me. I replied that I thought it likely, determined, if he did know me, to deny my identity, and to face him down that I had never heard of an individual of my name. He finally came to the conclusion that he was mistaken, and I thought it probable, inasmuch as he said he never had been in San Francisco. He said he had formerly been sheriff of San Luis County, and spoke to me of many of my acquaintances, among them Col. Parker H. French, who had represented the county in the legislature two years before. He soon reached his place of destination, and, taking a parting drink out of the jolly ex-sheriff's bottle, we bid him adieu, and galloped on our journey.

After riding between thirty-five and forty miles without drawing rein, we lost our way, and went at least two leagues off of the road. It was a very sultry day, and the fatigue and heat of the ride had again brought on my fever. Ramon, the guide, said the sun would have cooked an egg in our hands if we could have held it. We could absolutely see the heat in little waves conforming to the surface of the sandy plain. For miles around us, it was one scorching, unbroken series of sand-hillocks, reminding me of what I had read of African deserts. Not a spear of grass, nothing but the shining waves of sand as the wind had shaped them.

For hours I had not tasted water, and the heat and my burning fever made them appear days. My tongue became thick, my throat parched, and I felt a sensation like choking. Finally, to my great joy, after two hours' search, we again found the road, and about two o'clock, P. M., we arrived at a place, *Los Álamos*, distant about fifty miles from the town of San Luis Obispo. Here we changed horses, and endeavored to get something to eat, but without success. We got some water, however, which greatly refreshed us, and then rode on over a bad road to the Mission of Santa Inéz. Before we arrived there, I quite gave out with fatigue, fever, and thirst. I was two or three miles behind my companions, they having ridden on to encourage me to push my animal. I had neither strength to whip or spur him. As I was lagging along the road, more dead than alive, and suffering dreadfully from fever and thirst, I saw some cattle, that were ahead of me, leave the road, and at once knew they must be going for water. I followed them and found it, but, on attempting to dismount, my suffering was so intense that I fairly fainted by the side of the stream. How long I was in that condition I cannot say, but, on reviving, I found my horse standing beside me. He was very gentle at all times, but then much too tired to stray away. After bathing my wrists and face, I took a drink, which greatly refreshed me, and, again mounting my horse, I went back to the road and traveled on. After going some distance, the road led me to a crossing-place, higher up on the same stream from which I had drunk. Here I found Ramon waiting for me, who informed me that Dennison, fearing something had happened, had ridden back on the road in search of me. After some time he returned, and was furiously angry. I told him what had happened, and he swore like a trooper. I was too much exhausted to answer back. He had gone back six miles in search of me, of course passing me when I was off the road at the water. He told me that he had avoided telling me before a fact which he knew, viz., that the blacksmith to whom we had applied to get our horses shod at San Luis Obispo had once worked in San Francisco for a man named Blaisdell, and had recognized me, and he had been fearful all day that he would get up a party and follow us. He told me that he was responsible to my friends in San Francisco for my safety, and so long as that was the case, I must look to him for water or anything else that I wanted. All this was very true and reasonable, but I, also, not being in the best of humors, after a while found strength to quarrel back at him, and we had a regular swearing match, in which I was decidedly wrong, for the poor fellow *was* responsible for my safety, and was doing all that he could to secure it.

After our spat was over, he pointed to a mountain ahead of us, and told me it was Santa Ynez Mountain, and we must cross it that night if the horses could carry us. The quarrel had waked me up, and I had recovered strength. I told him I could cross it if the horse could, and could do anything else that he or any other man could do,—poor, weak boaster that I was,—and thus, refreshed with an hour's rest, and water, and *wrath*, we started to cross the mountain of Santa Ynez,—and what a mountain! To me, tired as I was, and not accustomed to anything of the sort, it seemed impossible, in the jaded condition of our horses, to cross that night.

Before commencing the ascent, Dennison told me to recall to my mind the worst hill I had ever traveled up, and then add a hundred per cent to it, and I would have some idea of the one before us. I laughed, and told him to "jog on." Each of us had to lead a spare horse, but in my exhausted condition I had to relinquish mine before we got half-way over. Dennison then led two. It was quite dark before we reached the summit, up to which point I got on pretty well; but in descending the other side I was less fortunate. I was twice unhorsed, probably from not letting my animal take his own way. Dennison laughed at me, and told me I was worse than an old woman, but presently he got a fall himself, and asked us, while he was picking himself up, "if we were going to leave him in that way." I told him he was worse than two old women. Ramon always assisted me, but suffered Dennison to shift for himself. My eyesight, which is miserable at night, came very near being rendered permanently useless in one eye, by a piece of wood that ran into it. It pained me so much that I thought I must have put it out; fortunately, however, I had not, though the wound was very severe.

At length, after stumbling and sliding down the tortuous trail in the darkness, risking, every moment, the necks of both riders and beasts, we reached the plain below, and rode toward the *Refugio Ranch*, where we arrived about nine o'clock in the evening, having traveled, that day, more than one hundred miles. Here, to our great disappointment, owing to the lateness of the hour, we could get nothing to eat or drink. I had not tasted a mouthful since morning, and, weak, sick, and disheartened, I threw myself down in the corral, spurs and all, and slept till daylight.

In the morning, it being the Fourth of July, Dennison brought me a bottle of bad brandy, and, after drinking some of it, I rubbed myself with the balance. We then got a good breakfast, which, as may be supposed, we relished exceedingly. After breakfast, we hired fresh horses with which to ride into Santa Bárbara, distant but a few miles, and left our own at the ranch to rest. After we had started, Dennison told me that his intention was to remain in Santa Bárbara three days, so as to thoroughly recruit the horses, and give ourselves an opportunity to rest and bathe in the hot springs. On reflection, I thought if that was the case, I had better remain at the *Refugio*. My eye was weeping blood and matter, and paining me very much, and I was otherwise very sick and sore. Besides, the rancho was a more retired place than the town, and there was less chance of my being identified by the sheriff of the county, or any sympathizers with the Vigilance Committee. Dennison agreed with me, and it was arranged that he should send back on the following Monday for me and the horses. Accordingly, we returned to the house to make the arrangements for my stay. He told them that I was sick, and desired to rest there for a few days. This was true, for I was almost worn out. They consented to the arrangement, and Dennison and Ramon rode on to the town.

I could not then speak or understand a word of Spanish, and, considering my condition in other respects, the day bid fair to be a dull Fourth of July to me. Situated as I was, however, I cared little for pleasure of any kind. I was playing the "game of life," and had to keep myself guarded at all points. Pleasures or comforts were secondary considerations with me. Mustering all my philosophy, I essayed to revive my drooping spirits by looking about me. At the *Rancho Refugio* there are three main buildings, all, of course, built of adobes, together with several small outhouses of the same construction. There are, probably, about the place from forty to fifty persons, all related to a well-known and generally respectable family in that county, by the name of *Ortega*. I became acquainted with many of them afterward, during my long stay in Santa Bárbara, which was destined to be much longer than I then anticipated. Little did I dream, that morning, that I was standing in a county whose boundary I would not again cross until I had roamed for seven months among its mountains, a hunted and despairing man, with scarcely life, and less of hope. Had such a vision crossed my mind, I should not, as I did, have endeavored to shake off my sadness, and enter into some sort of companionship with the people around me.

The *Refugio* is celebrated in the history of California as having, many years ago, been plundered by freebooters. And indeed, on looking around on the countenances of some of its residents and frequenters, I could not help thinking that, like our armies in Mexico, the freebooters had left their mark behind them; for many of them *looked* the freebooter still.

At one of the houses, they sold villainous brandy for a dollar a bottle, and an old fellow whom they called *Don Miguel Cota*, and who appeared to be a man of some consequence among them, had a decided relish for it. Seeing that I was possessed of the means of gratifying his *penchant*, he assiduously cultivated my acquaintance, and we struck up at once such a friendship as could exist when neither of us spoke a word of the other's language. However, we got on tolerably well, and, for want of better employment, I got the old Don as drunk as any patriot on that glorious day could have desired to see him. Without exactly understanding what there was particularly in the day to license unusual excess, he seemed to take it for granted that there must be something very glorious about it, and entered into the patriotism of the occasion with great spirit. Unhappily, however, in getting old *Don Miguel* drunk, I intoxicated with rage his better half, *Señora Cota*. She delivered herself of an oration to me, which, judging from the expression of her countenance — by no means beautiful even in repose — and her violent gesticulation, I took to be anything but complimentary. As it was couched, however, in the Spanish tongue, all, save the gesture which accompanied it, was thrown away. That, however, was sufficient, and, like the clown in the circus, I understood her *very well*, though I did not know what she said. She made me understand this much: that if I had anything to give away, I had much better present it to her, than spend it to purchase brandy with which to fuddle her lord and master. Finally, however, I managed to conciliate her by giving one of the children a piece of money, and, after a great deal of pretense of not understanding me, I prevailed on her to make me a cup of tea.

I was stopping with another branch of the family, who were apparently well off, and lived in the center adobe. Notwithstanding I paid well for all I got, when night came I found my bed made for me outside of the house. They appeared to have certain rules, from which they would not vary. All who belonged to the family, and had rights and privileges about the premises, could sleep within doors, but those who were not of the family, and had no rights in common with them, had to sleep out, notwithstanding there was abundance of room within.

The second day of my stay at the ranch, several personages, apparently not belonging to the household, made their appearance. Among them were two, who, as they will hereafter figure in this narrative, I may as well introduce to the reader now. One of them was perhaps thirty-five years of age, of medium size, well formed, of rather dark complexion, and was named Pedro Ortega, and resided at a place called *Arroyo Hondo*. The other was younger and smaller in stature than his companion, with rather a lighter skin; he was said to be well connected in Santa Bárbara, and resided at a ranch known as *Las Cruces*. Both of them spoke English very well. Pedro, as well as old Miguel, was very fond of his "*poco cognac*," and we very soon struck up an acquaintance. He, as well as his companion, asked me a great many questions concerning myself, all of which I answered as I thought proper. I could not help thinking that, in consideration of our short acquaintance, they treated me more like "down-easters" than the descendants of Cortés. I did not then, however, suspect their object. I told them that I was a drover, and was then on my way to Los Angeles to buy horses. They said they would like to sell me a horse, and

I replied that on my return I would probably purchase of them. Not long after this, the companion of Pedro told me that Don Miguel had said that I had told him I had five thousand dollars about me. I then began to suspect the character of my gentleman. I knew that he had told me a lie, and took it for granted that he must have some object in it. I asked him how it was possible that Miguel had said I told him so, when he spoke not a word of English nor I of Spanish. This appeared to confuse him, and he was for some time silent. I told him, however, in a very frank way, in order to throw him off the scent, that my money was to come down by the steamer to Santa Bárbara; that it would have been too unwieldy to have brought it along the road, and besides, I did not intend to make any purchases until I had reached Los Angeles, but that, on my return, I would probably purchase of him. They appeared very anxious to know how much money I had with me, and Pedro suggested the idea of my loaning him a small sum, only five dollars, and taking an order for it on a gentleman residing near Santa Bárbara, whom I knew very well by reputation. The five dollars was a matter of no consequence, but as I suspected it was only a *ruse* to get a sight at my purse, I politely declined. I bought them, however, as much brandy as they could drink, which was not a little, for they were decidedly good drinkers, and nothing more was said about the money that day. At dark I retired again to my bed outside the house.

CHAPTER III

*The Fatal Sisters hover round our birth,
And dash with bitter dregs our cup on earth.*
Trans. Ancient Poem.

I FORGOT to mention in the last chapter that I had received a message from Dennison, that he wanted me to meet him in the town of Santa Bárbara on Sunday, the sixth of July, instead of Monday, as had been arranged when we parted. I accordingly had my horses corraled the next morning while at breakfast, and, having hired a young Spaniard to drive the extra ones for me, was soon ready to start. I made signs to the *señora* to know how much I owed her, to which she replied, with a shrug of her shoulders, "*¿Quien sabe?*" and was apparently much pleased when I gave her six dollars. I then mounted, and, accompanied by my guide, started for the city of Santa Bárbara. I had now ridden nearly five hundred miles from San Francisco, and certainly thought I had a right to congratulate myself on my escape from all peril. As I rode along that lovely morning, excepting bodily fatigue I had no feelings but those of pleasure, and my heart was full of thankfulness to a merciful Providence for my deliverance from my enemies. Visions of future happiness and comfort in the bosom of my family, far away from the harpies from whose persecution I was fleeing, flitted through my mind, and I could already hear, in fancy, the welcome of my wife and the prattle of my children. Joy, resentment, the hope of vengeance, gratitude to my friends,—in short, almost every feeling, by turns, took possession of me, except apprehension; of that I was free. But, alas! how true is it that "Man proposes, but God disposes." How little did I imagine, as I reveled in the sweet freshness of that summer morning, that the heart then so lightly bounding with joy and hope would, ere that summer evening, be crushed and almost pulseless with despair! But to my story. We cantered gayly along the road, with nothing of interest occurring, except an ineffectual attempt to purchase some brandy for my guide, at a ranch which he told me belonged to *Señor Ignacio Ortega*, till we came in sight of the *Dos Pueblos*, the residence of Dr. Nicholas A. Den, an Irish gentleman, who has resided in California a great number of years, and is one of the wealthiest, as well as one of the noblest, men in the state. Of him, to whom I have done myself the honor to dedicate this poor narrative, I shall have more to say hereafter. The guide stopped to have a little chat with an *amigo*, the *mayordomo* of the establishment, while I rode on, not caring to be identified by any Americans who might be about the place. The guide soon overtook me, and informed me that the Doctor was not at home. I had been introduced to him by an acquaintance, the winter previous, in Sacramento, but at this time, not knowing his feelings in relation to the Committee, (God forgive me for such injustice!) I preferred not to meet him. It was seventeen miles farther to the city. We met no one on the road, until within a few miles of our destination. A great many persons were riding about on horseback and in wagons, and seemed to be enjoying themselves very much, apparently not having quite got over the hilarity of the glorious Fourth. I noticed a wagon coming toward me, containing six men, whom, from their appearance, I took to be Irishmen. They eyed me very closely as they passed, which I attributed to the fact that it was not customary to see a stranger loitering along the road with six horses. I must have looked very suspicious too: my beard was long and white, and I had a patch over my wounded eye, not giving a very agreeable expression to my countenance. I was sunburnt and travel-stained, and my weapons, too, were in sight. They stopped, and I heard one of them say, "I think he is an old horse-thief." I, at this, rode up to them, not wishing to have a hue and cry raised against me on a false accusation, which might as well have been true, as far as the consequences were concerned, if any of the Vigilance Committee were about. One of the party gave me a sign, which I understood, and returned to him. This man *must* have known me. He then said in a low voice, "I knew you had been there." He asked me to drink some brandy out of a bottle they had with them in the wagon, which I did. He then said to his companions, "He is all right," which I was very glad to hear. They asked me a great many questions, and in reply to one touching my business in that part of the country, I told them the old story about buying horses in Los Angeles. I knew the faces of two of them, but could not remember where I had seen them. One of them told me he thought he had seen me before. I told them that I was acquainted with their senator, the Hon. Pablo De la Guerra, and also with their representative, Gen. Covarrubias. One of them asked me if I knew the General's son Nicolas, to which I replied, "Yes; he is a clerk in the banking house of Palmer, Cook, & Co." They appeared satisfied that I was not a horse-thief, and after we had taken some more brandy all round, they drove off. I remained about the outskirts of the town some time, waiting for Dennison and Ramon to come out and meet me, but they did not come. I tried to make my guide understand that I wanted him to go into the city and find them, and tell them that I was waiting for them outside, but he either did not or would not comprehend me, and I, at length, very foolishly resolved to go at once into the town and find them myself.

I rode up to a hotel and restaurant kept by a Frenchman, and, before I dismounted, saw that I was recognized by one Albert Packard, formerly a shoemaker. He had resided a long time in Santa Bárbara, had married a native California lady and turned lawyer. My object in going to this place was to find Dennison, as it appeared to be the only hotel of note in the town, and I thought it most likely I should find him there. Packard was sitting on the porch, and finding I was recognized, I thought it best to put on a bold front; accordingly, I dismounted and took a seat beside him. We entered into conversation, and talked over pretty much all the topics of the day, including the Vigilance Committee, politics, &c. He told me that he was in favor of Col. Frémont for the Presidency. I tried very hard to sound him as to his connection or sympathy with the Vigilance Committee, but he very adroitly foiled me, and I could not judge from anything he let fall whether he was for them or against them. Fool that I was! Why did not common sense whisper in my ear that he was engaging me in conversation, merely to give time to the bloodhounds of Santa Bárbara to organize and arrest me, and that while I sat there I was perhaps talking my life away? I asked him to take a glass of something with me, thinking that a drink might make him communicative, but he replied that he seldom took anything before dinner. I had *heard* that he was a hunter up of fraudulent land claims, and a standing witness about the Land Commission; I *knew* that he was a humbug, and a libel on his adopted profession; he had *told* me that he was a Black Republican, and I might have *known* that he was a *Vigilante*. The fellow afterward wrote a letter to the San Francisco *Bulletin*, in which he gave an account of this interview, and made it appear that I did not think he recognized me. He knew very well that I knew he recognized me all the time. What his object was in telling so foolish and harmless a lie I do not know. I suppose, however, it was a cheap opportunity to gratify a natural inclination.*

---

* The following letter from Packard apppeared in the San Francisco *Evening Bulletin* [July 11th]: —

SANTA BÁRBARA, July 6, '56.

The usual tranquillity of our town has been disturbed to-day by the arrival of McGowan. The gent alighted at the Fonda at about midday, from a very tired horse, in company with a Mexican. McGowan straightway entered into a conversation with me, representing himself to be a cattle-drover, and in fact he somewhat resembled one, although I recognized him at once. But as he wished, apparently, to preserve an incognito, of course I did not interfere with his plan, and was very much amused with his views of matters and things in general. I could not help giving him the items of news as to what would probably be the fate of Judge McGowan if he should be taken to San Francisco. This caused him to give certain spasmodic jerks not very peculiar to cattle-drovers in general. He privately assured me

While we were conversing, a large-sized, well-dressed man approached, and, after regarding me intently for a moment, walked away. I asked Packard who he was, and he informed me that his name was George Parkinson, and that he had been, until recently, employed in the lighthouse at Point Conception. Packard expressed his surprise that I did not know him; I told him I had no recollection of ever having seen him before, and it was the truth. It was evident, however, that he doubted my statement. In a few moments, three other persons approached and looked at me very closely. One of them I had known for a long time. His name was A. F. Hinchman; he had called himself a lawyer in San Francisco in 1850, and had tried several cases before me when I held court in the old Plaza building. He was there only a short time, however; for so soon as men who were really lawyers began to be numerous in San Francisco, he found his level and migrated to Santa Bárbara, which county he represented in the assembly in the year 1852, and there distinguished himself by being the only member of the house who voted in favor of considering a foolish and somewhat insolent negro petition. He had married a native California lady, in order, it is said, to get a comfortable livelihood. He gave me a nod as he approached, but I did not return it, not being sure that he recognized me in the dress I wore. I was afraid of him, for his antecedents were such as to entitle him to full membership with the "purest and best," and I felt quite certain that he at least sympathized with them. Besides, he was opposed to me politically, and I had by this time come to the conclusion that politics had

---

that the great Democratic party would right all the trouble in San Francisco, and in the course of a few months all things would be in their old position. He allowed that Howard made a blunder in taking to the stump through the country. He was recognized by several people while he was conversing with me, and he appeared to be very nervous and uneasy. He complained bitterly about the hardships he had experienced since he had left San Francisco,—that the whisky was very bad on the road. The beds at ranches he voted as great nuisances, and said that the people would hardly be worth selling in Georgia. In fact, the old scamp appeared to be completely *used up* in both mind and body.

much to do with the crusade against me. Of the two others, Packard told me that the larger one was Russell Heath, Esq., the sheriff of the county. I afterward learned that these fellows had instigated this gentleman to arrest me and hand me over to the Committee. The smaller one was a red-headed, sneaking-looking cur named Harvey Benjamin Blake, a mischief-making, nose poking busybody, who had earned for himself, by his pe culiar gifts, the *sobriquet* of "*Cochi Gueri*" or white pig. I at once identified him as the former sweeper out of Ever ett's hatter's shop in Clay Street, San Francisco. He, too, had, in some unaccountable manner, made himself acceptable to a wealthy California lady, and is now one of the so-called merchant princes of the state. He was a tool and sympathizer of the Vigilance Committee, and he and Hinchman were partners in the firm of Burton, Blake, and Hinchman. The principal of the firm, Mr. Lewis Burton, is said to be a gentleman. It must be admitted, however, that he has the misfortune to be in horribly suspicious company.

Strange to say, I did not even yet suspect that anything was wrong, and when they went away without making any attempt to arrest me, I attributed their close scrutiny of me to a mere curiosity to see the "ubiquitous Ned," as the papers called me. I did not then know that they had been apprised of my coming, and were raising a larger party preparatory to making a demonstration. Gallant heroes! Four stalwart men did not dare to attempt the arrest of one old man, broken down by a ride of five hundred miles, and scarcely able to walk!

I afterwards learned that one Doctor S. B. Brinkerhoff, one of the "purifiers," had asked the Hon. Pablo De la Guerra if he could identify me. He told him that he could, if I was in the city, but he did not think I was there, not having seen me. The fact was, that, being under indictment for murder, I did not choose to call on any of my friends and run the risk of compromising them, but was only desirous of getting on to Mexico, and would have continued on my journey at once if I had only been able to find Dennison and Ramon.

When the above-mentioned parties had left, Packard

stepped into the house to dinner. I entered also, and was at once recognized by Capt. Bache of the Coast Survey, who was attached to the surveying schooner then lying in the harbor. He looked at me and smiled. I inquired for the room occupied by Dennison and Ramon. It was shown me, and I threw myself on the bed, and, notwithstanding I did not feel altogether easy, could scarcely keep awake. I fell into several "cat-naps," but suddenly something within me told me not to sleep. A sudden presentiment of danger took possession of me, and I became thoroughly alarmed. I rapidly ran over in my mind the conversation with Packard, and recalled the looks of the men who had stared at me so on the porch, and was thunderstruck at my stupidity in not having suspected my danger before.

Wondering why Dennison did not come to me,—for he must have heard of my arrival,—I took my knife and one of my pistols and laid them on the bed beside me. Presently I saw a man enter and fasten, on the inside, the door that led into the street. I grasped my pistol, determined, if he attempted to molest me, to shoot him. I said to him, "What are you doing?" Said he, "They are going to arrest you." "For what?" said I. He replied, "Jem"—meaning Dennison—"has told me all." I asked him where Dennison was, stating that I had been an hour and a half in town, and he had not come near me. He replied, "He will be here soon."

I now recognized in my companion the large, well-dressed man I had observed on the porch. He told me his name was George Parkinson; that he was formerly a partner of James Cusick, one of the expatriated, and that he would befriend me. He was an Irishman, and I thought I could trust him. In a moment more Dennison entered. "Come," said he; "there is no time to lose." Parkinson took one of my derringer pistols out of my belt, saying that we would go to his room, where he would give me another six-shooter, and we stepped into the street. The place was by this time alive with people running to and fro. We walked about two hundred yards before we reached the place for which we had started, and I noticed with gloomy forebodings that I was the object on which all eyes were turned. We found the door of our place of refuge

"Judge," said he, "there is no time to be lost. Vill you trust yourself to me? I will protect you as far as I am able."— *Page 72.*

closed! I heard shouts in the distance, and despair began gradually to steal over me. At this moment, when I was about giving up all for lost, a horseman came dashing toward us at full speed, mounted on a magnificent animal beautifully caparisoned. He reined up in front of us, and, springing to the ground, said to those who were with me, "The party is made, and the hunt is up for *him*," pointing to me. I recognized the speaker at once. It was Jack Power. Bandit and Destroying Angel though he may be, he was my guardian angel then, and may Heaven, which sent him to my succor, be merciful to him in his hour of need. I had seen him in San Francisco in 1849, and he recognized me at once. "Judge," said he, "there is no time to be lost. Will you trust yourself to me? I will protect you as far as I am able."

Parkinson and Dennison did not want me to leave them, but I knew Power's desperate courage well, and would have chosen him out of the whole state for a partner in a hopeless fight. Something prompted me to at once assent to his proposal, and I did so. In an instant we were gone, leaving my companions standing in the street, and in less than *three minutes* Dennison was arrested, but I had vanished. Jack ran with me about twenty yards up a street at right angles with the one in which he found us, passed me through the window of a house, rolled me up in about forty yards of carpeting he found lying on the floor, told the woman of the house, in Spanish, what he had done, cautioning her to say nothing, and then rushed out and joined in the pursuit after me, louder than the loudest, while the woman quietly took her seat in the doorway and commenced to sing. It was all done in less time than it has taken me to tell it. I had, in an instant, as it were, been snatched from certain death!

The pack was now in full cry, and, as I lay in the carpet, how wildly my heart beat as I heard them approach nearer and nearer, and how sweetly hope would whisper to me as the noise of the hunt receded! As I afterward learned, there were at least one hundred men in the pursuit, some mounted and some on foot, armed with guns, pistols, and swords. All the idlers, loafers, and scum of Santa Bárbara had joined in the "hue and cry." But an instant, and they thought their hands were on me; in another, I had vanished like a dream, and none, save two, in all that city, could say where. They could not realize, when they picked up my coat and waistcoat, which, a moment before, I had dropped in my flight, that I was not in them. The din was terrible; the tramping of hoofs and yells of the mob as the chase swept, pell-mell, up one street and down another, the men shouting, and the women (naturally prone to the side of the weak) bespattering them with most unsavory epithets whose bitterness can only be expressed in the Spanish tongue, now roaring past the very house in which I was lying, now dying away in the distance, — all contributed to make up the most fiendish and unearthly howl that ever had rung in my ears. And there I lay with palpitating heart. They ransacked Santa Bárbara, but came not to me. *Jack Power was leading them!*

At length, as I afterward learned, the Hon. Pablo De la Guerra, whose inherent chivalry of nature could not permit him to sympathize with such fierce persecution of an old man not yet proven to be guilty of crime, fearing that, if this hot pursuit was continued much longer, I must be captured and delivered up to the mercies of a ruthless mob, started the report that a man had been seen running into the *tules* adjoining the garden of his house, and that I was probably the fugitive. The bloodhounds, biting at once at the bait, surrounded the house and grounds, and set fire to the *tules*, the Sheriff of the county himself applying the torch.* Some one expostulated with the Sheriff, pointing

---

* McGowan at Santa Bárbara — Attempt to Burn Him out of a Swamp — Great Excitement. — By a gentleman who arrived yesterday from Santa Bárbara, we have been told all about the attempted capture of Edward McGowan.

It appears that on Sunday morning, the 6th instant, a stranger appeared in the town of Santa Bárbara, and was seen talking for a long time with Mr. Packard, a person well known in the city. At length the two were passed by Mr. Blake, who at once recognized in the stranger none other than the notorious McGowan. A short time afterwards, Ned went to the hotel and approached Maj. Bache, of the Coast Survey, who was eating at the table. The Major immediately knew the visitor, and Ned smiled as he neared Mr. Bache's seat, and withdrew. By this time everybody had heard that the runaway was in the place, and application was made to the Sheriff that he might

out to him, that, if I was really in there, now that the *tules* were surrounded, I could not escape, and by firing it he exposed me to the horrible death of being burned alive. The expostulation was of no avail, however: he did not stay his hand.

At least two hundred persons rushed into the garden to see my burned and blackened corpse taken from the fire, and more than one of them doubtless anxious to rob it. I had forgotten to mention that the miserable reptile called the "white pig" had circulated, in order to whet the fangs of my pursuers, the ridiculous story that the Vigilance Committee had offered ten thousand dollars for my body, *dead or alive*, the Governor five thousand, and that I had five thousand *about my person*. The mob, in their anxiety to capture me, had done immense damage to Don Pablo's garden, breaking down fruit-trees and trampling the flowers underfoot, and, indeed, at one time the premises of my friend were likely to be destroyed by fire. Finally, becoming convinced that they had been on the wrong scent, and reluctantly coming to the conclusion that I had got

---

be arrested. But, while this officer was satisfying himself that there really was an indictment against McGowan for murder in San Francisco, Ned's friends became alarmed, and ran him off to the fastnesses of a swamp. The Sheriff collected a posse and started in pursuit; but, it being near night, it was not possible to enter the swamp to make search with any prospect of success, so he spread his posse around and set fire to the tules. Meanwhile the darkness approached, and the search was given over.

It was now ascertained that the fugitive had been accompanied to the place by two men, one a Californian, and the other an American named "Jim Dennison," who had acted as guides either from the Mission of San José or Dolores. Dennison, who is a butcher, and has a ranch at Halfmoon Bay, stated that he was on his way to San Diego to buy horses for the Governor. (?) The two were arrested, and were being examined amidst great excitement as our informant left; and about twenty Californians were started to scour the country for the so long invisible Ned.

Is it possible that the scamp has been out here this while or at the Mission of Dolores, and read and heard all that has been said about him? The three were, according to Dennison's own statement, five days in reaching Santa Bárbara, and McGowan was so much wearied by the journey that they were forced to stop for a time at a ranch twenty-five miles north of Santa Bárbara to recruit muscle. — *Alta, July 10th.*

clear away from the town, they slunk back to their kennels, followed by a parting malediction from the women.* All this time, I, of course, was ignorant of what was going on, and from the glare and smoke which I could see in the sky through the breathing-aperture of my carpet, I thought the town was on fire. I lay still, though, preferring to be scorched a little, and even burned, rather than fall into the hands of that cruel mob. I had also been represented to them, by the "white pig," as a desperado, a perfect demon; they only hunted me in fifties and hundreds; and, I doubt not, had they seen me, death would have been my portion on the instant. It sometimes seems to me unaccountable how such bitter malignity could have been so suddenly engendered in the hearts of men whom I had never wronged or injured; but the whole history of our race shows that a taste for cruelty, and a delight in the misery of others, are moral diseases, easily contracted by minds not naturally ferocious, and, when once acquired, are as strong if not stronger than any of the propensities with which we are born.

I cannot say that I forgive that "white pig" and his

---

*The following letter appeared in the *Bulletin* of July 10th:—

SANTA BÁRBARA, June 6, 1856.

EDITOR BULLETIN:—Thinking a few items of intelligence from this remote quarter might not be uninteresting, I avail myself of the departure of the steamer to-morrow to drop you a few lines.

Well, sir, who do you suppose honored this little town to-day with his presence? No less a personage than the "noble-hearted, generous, and brave" (see a certain senator's speech in the last legislature) NED MCGOWAN! He arrived in this place early this morning. The rascal had the impudence to put up at the best hotel in the place, and ordered dinner. He was recognized by three or four gentlemen who had known him, in times gone by, in San Francisco. Information was given to the Sheriff, who, after an unaccountable hesitation, summoned a posse and proceeded to the hotel, at which place his (the Sheriff's) informer had left McGowan but twenty-five minutes before. On his arrival at the hotel, he found the bird had flown, under the protection of some two or three notorious individuals who are at the head and front of all the disturbances in our otherwise quiet little city. Diligent search was made all the afternoon, and a large patch of "tules," where it was supposed he had secreted himself, set fire to; but all in vain. So we returned, very much disheartened at our failure.

associates their murderous persecution of me; that, of course, I will never do. But I will freely say, that I rejoice from the bottom of my heart, on their account, that they have escaped the frightful responsibility to which they would have been held at the judgment-bar of the Almighty if on that day their myrmidons had found me.

But to return to my story. It was one of the hottest days I ever experienced. The heat of the carpet and the excitement nearly killed me. I was tormented, too, by myriads of fleas, of which the carpet was full. I lay still, however, for I considered that to move was death. After I had lain there about an hour and a half, I heard footsteps in the room, and presently Jack's voice. I implored him in mercy to give me some brandy and water, for I was nearly fainting with suffocation. He replied, "Lie still, or directly you won't have a throat to drink with!" and immediately passed out again. I suffered on for another hour and a half, and by that time it was quite dark. The woman of the house lit a candle, and commenced washing her children and putting them to bed. Presently I heard voices at the door, and could distinguish that of Power speaking in English. A party wanted to enter the house and search it. My protector told them there was no one there, and it was of no use to disturb the children. They said they had searched every other house without opposition, and they did not intend to make an exception of this. I now thought that my time was come, and, slipping out of the carpet, I silently cocked my pistol, grasped my knife, and, making a short prayer to Heaven, stationed myself just inside the door-post, within *two feet* of the man who was asking admittance, determined to sell my life as dearly as possible. Power, however, as Providence would have it, managed to make such resistance to their entrance that they finally walked away.

I had forgotten that there was an open window behind me, and, as there was a light burning in the room, they had only to turn the corner of the house to see me standing against the door-post. The instant they had turned from Jack, he turned his face to me and whispered, "Under, for your life!" I dropped, and crawled under the bed, and in the same moment they passed the open window. I again begged for water, and he pushed to me with his foot the basin in which the children had been washed, and I plunged my face into it and drank it all, and never in my life before did I taste so refreshing a draft as that filthy water was to me.

As soon as the footsteps of my pursuers had died away, Jack assisted me to get out of the window, and, getting out after me, ran with me some thirty yards and laid me down on my face in a sort of garden, telling me that when the moon went down he would come and take me to a place of safety. When he left me, it was about half-past eight o'clock, and the moon was then two hours high. The town of Santa' Bárbara had gone back to its wonted quiet, and the excitement of the day had been forgotten in the general conviction that I had managed to escape from the trap into which I had that morning entered. Music and dancing were going on, and all the world seemed happy but me. There I lay, with trembling limbs and beating heart, almost unmanned. My escape from death seemed to me a dream which I could not realize, because I dare not believe that I would ultimately be spared from the dreadful perils that surrounded me.

And who shall describe the agony I underwent in that long, lonely watch? He who has not stood, as it were, in the full flush of life and gazed into his tomb; he who has not felt that a breath, a shadow, the cracking of a twig, might open to his burning eye the mystery of his HEREAFTER,—can form no idea, from mortal pen, of the weird phantoms that peopled those two dreadful hours!

It was a heavenly night. A cool breeze played gently round my throbbing temples, but it brought no balm to me. I could only feel in its freshness the icy hand of death, and mistook its fragrance for the odor of the charnel-house. Flowers were springing round me, but, as they waved in the pale moonlight, I only saw funeral-plumes. A little stream was trickling near me, and its gurgling ripple broke like a death-rattle on my ear. I heard the guitar and tambourine in the distance, and, as the sighing night-wind brought them down to me accompanied with light-hearted beauty's laugh, I only heard a death-wail and a dirge. All around me spoke of death. So fearfully had my mind been wrought upon by the horrors of that day, that I really *was*, in fancy, on the confines of the spirit-land, and, as is always the case when the spirit either is or fancies itself about to wing its flight from earth, the phantoms of the dim past floated before me as vividly as if but yesterday I had passed them on the stream of Time, instead of years and years ago. I saw my poor old mother (who died during this persecution of me) as I had seen her in my childhood; and so startlingly distinct was the vision, that but a day appeared to fill the gap which years had made. Wife, children, brothers, sisters, and all my kindred, and long-buried friends of other days, passed in bright review before me; and as the clear, cold moon looked down into my very heart, every action, good or evil, of my past life seemed to be searched out from the rubbish-closets of memory, and held up before me as vividly as though each one was but the event of yesterday. And as I watched that weary moon sink gradually to its setting,—that moon whose light had often seemed to me, in youth, so lovely, but for whose waning now my throbbing heart so longed,—I could look it bravely in the face and declare to the Being who placed it there, by all my youthful joys that moon had witnessed, and by the agony of soul which its departure would take from me that night, that I was, in heart and in deed, innocent of the crime for which I was persecuted.

At length that dreadful watch was over. The moon had sunk below the horizon, and, under the pall of darkness which its setting left, I thanked a merciful God that he had guided no enemy to my place of concealment. It was not long before I heard footsteps, and presently Power appeared, accompanied by two Spaniards. He told me, in a whisper, that, for the present, they would take me to a hiding-place, and then, for a consideration in money, which I there agreed to pay them, they were to return for me at three o'clock in the morning and conduct me to a place of safety. I grasped Power by the hand, and went with the Spaniards. They conducted me to a long, low adobe building with a balcony in front of it, on the outskirts of the town, and there left me, promising to return, as had been agreed upon, at three o'clock. Not long after they had gone, I was joined by two others. They entered the house apparently as though they had a right there, and, indeed, the place looked as though it might be their den. It was a villainous-looking hole, and if ever *robber and assassin* was written on the human countenance, it was written on the faces of these two men. They had a lamp with them, and by its light I saw that one of them had been drinking. They had apparently been informed of my being there, and, after scrutinizing me very closely, endeavored to enter into conversation with me. I could only reply to their questions by signs, and here and there a word of broken Spanish. One of them at length espied a very pretty scarf about my neck (it was about the only piece of decent apparel I had left, and was the gift of a lady), and, taking hold of it, jerked it from me, saying, "*¿V. no quiere presente me este?*"* It was useless to remonstrate with the scoundrel for such a trifle, and of course I let him keep it. He then made me understand that he wanted to know if I was armed, whereupon I showed him that I was. He then wanted to know where my money was, and I told him that my *amigo* had it. He next proposed to exchange coats with me. Mine was a policeman's uniform, buttoned up in front. He gave me to understand that his old coat, which was in rags, was a much better disguise for me. I would have given the rascal the coat rather than had a noisy difficulty with him just then, but in the breast pocket of it I had a purse of gold, which I was determined he should not see, and, of course, to exchange coats without taking it out was out of the question. After considerable palaver, he said to me, "*¿V. no quiere presente me uno peso?*"† I took out a handkerchief in which I had some silver and a few gold pieces tied up for my current expenses,—as I did not care to exhibit my purse on all occasions,—and handed him a dollar. He let it fall on the floor, either by accident or design, and did not stoop to pick it up, saying, "*Yo no quiere para plata, pero mucho para oro.*"‡ I gave him a two-dollar-and-a-half piece, and then made him pick up the

---

* Don't you wish to present this to me?

† Don't you wish to give me a dollar?

‡ I don't want silver; I want gold.

dollar, being fearful that, if I did it myself, he would stab me as I stooped, either in the back or neck, and then rob me. He at first refused to do it, but, being determined to be trifled with no longer by the scoundrel, I covered him with my pistol and made him pick it up. I then gave him to understand that I wanted no more to say to him, and, making him take what few old clothes he had hanging on a line in the building, I drove him into another room and fastened the door.

This fellow doubtless thought I was a robber or highwayman like himself, and that the object of that day's pursuit of me had been to deliver me up to justice for offenses in that line; consequently that I was a legitimate subject to demand toll from, in the way of "hush-money." Indeed, I am not astonished that the wretch should have taken that idea into his head, for the Santa Bárbara mob had been taught to regard me as the fiend incarnate, guilty of every crime in the decalogue, and, instigated by the hope of reward, had pursued me on "general principles," utterly ignorant of the real object of my persecutors.

It was now getting quite cold, and I sat myself down on the earth floor of the house, anxiously awaiting the coming of the Spaniard whom Power was to send to conduct me out of danger. Their signal was to be three raps at a back window.

Three o'clock came, as nearly as I could judge, and yet no one rapped. I still anxiously waited, thinking that perhaps something had occurred to change Jack's plan, and that I should shortly hear from him. At length day began to break, and I could see, through a crack in the windowshutter, that it was very foggy. I now made up my mind to remain no longer where I was. From the treatment I had received since entering the house, I knew that I was in bad hands, and feared that if I waited there during the coming day, the villains would betray me for money. I also knew that the steamer from San Diego would pass up that day, and was, of course, aware that, if captured, I should at once be sent to San Francisco and delivered over to the Vigilance Committee. I considered, therefore, that I ought, by all means, to get into the mountains at once, and remain there at least until after the steamer had passed up, even if I then had to return to the town. By that means my friends would have time to sue out a *habeas corpus*, as it would take at least a week or ten days to send down after me, which I knew would be done, now that they had got on my true track. They had been egregiously humbugged by all the other reports my friend had started as to my whereabouts, and having spent many thousands of dollars in various "wild-goose chases," I supposed that they felt sufficiently sore to be very anxious to lay hands upon me. Accordingly, I went to the window and endeavored to open it, but found that I had not sufficient strength to do so. I then went into the apartment where the two Spaniards were sleeping, and my entrance awakened one of them. The one, however, who had attempted to rob me had not yet slept off the fumes of his drunkenness, and I, of course, took no pains to awaken him. I made the other one understand that I could not open my window, and wanted his assistance. He came and opened it for me, and I waited till he had gone back to his bed, and then I got out. I threw my boots out before me, and it was with the utmost difficulty that I could follow them.

I was so stiff and sore that I could scarcely walk. It was now daybreak, and I could hear the musical bells of the Catholic church chiming for matins. The fog was so dense that I could not see twenty yards before me. I did not know the direction of the mountains, and was compelled to strike out at "haphazard." Presently I found myself getting into soft clay, and saw, looming through the fog, the binnacle-light of the surveying-schooner, which was anchored abreast of the town. I knew from this that I was getting onto the beach, and fearing that if I continued along it my footprints would lead to my capture, I at once turned and groped in the opposite direction. After walking some time, I reached the foot of the Coast Range, to the eastward of the city, and commenced ascending it.* After I had gone

---

* NED MCGOWAN AT SANTA BÁRBARA — THE PEOPLE IN PURSUIT — EXPECTED APPREHENSION. — We are indebted to the purser of the steamer Sea Bird, which arrived here this forenoon from the southern coast, for the following important and interesting information in regard to the notorious Ned McGowan. Ned had been tracked at last. We trust that by the next arrival from Santa Bárbara the

up some distance, I ensconced myself in some thick furze, determined, before proceeding farther, to take some rest. The sun was now fully up, and as the mists melted before his rays, it bid fair to be a beautiful day.

As I sat looking down from my eminence, my eye fell on the cross on the little Catholic church at the lower end of the town, and I was reminded of a religious duty too often neglected by me in bygone days of comfort and luxury. I had been instructed by my poor mother in the religion of the Church, and, falling on my knees, I made the sign of the cross and thanked God for his merciful kindness.

---

scoundrel will be brought hither to meet the fate he so richly deserves, and which his companion in guilt, Casey, has already suffered. The purser's memorandum says:—

"Great excitement was created at Santa Bárbara by the arrival there of *Ned McGowan*, who made his appearance last Sunday, the 6th of July. Upon being recognized, which he immediately was, Ned took to the mountains in the vicinity, closely pursued by the citizens, but, up to the time of the steamer sailing (the 7th), no clew has been found of him. The people, however, were in hopes of taking him before evening. Mr. Russell Heath, Sheriff of Santa Bárbara, had arrested a California boy and an American who accompanied McGowan from Santa Cruz to Santa Bárbara. They stated that McGowan left San Francisco about the 23d or 25th of June, and they joined him at Santa Cruz, he representing to them that he was a cattle dealer, and on his way to San Diego to buy cattle. They arrived at the Rancho de Refugio, about twenty-seven miles from Santa Bárbara, on the morning of the 4th of July. McGowan was then so exhausted that he could proceed no farther, and had to go into Santa Bárbara, where he arrived on the morning of the 6th. He was immediately recognized by those who knew him. Upon hearing of this, McGowan left his horse and took for the mountains, followed by the citizens. The majority of the people think he is secreted within the town of Santa Bárbara, as there are many seeking to aid him in his escape.["]—*Bulletin, July 9th.*

CHAPTER IV

*Creation slumbered in the cloudless light,
And noon was silent as the depth of night.
O what a throng of rushing thoughts oppressed,
In that vast solitude, his anxious breast!*
                                        Moore.

I HAD remained for two or three hours where I had halted on the mountain-side, looking out on the vast ocean glittering like a burnished mirror beneath the rays of the morning sun, and down on the city of Santa Bárbara, which lay like a little social pebble on its sounding shore, thanking Heaven for my recent escape, and revolving in my mind plans for my future action. By that time I became materially rested, and mustered strength to penetrate the mountain wild still farther, deeming it to be but prudent to place a little more distance between myself and my pursuers, and accordingly commenced a farther ascent. After proceeding some distance, I came to a very precipitous "bench" overgrown with a thick and impenetrable "*chaparral.*" Into this I cut my way with my knife until I came to some rocks that afforded shade, and near by I found some water. Here I halted, and remained behind the rocks the entire day without seeing a living creature of any sort. Strange to say, either from extreme excitement or some other cause, I felt no hunger, although the last meal I had eaten was my breakfast on the preceding morning at the *Rancho de Refugio*. I drank a great deal of the water, however, for I still suffered from fever. Before reaching this spot, I had thrówn away my flannel under-

Finding no safe place to sleep immediately about them, I at length got into an oat-field in which the straw had been cut and stacked up. *Page*

clothes, owing to the excessive heat, but toward evening it became quite cool, and I discovered I had done a very foolish thing. I had lost my overcoat and waistcoat the previous day, as before mentioned, and suffered greatly for the want of them. I may as well here state that in the pocket of the overcoat were all my papers of a private nature, but, fortunately, they fell into the hands of Don Antonio María De la Guerra, mayor of Santa Bárbara, and brother of the present senator, through whose kindness they have been restored to me. Among these papers were letters to the different Missions in lower California and Mexico, stating that I was a good Catholic, and not traveling through those countries on any political errand. This, as I afterward learned, was told to the good Bishop Amat, and he sent messages to the various Missions, instructing them to give me shelter if I visited them. He also had mass said for me. Had I known all this at the time, I would have been spared the painful pilgrimage I was then about entering upon. I should have at once sought an asylum at one of the Missions, and been safe.

When it was quite dark, I prepared to come down from the mountain and sleep in the plain, being afraid of the bears, in which the country abounds. I got into a canon in which was an aqueduct built of stone. It is many miles in length, and supplies the Mission of Santa Bárbara, which is distant a few miles from the city, with water for irrigation and other purposes. I followed the course of this aqueduct till it brought me near to the old Mission church and buildings. Finding no safe place to sleep immediately about them, I at length got into an oat-field in which the straw had been cut and stacked up. Here I made a very comfortable bed, and slept soundly till just before day, when I heard a man driving some cattle into the field. I remained quiet till he went away, and then got up and again ascended the mountain back of the church. As may be supposed, by this time I had become quite hungry. I saw some fish swimming in a kind of basin in the watercourse, and thought I would try to catch some of them and eat them raw. I cut some holes in the crown of my hat, so as to make a kind of net of it, and then, fastening it to a pole, endeavored to get some of them; but, either

I was too unskillful a fisherman or fate had determined I should not succeed. After trying a long time in vain, I was compelled to give it up and remain hungry. I continued up the cañon a mile or two, keeping all the time in the watercourse and walking barefooted. Still having fever, I drank every half-hour. I endeavored to cross the mountain, thinking that I might find some friendly ranch in the plain on the other side, but, after I had traveled till I could advance no farther even in the watercourse, I was obliged to give it up, and sat down to rest. I have since been informed that, in endeavoring to cross that mountain, I was undertaking an impossibility, it never having been crossed at that point. I remained there in solitude the entire day, and at night again descended to the Mission, and slept in the same oat-field, without interruption, till day. When I awoke, I found myself suffering intensely from hunger. I had now been three days without eating, and was perfectly ravenous. I determined to go to the first rancho I could find and ask for food, concluding that I might as well be captured and killed as starved to death. Accordingly, I got out into the road, and walked on without knowing which direction I was going. Presently I came to a house. I should judge it was then about seven o'clock in the morning. A young man was standing in the door, whom, from his appearance, I took to be an American, but, on accosting him, I discovered that he could not speak English. I then addressed an old woman, who appeared to be his mother, but with no better success. I managed, however, to make her understand that I was hungry, and showed her a five-franc piece. Her breakfast was nearly ready, and she soon invited me to sit down and fall to, which I did with a will. After breakfast, I got the old lady to give me some beef, hard bread, and a bottle of milk, for which I paid her three dollars. As no one spoke English about the premises, I thought there was no fear of my being betrayed by them to my enemies, and continued my walk along the road. I had got my head so "turned round" on the mountain, that I did not know the direction of the city of Santa Bárbara, till suddenly, to my horror, I came right upon it. As soon as I espied it, I turned and ran off the road about a mile, when I came to a small cañon filled with very thick bushes. Into these I crept, and lay there all day without molestation. And better need I had to be well concealed than I was then aware of; for it turned out that the woman at whose house I breakfasted was a Mrs. Robbins,* and, though a native herself, the widow of one Captain Robbins, an American, and, moreover, she was the mother-in-law of none other than Harvey Benjamin Blake, alias the "white pig," who had instigated the Santa Bárbara mob to hunt me so savagely two days before. He was in the habit of almost daily visiting his mother-in-law, and, as I afterward ascertained, did actually, on that day, pay her a visit, and was telling her about the hunt of the preceding Sunday, when she informed him that I had breakfasted with her that morning. At this "the pig" became almost frantic. He mounted his horse and rode back to town, where he communicated his news, and, getting up another party, they gave me another hunt. All the while, however, I, unconscious of what was going on, lay safely ensconced in the bushes, and their search was fruitless.

As soon as night came on, I watched the moon and stars to ascertain which way I should go to get north of the city of Santa Bárbara. I had determined to abandon my project of going to Mexico, and to return toward San Francisco, knowing that I should be more rigorously pursued in lower California than elsewhere.† I thought that I was south of

---

*THE CHASE AFTER MCGOWAN.—By the extract from the Santa Bárbara *Gazette* on the outside page, it will be seen that McGowan had disappeared from Santa Bárbara, and that a sheriff's posse was after him. Another posse is also on his track, and it is not probable he will escape.

McGowan left Santa Bárbara on the 6th instant, and on the 17th he was seen a short distance from town, where he paid a dollar for a glass of water, and the next day, at the ranch of Mrs. Robbins, about two miles from town, he paid three dollars for his dinner. At this time he had no hat on, and was badly scorched and blistered with the sun. It is said that he had $900 on his person, and in roaming about that section of country it is not improbable that he may be murdered for his money. Indeed, there was a report in Santa Bárbara that he had been murdered, although passengers from there by the Sea Bird say there was nothing to confirm the report.—*Alta California, July 20.*

LOS ANGELES, July 16th, 1856.
† EDITOR BULLETIN:—The Vigilance Committee boys are now

the town, toward Los Angeles; but in this I was mistaken. When I fled to my present hiding-place, I had come at least a mile and a half in the direction I wished to travel. I came out of my retreat and traveled on, getting, as I supposed, to the northward of the city. I kept two or three miles off the road, and walked for nearly three hours, when I came to a ranch. By this time I had become sleepy, and, as I preferred to rest near a habitation on account of the bears, I determined to halt here. I laid down by the side of a fence, but, notwithstanding my fatigue, it was so cold I could not sleep. One of the greatest annoyances I found during my pilgrimage in Santa Bárbara was the California watch-dog. There are always eight or ten of them about a ranch, and they invariably gave the inhabitants notice of my presence by barking. They soon found me out in this instance, and at once became very noisy. Presently I heard a man speaking to the dogs, in English! I started up in alarm, knowing that if he was an enemy, and recognized me, escape was impossible while he had his dogs to assist him. Presently he came out to see what they had discovered. I boldly accosted him first, saying, "Your dogs are barking at *me*, sir," following up the information by asking him how far it was to the city of Santa Bárbara, pretending that I was going in that direction. Without answering my question, he replied, "Are you from above?" I replied in the affirmative, and he asked me, "From how far?" I told him, "From San José." He asked me how long I had been

---

close on Ned McGowan's trail, and you may expect them up with him by the next trip of the Sea Bird. When last heard from, he was on foot, and hardly able to walk. He stopped at the Mission of San Buenaventura, on Wednesday morning, 16th inst., to get his breakfast. They immediately sent news into Santa Bárbara to that effect. Eight good men, on picked horses, are now on his track, and he cannot long escape.

By the inclosed bill you will perceive that the authorities have offered a reward of $300 for his body, dead or alive. The vaqueros and Indians are scouring the country between Santa Bárbara and Los Angeles. At Los Angeles, Judge Hayes has issued three bench-warrants for his arrest, and sent one to San Diego, one to San Bernardino, and one to the Ferry on the Colorado River, thereby closing every avenue of escape. Ned's race is run; the fox is earthed at last. *Nada mas.*— Bulletin, *July 19.* M.

on the road, and I told him about a month. He then said, "It is only about four miles to the city, and a good road. You can soon make it." I judged from his accent that he was, as we familiarly say, "from Pike." I imagined, too, that he did not wish to give me shelter for the night. However, he was not aware that, had he offered me his hospitality, circumstances would have prompted me respectfully to decline it. I left my friend "from Pike," and, after walking a short distance farther, came to a sheep-ranch, where I saw some large stacks of oats. I was now glad that the dogs had roused me from my last uncomfortable resting-place, and, crawling in between two of the stacks, I enjoyed a sweet and refreshing sleep until morning.

I arose before it was fully daylight and continued my journey. I had no fixed plan of operations; nothing more than a general idea of getting northward as quietly and as rapidly as possible. I had not gone far before I saw a Spaniard on the road. He did not approach me, however. He was a vaquero, and was watching some cattle. After proceeding some five or six miles, I saw some horsemen on the road, coming toward me, on their way to the city. At the same time I observed two men at work in a field. Immediately it struck me that the best way to avoid meeting the men on the road was to join those in the field. I accordingly approached them, while the horsemen passed on. I remained with the two men some time. They were engaged in making a fence, and preparing the ground to put in a crop. I ascertained that I was upon the land of Daniel Hill, Esq. He is an old Californian, having resided in the county of Santa Bárbara thirty years. He had married into the Ortega family, and is the father of Mrs. Nicholas A. Den, the wife of the gentleman to whom I have before referred. I learned these facts from one of the men, who was a Chileño and spoke English. He informed me that he had been a long time in the employ of Grogan & Lent, of San Francisco. He said my face was familiar to him, and asked me what countryman I was. I told him that I was French, but had been a long time in America, and was then on my way to the Mission of Santa Inés, to act in the capacity of teacher of English. He asked me if I had seen anything of "the man the people were hunting." I told him that I had not, but that it was supposed that he had gone to the lower country. I told him that I was one of the party who had pursued him, and regretted that he had escaped us, and further informed him that, during my stay in Santa Bárbara, I had been the guest of Don Pablo De la Guerra. This appeared to satisfy my *Chileño-Yankee* friend, and he annoyed me with no more questions. They asked me into their tent, which they had pitched in the field, and treated me to a cup of good warm coffee, and exchanged some of their soft bread for my hard biscuit. They also gave me a drink of *aguardiente*, for which I paid a dollar to the one who did not speak English. I told them, as I left, that I was going no farther than Dr. Den's house that day, and the next day I hoped to reach the Mission of Santa Inés.

As soon as I left them, I got into the mountains, it being then about eight o'clock, and entirely too late for me to travel any longer on the road. I lay concealed in the mountains all day, and at night came down again. Finding no straw at hand, of which to make a bed, I continued my journey until the moon went down, which was at about midnight, and then fell asleep under a tree. I awoke in the morning very cold and stiff, and suffered greatly until the sun came out. The warmth then restored me to a comparative degree of comfort, and I pursued my journey. I passed the residence of Dr. Den before any of the household were stirring, and, after walking some five or six miles farther, came to the ranch of one *Don Ignacio Ortega*, where I had made the unsuccessful attempt to get some brandy for my guide after leaving the *Refugio*. After I had passed this place, I again went into the mountains. Here I remained all day, and, after having eaten all that remained of the provisions I had bought of old Mrs. Robbins, I enjoyed a good sound sleep until about five o'clock in the evening, when I awaked. I was on a very high mountain which commanded a view of the road for some distance both ways. Not seeing any one, I descended to the road which led to the Refugio Ranch. It ran through a deep cañon which I remembered having passed on my way to Santa Bárbara, and I knew that now I must be at least thirty miles north of that town.

As I was making the best of my way along the road, I suddenly heard the sound of hoofs, and, looking up, I saw a horseman approaching me at a full gallop. He was so close upon me that it was impossible to hide from him, and besides, he had seen me, and it would have been foolish to attempt it. I loosened my pistol and my knife in my belt, to be ready for service in case he attacked me, and awaited his coming.* When he reined up in front of me, I at once identified him as one of the two men who, it will be remembered, were so curious about my money at the *Refugio*, on the Fourth. This was not Pedro, but his companion, who lived at *Las Cruces*. He was also a brother of the guide who had gone with me into Santa Bárbara. After the first recognition, I tried to deceive him as to my situation, and told him that the Indians had stampeded my horses; but I soon found that he knew all about me, and everything that had befallen me in Santa Bárbara. He told me, furthermore, that Dennison had gone on back to Halfmoon Bay, taking with him all the horses. I suspected this man to be a robber, and of course was anxious to get rid of him. How to do it, however, without any difficulty puzzled me. In the event of his attempting to rob me, which I thought it not unlikely he would do, I did not want to kill him, for it would have caused me a great deal of trouble to bestow his body, and horse and saddle, in such a manner as to prevent discovery. I had a fierce

---

* NED MCGOWAN NOT YET CAPTURED — EXPECTATION OF SOON CATCHING HIM. — By the steamer Sea Bird, which arrived this morning from ports on the southern coast, we have Los Angeles papers to July the 12th, and the Santa Bárbara *Gazette* to July 17th.

The news all relates to the movements of the *Hon.* Judge Ned McGowan and the chances of his capture. In another column, we give a letter from a Santa Bárbara correspondent, which contains the latest intelligence on this subject, from which it would appear that McGowan cannot escape the hot search after him. In all probability, this noted veteran scoundrel will be in this city, in the hands of the Vigilance Committee, within the next ten days. We may add here, that McGowan is ill of the piles, and is physically unable to move onward. The Indians and vaqueros who have seen him report that his bowels are protruding. The letters of our Santa Bárbara and Los Angeles correspondents show that the whole southern country is up and in eager chase after the fugitive. — *Bulletin*, July 19.

enough pack at my heels already, without wishing to do anything which would render them more savage than they were; and yet, to suffer myself to be robbed by him was out of the question.

He told me he was going into town to get some medicine for a sick brother, and when he returned he would sell me a horse he had at his place. It occurred to me to ask him if he would take a message for me to General Covarrubias, telling him where I was. He at once agreed to do it, and I gave him a four-dollar piece. At first he refused to accept it, but after a while he did so. After conversing a few moments longer, he started off, as I supposed, to go to the city. Presently, however, he returned with a bottle half filled with brandy which he had procured at the *Refugio*, and offered it to me to drink. I suspected it was poisoned, and very politely told him, "After you, senor." He drank, as I thought, very sparingly, and handed the bottle to me. I took a mouthful of it, but did not swallow any. Indeed, the liquor was poison enough, of itself, without any "doctoring."

He now asked me to give him ten dollars more, which I would have done had I have had it out of my purse. I had no idea, however, of letting him see my money, and therefore told him that all my money was in twenty-dollar pieces, and on his return from General Covarrubias I would give him one of them instead of a ten. My object was to get rid of the fellow, and of course I never intended, after he had left, to wait for him, or ever let him see me again if I could help it. I contemplated crossing the mountain of Santa Ynez, and then leaving the Coast Range. He appeared satisfied with my answer to his demand, and was about riding away when something put it into my head to ask him if he knew Jack Power. His eye brightened in a moment, and he replied in Spanish, quickly, "¿*Jacky Power V. amïgo?*" I told him "Yes." His whole manner at once changed; he appeared very much pleased to know it, and, taking a long pull at the suspected bottle, he said to me, "If Jacky Power is your friend, I will have him at this place to-morrow at twelve o'clock." It was then sundown, and he immediately started for Santa Bárbara, distant thirty miles. I had not the remotest idea, when he rode away, of being there the next day, for I had no faith in him; I did not believe he could bring Power to me, as he had promised, and I was very anxious to be clear of him. As soon as he had gone, I bent my steps towards the *Refugio*, in search of a place to sleep. I waited until it became quite dark, and then attempted to get into one of the small houses adjacent to the main building, which, when I was last there, I had observed to be unoccupied. In this at tempt I failed, the door being fastened. I managed, how ever, at length, to stumble upon a sort of little outhouse, built of *adobe*, with a tile roof, and laid down inside of it to sleep. I had lain there but a few moments when I heard voices, and presently two men approached, conversing in Spanish. One of them entered the house. I lay perfectly quiet, and directly he lit a match, which for a moment lighted up the place, but he did not see me, and immediately his companion went away, whereupon he fastened the door on the inside and laid down. Soon afterward, another came to the house and tried to gain admittance, but my companion refused to let him in, and he went away. I waited till I thought my fellow-lodger was asleep, and then stole softly to the door, unfastened it, and went to the garden of the establishment, and laid down under a row of willows which were planted inside of the fence.

I subsequently learned, before I left Santa Bárbara, that the man who entered the building in which I was secreted was a prisoner who had broken jail in Santa Bárbara while the Sheriff and the mob were hunting me, and made his escape. He either had a wife or friend at the *Refugio*, which accounted for his coming there. I managed, notwithstanding the cold night air, to get some sleep, but I awoke at daylight shivering, and nearly chilled through. I got up, however, and continued my journey toward the mountain of Santa Ynez, and before long the warmth of the sun relieved me. I tried very hard to discover the pass by which Ramon, Dennison, and I had crossed it, but, after two hours of fruitless search, I had to give it up. Having thus abandoned all idea of crossing the mountains alone, I determined to await the result of my message to Power. I did not go to the spot where I told my messenger I would await him, fearing that he might play me false, and, tempted by a reward, bring my enemies upon me. So I moved about a mile and a half down the road, nearer the city, and, taking a position which commanded a view both ways, secreted myself in the bushes and awaited his arrival. When it had got pretty well on toward noon, I spied two men in the distance, coming from the direction of Santa Bárbara, and on their nearer approach I was delighted, and at the same time surprised, to find that it really was Jack and my messenger. They had to ride around the foot of a steep hill before they could pass me, and, seeing no one else on the road, I descended from the mountain to meet them. Jack was very glad to see me safe, and told me all my friends in town had come to the conclusion that I was killed. He asked me why the devil I did not remain with the men he had sent to me in the adobe house, and explained that all my friends thought it would be better for me to remain in town a day or two, as there was very little fear of my being discovered where I was, and hence I had not heard from him at three o'clock that morning, as had been agreed upon. I reported to him how one of them had attempted to rob me, and told him that I, of course, thought myself much safer in my own keeping than in such hands, and therefore had left. I then narrated to him my adventures since I had started out on my own account. He swore furiously at the scoundrel who had treated me so ill, and declared that he would cut the rascal's ears off when he saw him. He, however, asked me if the fellow was not drunk, and I told him that he was, which appeared to account to him for his conduct.

He told me that he had had several persons busy the last four days hunting the mountains for me, and when the messenger told him where I was he did not believe that he had seen me till he had shown him my name which I had roughly scratched on a piece of paper when I sent him. Power and I stepped a little aside from the Spaniard and had a long conversation. He told me that it was suspected in the city that he knew of my whereabouts, and a large sum of money had been offered to him to reveal it, but of course in vain. He told me, that, though he was poor, he would not have the blood of a helpless man upon his hands, and I might feel quite certain he would never betray me.

Of this I was very sure, and, although he did not ask me for any money, I gave him one hundred dollars for his kind services to me thus far. When I took out my purse to give him the money, he asked me if the Spaniard had seen it. I assured him that I had been too cautious for that, and he replied that it was well I had been, for the fellow was a robber, and would at any time have murdered me for much less than what I had with me, as would many others of his stamp, who were very plenty in that section of the state. He added, however, that there was no danger now of any of them betraying me, because they had learned that I was a good Catholic, and they would not have the reputation of having *sold* my life to my enemies. Besides that, he told me, with a significant expression of the eye, that he was a "*medicine-man*" among them, and they would not provoke him. He then called to the Spaniard, and, giving him twenty dollars out of the money I had given him, to which I added five or six dollars more, he bade him go to the Refugio and procure for me a horse, saddle, and bridle.

While the Spaniard was absent, Jack told me that his original intention, on learning where I was, was to take me to "Los Álamos,"—one of the places at which I had stopped, as the reader will remember, before crossing the mountain of Santa Ynez,—but that, on reflection, he thought it best that I should go to a place called the "*Arroyo Hondo,*" being the same place where resided my friend Pedro, who had been so inquisitive about me on the Fourth, when in company with the Spaniard who was then with us. He told me that it was but five miles distant from where we were, and that, though the Spaniard could take me there, as he knew the place and the friend to whom he intended to send me, he did not intend to trust him, but to go himself. It was not long before the man returned from the Refugio, bringing only a naked mule, with the information that that was the best he had been able to do. Jack looked suspiciously at him for a moment, and then, telling him to dismount from his horse, he coolly took the saddle from the animal and placed it on the mule. The man then spoke in Spanish to Jack, who afterward told me that he wanted him to let him take me to his place at Las Cruces. Power told him that he intended to take me to Los Álamos, and that he might either stay where he was, or go to the Refugio and wait till his return. I then mounted the mule, and Jack his steed, and we proceeded along the road, leaving the Spaniard and his unsaddled horse to keep each other company. As soon as we were out of his sight, Jack exchanged animals with me. Being a fine rider, he could get along with the mule much better than I, and besides, in case of an unexpected pursuit, his magnificent horse would take much better care of me than the miserable little animal I was on. The horse was very fleet and powerful, and, withal, perfectly gentle, with a gait as easy as the rocking of a cradle. After making the exchange, we got in the road, and took the direction of the *Arroyo Hondo*, at which place we shortly arrived.

Here I at once discovered that the master of the place was, as I had suspected, none other than my inquisitive friend of the Fourth, Don Pedro. Power appeared to have a mysterious influence over all these people. They all respected him, and, while many of them would have cut my throat at any time for my money had I been alone and unfriended, his name seemed a talisman which converted them from enemies into hospitable friends. He frankly told Pedro who I was, and what were my troubles, as also who were my friends at Santa Bárbara. He informed him that he had brought me to his house for refuge, and as he delivered me to him safe and sound, he expected me to be returned to him in the same condition when called for. He told him to take charge of me for a few days, until the hunt after me had begun to flag, or some other and safer place could be found for me. He further charged him to tell no one that I was there, to let no one see me, and particularly to keep my hiding-place secret from the Spaniard whom we had just left on the road, calling him by name. All of this Pedro willingly agreed to, and Power then stated the case to his wife, and exacted and obtained from her the same pledges. It will be seen that she faithfully and honorably kept her trust to the last, and took care that her children did the same; but the sequel will also show how far her husband kept his.

CHAPTER V

Thou art a wanderer, it is said;
For Mortham's death, thy steps waylaid,
Thy head at price — so say our spies,
Who range the valley in disguise."
Rokeby.

IN order that the events which occurred during my stay at the *Arroyo Hondo* may be fully understood, it is perhaps not amiss here to give some description of the place and its inhabitants. The Arroyo Hondo is a mountain stream which runs for several miles through a narrow mountain gorge or canon, and empties, without any bay or indentation in the coast, directly into the sea. The house of my host is situated in a very wild and romantic spot at the bottom of the canon, and within sound of the ocean surf. It is a new structure, built of adobe, with two stories, and very comfortably finished inside. A short distance from the house, and lower down the canon, is an old hut, built of reeds. There is a garden and orchard on the premises, and also the ruins of a vineyard which once was cultivated by the people of the Mission of Santa Inés, and sufficient plateau, or level land, to herd quite a number of cattle. The inhabitants of the place consist of *Pedro*, his wife, and six children, — *Chino*, the eldest boy, *Juan*, the second, and *Avellino*, the third; also two little girls, and an infant, whose sex I never knew.* In the old adobe hut above mentioned, there lived an old Santa Inés Indian whom they called *Konoya*. He was bent with age, and must have numbered nearly ninety years. His sole companions were two black dogs. I became, in the course of my sojourn there, quite friendly with old *Konoya*, but all my attempts to cultivate the acquaintance of those dogs were in vain. They ate at the same table with their master, who always cooked his frugal repast of jerked beef and *pinole* with his own aged hands, without assistance from the family at the house.

Old *Konoya* was as black as a negro. He probably had never known what it was to have his head or feet covered, or a coat on his back. His sole raiment was a flannel shirt, and a cloth tied round his loins; he also wore his hair in a long queue, fancifully decorated. He never moved on the most trivial occasion without his two dogs following like shadows at his heels. Their sole errand on earth seemed to be to guard that aged Indian, and no persuasion or coaxing could ever produce any other effect than a sullen growl and a closer crouching at their master's feet. The old man's occupation appeared to be to keep the garden fence in repair, and that of the dogs to drive the squirrels out of the corn. Whenever *Konoya* spoke, the dogs would fly like lightning to do his bidding; but at the sound of any other voice, they would only growl, and look into the old man's face for instructions. During the two weeks I was at this place, I never succeeded in patting one of them on the head, nor could I have ever crossed the threshold of the Indian's hut without his permission. The old man was a very devout Catholic, and counted his beads every morning. When he ascertained that I also was of his religion, he became very friendly with me. He knew that there was some mystery connected with my being there, but never thoroughly understood what it was. He was made aware that men were hunting me, and that no

---

*The *señora* was a very pious woman, and made it a practice every morning to call her children around her to say their prayers, and then send them out to their father, Pedro, to receive his blessing. He generally sat out on the porch during the family worship, in which he never participated.

He had a little pony of his own, the gift of his grandfather, and he rode him without saddle or bridle.—*Page 100.*

one was to know of my presence there. He frequently brought me warning from the *señora* to go farther into the woods, when strangers were about the premises.

Of the children of my host, *Chino*, the eldest of the sons, was, I should judge, about seventeen years of age. He was looked upon as a sort of *mayordomo*, and had a general supervision of the ranch. *Juan*, the second son, was about twelve years old, and his business appeared to be to let the water in on the crop from the Arroyo, herd the stock, milk the cows, etc. Little *Avellino*, the youngest, was his mother's pet and my favorite. He was a beautiful boy, not more than eight years old, and a perfect child of nature. When, in the course of my sojourn at his father's house, it became necessary for me to hide in the mountains, it was the faithful little Avellino that brought me my food and he was generally the unsuspected little messenger sent by his good mother to warn me of danger, when my pursuers were about her house. He had a little pony of his own, the gift of his grandfather, and he rode him without saddle or bridle. He would take the sash from his waist, and, calling the pony to him, who minded him like a dog, he would fasten the end of it around his nose, and then, throwing the rest of it over his neck, would seize it in his hand, and thus sway himself onto the pony's back, where, when once seated, he was as much at home as if he had been on his feet. He knew that it delighted me to see him ride, and when I would applaud him with "¡*Bravo, Avellino!*" away he would fly like the wind, cutting all manner of capers, and rolling about on the back of his pony like the circus rider in "the drunken-sailor scene." When *Pedro* was away, which was pretty much all the time, he would ride races with his brothers, of which *Paisano*, as they called me, was always chosen judge; and, notwithstanding he sometimes came out behind, I generally found some excuse to decide in his favor.

Dear little *Avellino!* The remembrance of his warm and faithful little heart will never fade while I live. Neither he nor any of his brothers had ever been to a school or could read a line of their own language, yet nature had endowed that child with attributes which are wanting in the bosoms of thousands who wear the highest lit erary honors of the earth,— sincere sympathy with the distressed and helpless, hatred of the persecutor, and fearless fidelity to those who reposed confidence in him. I cannot refrain from relating, at the risk of being tedious, one little incident with regard to him, and then I will resume the thread of my narrative.

The little fellow was a frolicsome, laughing child, and very full of what boys call *fun*. One day, when I was secreted in the mountain, he came to my hiding-place and shouted, "*¡Paisano! ¡Vamos, vamos! ¡Los Vigilantes!*" I immediately sprung up, and was hastening up the mountain in double-quick time when I was arrested by a loud laugh from the urchin. On looking round, I perceived that I had been "sold," and the little scamp was enjoying my fright immensely. I was vexed that he should thus make a sport of my miseries, and I have no doubt my features showed it. The child stopped laughing, and, approaching me, put his arms around my knees, and looked up into my face with his large, dark eyes, in which I could read sorrow for having caused me unnecessary alarm, and, murmuring "*¡Pobrecito!*" he took some pears out of his little pocket and gave them to me. I could scarcely refrain from tears. He never gave me a false alarm again. With this description of my retreat and its inhabitants, I again return to my story.

As soon as Jack had finished his explanations with regard to me, the *señora* cooked some jerked beef and made us some warm tea, and we enjoyed a hearty repast. After dinner I offered the *señora* a Mexican doubloon, but she refused to accept it. Power told me she would not accept money for her hospitality, and advised me, if I wished to make her a present, to take some other mode of doing it; which I determined to do on the first opportunity. Jack and I then went upstairs to take some sleep, as it would be necessary for him to remain with me until night in order not to return too soon to the *Refugio*, and thus undeceive the Spaniard as to his having taken me to *Los Álamos*. As soon as it was dark, Power saddled his horse, and, before he left, told me that he was going in a few days to Los Angeles, in order to be followed there by my pursuers, if he could succeed in making them believe he had taken me in that direction. He told Pedro to send a packmule into town the next morning, and he would load him with some coffee, sugar, and other necessaries; then, taking with him the mule that we got from the Refugio, he bid us good by and rode away.

Let the world say what it will of Jack Power, he is not a bad man *at heart*, and his conduct toward me proved it. I am not the apologist or the *friend* of any man who lives at open war with society, and bids defiance to the laws, whether in the character of a highway robber or that of a hypocritical reformer who, under the protection of *Vigilance Committees*, sets our constitution at naught and saps the foundations on which rest our prosperity and respectability as a people; but, admitting all that the newspapers may report concerning this man to be true, he certainly did, in my case, exhibit traits utterly foreign to the character of an unscrupulous ruffian, such as he has been represented to be; and it would be an act of base ingratitude on my part to leave unimproved an opportunity of rescuing from universal odium the name of one to whom I am indebted for the opportunity of laying this history of my wrongs before the world, so far as a truthful statement of facts as to his conduct can so rescue it. He knew me only by reputation and sight. He saw me for the first time in many years, at a moment when my life hung so nicely in the balance that a feather's weight would have decided it. He knew not how justly I was pursued; he only knew how ruthlessly. He saw that in an instant more, perhaps, my life would have been sacrificed, and, prompted by some feeling *not to be found in the heart of an assassin*, he saved me. Having saved me, he remained true to me. I had no claim upon his friendship; I had no feelings or associations in common with him; I had never even spoken to him, that I remember. He knew that a price was set upon my head, and he knew that it was in his power to earn it, and that, too, without being suspected of having done so; and, again obeying the mandates of a voice *that never whispers into the ear of a robber*, though poor, he loftily scorned to better himself by such baseness; and, not content with being true to me himself, he exercised all his energies, influence, and ingenuity to keep others so. He may be a "robber chief," as the press has designated him, or he may not. I know nothing of his offenses against society; I only know that, in his intercourse with me, I found him a brave and noble hearted man, willing to risk his life on the side of a persecuted and outraged stranger; and I fervently hope that for *that* the Recording Angel will drop a blotting tear upon the page of his misdeeds.

Early the next morning (the twelfth of July), Pedro was ready to start with the pack-mule. I gave him eight dollars to buy his children some "*dulces,*" also money to get his eldest boy, *Chino,* a hat, and some brandy for himself and me, and off he started to town. I remained about the house all that day and the next without anything of interest occurring, and in the evening of the second day Pedro returned with everything, including a pair of shoes, blanket, and checked shirt, which Power had sent to me. I, however, discovered that, though the brandy had arrived with the other things, it was not in its "original package," but was contained in Pedro's skin. He had left town with it, all right, but, it being a very hot and dusty day, he became dry, and then drier, and at length *very* dry, and had finished by emptying the jug, which he left upon the road as a useless encumbrance. He endeavored to excuse himself by telling me that my friend General Covarrubias had instructed him not to give me any brandy, as I was imprudent when drinking, and might bring trouble on myself. This appeared all very well, but I was compelled to doubt the statement, knowing that the General could appreciate a good glass of brandy himself, and was not likely to wish to deny me the same comfort. However, I made up my mind to do without it, and, indeed, it was much better for me. During my stay at the Arroyo, my corpulency began to diminish, and I perceived that I was again getting into some sort of shape, while my general health was never better.

During the first few days of my stay at the Arroyo, I slept in the house, amusing myself in the daytime with the children. Nothing of note occurred until about the fourth day, when my friend the Spaniard who had been deceived by Power about my whereabouts called at the house. I was upstairs while he was there, and overheard his conversation with the *señora* and Pedro. He had discovered that he had been deceived by Power, and had been hunting me up. He asked Pedro if he had heard or seen anything of me, to which Pedro replied that he had not. I had by this time picked up enough of Spanish to understand the general drift of their talk. The Spaniard expressed it as his opinion that *Jacky Power* had killed me for my money, and hid my body somewhere. Pedro appeared to be very much astonished at such a suspicion. The wretch little knew that I was then safely listening to him from a place of refuge which Jack had provided to save me from being murdered and robbed by him. After some further conversation with the family, he went away as wise as he came, so far as my matters were concerned.

On the twelfth day of July, a relation of Pedro came to the Arroyo. He was driving a band of cattle, and made that point his stopping-place for the night. While he was there, I, of course, kept myself out of sight. He was, I think, the godfather of Avellino, and, before he left the next morning, presented him with a fat three-year-old steer. The gift was a very welcome one, as there had not been any fresh meat about the place for several days. The day of his departure, while I was lying in my room, I heard a voice that struck me as being very familiar. The speaker was talking Spanish, however, and I did not understand what he said. After he had gone, I looked after him, and at once recognized him. It was Robert Hays, Esq., the brother of the present U. S. surveyor-general for California. Although I knew him very intimately, I did not hail him, as he had several persons with him. Poor Bob! It was to be the last time I ever saw him on earth. He has since died. He had a six-mule team with him, and had stopped to inquire the road of the *señora*, who informed me that the party were from the lower country, and were inquiring the road to San Luis Obispo.

Toward evening of that day, I suddenly entered the house, and, seeing a woman standing in the door, mistook her for the *señora*, and was about to address her when I discovered that I was mistaken. It was a daughter of old *Miguel Cota*, of the *Refugio*. She was accompanied by a young brother, a lad about seventeen years of age. She at once recognized me, and I knew that I was now subjected, by this mischance, to real danger. The very people, of all others, from whom I wished to keep my hiding-place a secret, were the inhabitants of the Refugio. As has been before stated, it was a public drinking-place, and general *rendezvous* for all the idlers, newsmongers, and rascals of the neighborhood; and besides, my anxious friend, the Spaniard of Las Cruces, who, I knew, was endeavoring to discover my whereabouts, was a frequent visitor there. It was a bad business, but I had to make the best of it. She did not remain long, and, after she had left, the *señora* expressed her anxiety lest my secret should become known. I tried to reassure her, telling her that I did not think she would tell of my whereabouts, though I felt quite sure that either she or her brother would certainly do so; and it turned out that I was not mistaken in my opinion.

The very next morning, before I was up, old *Miguel Cota* was in the house, and the *señora* had great difficulty in getting me out of it without his seeing me. He told her, as I afterward ascertained, that he had heard of my being there, and was very inquisitive about me. The *señora* told him that I had left her house that morning, and gone to the lighthouse at Point Conception. The old fellow remained all day at the house, while I kept concealed in the cañon. The *senora* sent me, by *Avellino*, some nice fresh meat, they having killed the steer that day, and some warm tea. Several other persons visited the place during the day, but at night they all left, and I returned to the house. The *señora* told me, before I retired, that she thought old *Miguel* really believed that I had gone to Point Conception, and I felt greatly relieved to hear it.

Things went on very quietly for two or three days after this, and nothing of importance occurred until the night of the fourteenth of July. I still slept in the house, and was enjoying a pleasant rest when, at about two o'clock, A. M., I was awakened by the sound of horses' hoofs approaching the door. The visitor proved to be General Covarrubias. He had ridden all the way from Santa Bárbara to inform me that a deputation of twenty or twenty-five of the Vigilance Committee had arrived that evening, in the steamer from San Francisco, and would, without doubt, begin the pursuit after me at daylight. He had therefore kindly come to give me timely warning, in order that I might put myself out of the way. He could not give me the names of the deputation, but was enabled to inform me that *Selim E. Woodworth* was one of the leaders. I thought this was very strange, for both Selim and his brother had told me, a few days after the organization of the Committee, that, although they had been members of the Vigilance Committee of 1851, they were not of this one, and saw no necessity for its organization. What had worked this wonderful change in two months, I am unable to say; nothing had occurred since the organization of the Committee more likely to lead them to join it, than the event which brought it into existence. One significant fact, however, is, that Frederick A. Woodworth was elected to represent San Francisco in the state senate, last winter, by the vote of the Vigilantes.

General Covarrubias did not remain long with me, as he had to return to Santa Bárbara, a distance of thirty-five miles, before day, to prevent his visit to the Arroyo from being known. Thus that generous-hearted old gentleman had taken upon himself a ride of *seventy miles* in one night, to give warning to a poor outcast, against whom it seemed the whole world was in arms. May years of honor and happiness be still in store for him, and his old age as green as will ever be my grateful recollection of his kindness. He gave me a bottle of really *good* brandy, which he brought from Santa Bárbara for me, and, after telling me to be sure to get out of the way as soon as it was light, he rode back to town. I have been since informed that he was seen, that night, going to the Arroyo Hondo by one of Don Pablo De la Guerra's people; on being informed of which, that gentleman immediately sent the man to one of his ranchos in the interior, to prevent his telling it.

As soon as it was light, I took my blankets and water, with provisions sufficient to last me several days in case circumstances should cut off my communication with the house, and went out with little Avellino, who carried the things on his pony, in search of a good hiding-place. I selected one at no great distance from the house, on the mountain-side, where, from its steepness and the thick growth of chaparral, it was impossible for a horseman to approach me. No one but *Avellino,* who was to visit me as often as possible, knew the place of my retreat. I remained in this place five days without interruption, Avellino visiting me every day, and bringing from his good mother warm tea, eggs, etc. During the first part of my sojourn here, Avellino, who daily brought me the news, informed me that several of "*Los Yankees,*" as he called them, had been riding about the neighborhood, but, as yet, none of them had approached the house. One morning, however, he brought me the intelligence that a stranger, who was an American, and armed with a six-shooter, was at the house. Avellino said he talked a great deal about me, and professed to be my friend. The little fellow did not return to me that day, as usual, with my dinner. From this I suspected that there must be something wrong. About the middle of the day, I heard loud shooting in the vicinity of the house. First there were six shots fired from a pistol, in rapid succession, and then no more shooting for a long time, when I heard three or four tremendous reports, nearly as loud as would have been made by a cannon. This threw me into great consternation. I did not know what on earth to make of it. I surmised all sorts of things. I was in a dreadful agony of suspense, and sometimes fancied that perhaps the Committee had received proof that *Pedro* had sheltered me, and, not finding me on his premises, had battered down his house, and killed him and the *señora*, and possibly the little children, and old *Konoya* and his two black dogs, and everything else about the place. I lay still, however, in my hiding-place, without stirring out of it till night came. Still no one came near me, and I now made quite sure that something unfortunate had occurred. I slept none the whole of that anxious night, and the morning found me still unvisited. At length, about noon, to my great relief and joy, I saw little Avellino coming to me with my food, and so great was my delight that I could not refrain from taking him in my arms and kissing him. I tried to learn from him what had happened, but, though the child did his best to make me understand him, he could not succeed. I could only learn from the Spanish word which signified it, that something had been *killed*, and could also make out that everybody about the house was safe. I made him understand that I wanted to see his father, to which he replied, "*Poco tiempo*," and gave me to know that the American was still at the house. Avellino left me, and toward evening he guided Pedro to my hiding-place. The whole mystery of the preceding day was then explained. Pedro told me that the American was traveling from Santa Bárbara, according to his own story, to San Luis Obispo, and had stopped at his house to rest himself for a day or so. Shortly before dinner-time, the dogs had started a California lion in the orchard, and ran him into a tree. The stranger had expended all the shots of his six-shooter on him without killing him, and they had then sent over to the Refugio for an *escopeta*, with which he was finally dispatched. This accounted for the loud reports I had heard. Pedro gave me a copy of the San Francisco *Herald*, and another of the New York *Spirit of the Times*, which the stranger had left behind him. Whoever that *Vigilante* was, I beg leave here to return him my thanks for the news with which he so kindly supplied me. Pedro told me that the fellow talked a great deal about me, and professed to be my friend, telling him that I could return to San Francisco, after the excitement had died away, without molestation, etc. I told Pedro that the man was a spy, and had only been endeavoring to draw from him some information as to my whereabouts. There was no good reason why he should require to rest nearly two whole days after riding only thirty-five miles, the distance from Santa Bárbara, and I, of course, understood that his protestations of friendship for me were only intended to throw Pedro off of his guard, and induce him to be communicative. Pedro agreed with me, and, after some little further conversation, returned to the house. Two days after this, and after the steamer had gone down the coast, I came down from the mountain and prepared to sleep in the cañon, which was much warmer and pleasanter. After I had spread out my blankets, it being quite dark, I went to the house to pay a visit to the senora. I stayed some time there before I returned to my sleeping-place. It was very dark when I got back, and, as I was about getting under my blankets, I felt something crawl along my body and coil itself up beside me. I, of course, knew what it was, and as I was springing from the blankets the reptile began to rattle. I ran off a short distance, and, peering through the dim starlight, I could see its outlines as it lay coiled near the blankets, rattling its tail. Thank Heaven, however, it had given me warning, and I could not help thinking that, in that respect, it was more chivalrous than the bloodhounds of the Committee, who were trying to steal upon me, night and day, to murder me. This was really one of the worst

I ran off a short distance, and, peering through the dim starlight, I could see its outlines as it lay coiled near the blankets, rattling its tail.

frights I had during my campaign. I did not go near my blankets again that night, but returned immediately to the house and informed them of my narrow escape. The senora put me upstairs, in the bed with her oldest boy, *Chino.* After I had got into my little friend's bed, I could not sleep. It was not half as comfortable as my blankets on the ground; and I had been sleeping in the open air so many nights, that the air of the room was disagreeably close. The bed, too, was full of fleas, which were devouring me. Toward day, however, I succeeded in getting to sleep, and so remained till about eight o'clock in the morning, when Avellino came to call me to breakfast. It had been ready some time, and waiting for me. I got up and dressed, but felt so badly from the loss of sleep and the bites of the fleas, that I told the senora I would take a bath before I breakfasted. About an eighth of a mile from the house, there was a clear, cold spring, in which I bathed every day, to make myself tough and hearty. To this spring, then, I went, and enjoyed a most delightful bath. I had just got out of the water when I heard the voice of Avellino calling out to me, "*¡Paisano, Paisano!*" I replied, "*¡Aquí, aquí, muchacho!*" He came running up to me breathlessly, exclaiming, "*¡Los hombres en el casa! ¡Mucha mala! ¡Vigilantes! ¡Escopetas! ¡Vamos, vamos!*"—making motions with his hand to me to run up the mountain. At the same time, he gathered my blankets, which lay where I had spread them the night before, and put them in a hollow tree. I knew that the little fellow was in earnest, and, hastily throwing on my clothes, I moved off as fast as my legs could carry me, while Avellino ran back to the house.

I had not been long on the mountain before *Pedro* came and informed me that I had scarcely left the house before two men, armed with guns, rushed into it, and went directly upstairs to the bed where I had slept. Then they searched the house thoroughly, and afterwards old *Konoya's* hut. While they were ransacking the hut, the senora, fearing that I would come back, dispatched Avellino to warn me of my danger.

He told me that one of them was known to him, and that he was a keeper of the lighthouse, named MEACHAM. The other one, he said, was a large man, with sandy whiskers, probably from San Francisco, and a stranger to him. They told him they had ridden from the lighthouse that morning, a distance of twenty miles, Meacham acting as guide. He said that *they were then eating the breakfast that had been prepared for me.* Here was an unexpected state of things! As there were only two of them, I suggested to Pedro the idea of capturing them. Pedro having no gun, however, I concluded that if we took them at all, it would have to be done singly. One of the men, Pedro told me, had left his gun leaning against the house, outside the door, when he went in to breakfast. I proposed to Pedro to walk into the house and engage them in conversation while I should manage to get the gun and shoot the San Francisco man, and we would then capture Meacham.

Reader, be not startled at this avowal of so bloody an intent. I deliberately declare to you, that, if it had been feasible, I would have done it, and felt now no pang of remorse or upbraiding of conscience on account of it. A cruel and relentless war was being waged against me by a set of lawless miscreants; I was myself hunted with guns, like a wild beast; and it was as much my natural right to turn and rend my pursuers, if I could, as it is that of a bear or a wolf to destroy, if he can, the huntsman who has wounded him. The question of murder or manslaughter, or any other legal phrase which designates the killing of man by his fellow, enters not into the consideration of what I was about to do. These men had placed themselves outside the pale of the law, and even of civilization, by their barbarous persecution of me, and I would have killed one of them with as little compunction as I would a wild Indian who was pursuing me in a hostile wilderness. I offered Pedro half of the money I had if he would assist me to carry out my plan, but he would not listen to it. He said that Meacham was his friend, and harm might befall him in the melée, and besides, it would be very sure to bring trouble on himself.

Finding that there was no chance of carrying out my design, I was obliged to give it up, and let the bloodhound live, and bitterly do I still regret that it had to be so. I was anxious to get a look at them, and Pedro and I walked cautiously down toward the house. The gun had by this time been taken indoors, and I did not see it. Pedro said that the San Francisco man talked a great deal to Meacham about me, expressing his surprise that I had not yet been taken. He would have talked on about the plans of my pursuers, but Meacham checked him by telling him that Pedro understood English. Meacham himself spoke Spanish. They asked the señora a great many questions about me. She told them she did not know who the man was that had been to her house (the *Refugio* people had given the information of my having been positively seen there), nor where he had gone, and asked Meacham if he had not been to the lighthouse, where he started to go when he left her house. They evidently suspected that she knew more than she chose to tell, and finally they told her that if she would tell them where I was, they would give her three thousand dollars. But the faithful woman, though very poor, and with a large family of children and a drunken husband, persisted in denying that she knew anything about me.

Finding that they could make nothing out of her, and probably giving up the idea that I was about the premises, they finally mounted their horses and rode toward Santa Bárbara; Meacham stating, before he left, that he would be back the next day, on his way to the lighthouse. As they rode away, I had a full view of them, but they were too far off for me to distinguish the features of the large man from San Francisco, with the sandy whiskers. After they were gone, I did partly persuade Pedro into a plan by which, if they came back, I could get a chance at the large man from San Francisco. Meacham only returned, however, and he did not stop at the house, but rode directly on.

The occurrence of the morning convinced me that there must be something foul going on about the premises, and I confess I had begun to suspect that Pedro's avarice could not stand much more temptation. The fact of those two men rushing directly to the bed I had occupied, and one of them being a great friend of Pedro, looked very badly. However, I did not communicate my suspicions to any one of the family, and determined to keep a sharp lookout, and, at least, not come so near being caught napping again.

About the time of this attempt to kidnap me, another cargo of "reformers" landed at Santa Bárbara, in the schooner "Exact." They were under the command of T. D. Johns, a colonel of one of the Vigilance Committee regiments. Whether this man's antecedents in California peculiarly fitted him for the task of reforming the morals of his fellow-citizens or not, is a question which, at some future day, I propose to investigate for the enlightenment of our own day and generation, as well as of posterity. This immaculate "purifier" had under his command James F.

Curtis, now chief of police in San Francisco,—an office bestowed upon him by the Vigilance vote as a reward for his zealous and self-sacrificing efforts to subvert the constitution and insult the laws. There were also in the party D. W. C. Thompson, Charles H. Gough, and a score or two of obscure lunch-eaters, hired by the day to do the Committee's dirty bidding, whose glorious names I regret to be unable to hand down to posterity with befitting honor. They landed part of their force at the lighthouse at Point Conception, and placed them under the command of Meacham, who, enjoying the position of lighthouse-keeper merely to vary the monotony of his existence, amused himself by perpetrating treason against the government, upon whose bounty he lived. They landed in a small boat, which they presented to Meacham, and I afterward understood that he had promised to give it to Pedro. As they never found me, however, at Pedro's house, I scarcely think he made good his promise.

The "Exact" remained but a short time at Santa Bárbara, and then proceeded down the coast, stationing men at San Pedro, San Diego, and all the important points on the coast, even as far down as the Rio Colorado. I have reason to believe that by this time my friend Jack Power had managed to get most of them on the wrong scent, for by far the greater portion of the party in the "Exact" went down the coast.*

---

* THE VIGILANCE COMMITTEE POLICE ARRIVED AFTER THE BIRD HAS FLOWN.—The *Gazette* of the 17th says: On Sunday last, the schooner Exact, from San Francisco, arrived at this port. She had a large number of passengers on board. Some of them came on shore, and are still in the county. The schooner set sail on Tuesday last.

MEANWHILE NED VISITS LOS ANGELES.—The Los Angeles *Star*, after narrating the events which transpired at Santa Bárbara, gives us the following further information as to the subsequent movements of this modern "will-o'-the-wisp":—

After this miraculous escape, (the Santa Bárbara affair,) we next heard of him, on Thursday evening, being in Los Angeles. The report was general that he was here,—nobody seemed to doubt it,—yet we could not discover any one who had seen him; although a certain party—somewhat of a wag, however—went to the express-office inquiring for letters for McGowan.—*Bulletin, July 20th.* [?]

Most of the above information as to the movements of my pursuers I received from a nephew of Don Pablo De la Guerra, who visited me at the Arroyo a day or two after the visit of Meacham and his San Francisco friend. This young gentleman spoke English very well. His father was an Englishman named Hartnell, who had married into the De la Guerra family. He informed me that the San Franciscans reported all sorts of stories as to my whereabouts.*

I had forgotten to state, that, while General Covarrubias was making the night-ride to give me warning of the arrival of Woodworth's party in the steamer, Don Pablo, not being very anxious for them to commence the hunt after me that night, entertained them at a sort of evening party at his house. This young gentleman had been present on that occasion, and gave me an account of it. He said that Dr. Den was present, and asked *"Little Woody,"* as his friends called him, if he had turned "rat-catcher." Wood-

---

* NED McGOWAN NOT CAPTURED.—There is an old legend related somewhere about the king of the French who, with a large army, on a certain memorable occasion, marched up a hill, the name of which has not yet been rescued from oblivion, and, after having performed this feat, marched down again. So with the schooner Exact. It spread all sail about ten days ago for Santa Bárbara—arrived there—anchored there—landed the Vigilance Committee police there—waited for their return—took them again on board, and steered for this port, where she arrived yesterday. The cruise of the Exact may be summed up in a few words. She sailed for Santa Bárbara, and sailed back again. It was rumored, when she cleared, that a large number of the Vigilance Committee police took passage upon her for Santa Bárbara, for the purpose of taking Ned McGowan, who, according to the reports circulated in this city previous to the sailing, was completely run down to the heel, his face covered with black patches, and his hat—even that white hat—missing. But, notwithstanding that he was supposed to have been reduced to this deplorable condition, he again "dodged," and has not been heard from since. It must be admitted that he is an eccentric genius. After his flight from this city, we first hear of him at Carson Valley, and scarcely sufficient time has elapsed to form a correct idea of the celerity of his movements, when he turns up at Santa Bárbara. At this point a vigorous search is instituted, but no traces of the fugitive can be found. Meanwhile he dies, and the sheriff of Santa Bárbara offers a reward for his body, and it is by no means certain that McGowan may not yet claim, *in propria persona*, that reward. Where he will turn up next is beyond the range of conjecture.—*S. F. Herald, July 26th.*

worth replied, that he was there in the capacity of a deputy sheriff, and that, if he succeeded in capturing me, *he should, of course, hand me over to the officers of the law* (of course he would!), and actually exhibited a bench-warrant. Here, then, was the first gun fired at me from a legitimate quarter. How these persons came into possession of those warrants is a mystery to me to this day. I have ascertained that David Scannell, the sheriff of San Francisco, did not depute them, and he alone had power to do so. Thomas Hayes, the county clerk, has assured me that there is no record in his office of the issuance of any such warrant, and none of the newspapers of San Francisco appear then to have known that any members of the Vigilance Committee were in the possession of authority to arrest me, under the law.* Probably Mr. District Attorney Byrne is able to

---

*PURSUIT OF NED MCGOWAN.—Yesterday, after the arrival of the steamer Sea Bird, and the spreading of the news that the notorious *Judge* Ned McGowan had been discovered in the neighborhood of Santa Bárbara, several members of the Vigilance Committee went to Sheriff Scannell and asked him to deliver to them the warrant for McGowan's arrest, which had been issued from the court of sessions when, as will be recollected, McGowan was indicted for the murder of James King of William. The Sheriff refused to give up the warrant, but assured them that he would send Deputy Sheriff Harrison with the warrant after McGowan on the next steamer, which goes to-morrow. The Vigilantes retired, and as the affair seemed to them to require dispatch, they immediately took measures for pursuing, and if possible capturing, the fugitive on their own responsibility. The schooner Exact was chartered by the Committee, made ready for sea, ten members of the Vigilance police placed upon her, and, last evening, about ten o'clock, all arrangements having been completed, she was towed out beyond the Heads by the steam-tug Hercules, and pro ceeded on her voyage with all the sail that she could spread upon her masts.—*S. F. Bulletin, July 10th.*

THE ARREST OF NED MCGOWAN.—The Sheriff, it is stated, has sent one of his deputies on the Sea Bird, empowered to arrest McGowan if he should be found at Santa Bárbara. This is a very proper proceeding, although it would have been better to have authorized the delegation of the Vigilance Committee, who went down on the Exact, to arrest this man. We suppose that a delegation of the Committee also went down on the Sea Bird, as it would prevent future difficulties with the authorities to obtain possession of McGowan previous to his arrival in this city. McGowan *must be tried by the Committee.* The people will be satisfied with no other mode of trial, and we are confident that no other mode of trial will secure the ends of justice. There is no body so fit for the investigation of this

solve the mystery. His brother, Lafayette Byrne, was the deputy sheriff attending on the court of sessions, and it is a little remarkable that when Mr. District Attorney Byrne was called upon to give new bonds under the Consolidation Act, Selim E. Woodworth and his brother, the senator, became his sureties. Since my return, I have endeavored in vain to discover who it was that deputed these people, and thus put an additional weapon into the hands of my enemies. It is almost as difficult to solve this matter as it was for my enemies to discover the "white hat" which was supposed to cover the head of the ubiquitous author of this narrative. One thing is very certain: they had the warrants; and it is equally certain, in my mind, that, had either Mr. Selim E. Woodworth or any of his gang succeeded in capturing me, the officers of the law would have had very little chance of exercising their functions in my case. Under the circumstances which so notoriously surrounded me, it can scarcely be insisted that giving me aid and comfort, even against these warrants, could be construed into the compounding of a felony. On the contrary, all aid extended to me, under the circumstances, was only so much done toward preventing the perpetration of a felony on me.

I also learned from Mr. Hartnell that placards offering large rewards for my body if, as was by some supposed, I was dead, were posted in conspicuous places throughout Santa Bárbara. They were printed in both English and

---

man's case as that which has ferreted out the crimes of his accomplices and punished their perpetrators.

Now, in advance of any action in this matter, we wish clearly to give the authorities of this city notice, in the name of the people, that no tricks or quibbles of law will avail to save this man from his deserved doom. No *habeas corpus* writ, or other means of exciting a public disturbance, need be resorted to. The people are determined to carry out their purposes, in spite of any opposition—and opposition will therefore be useless. McGowan must not be left to the law to deal with him. We trust, therefore, that either the Exact will arrive at Santa Bárbara in time to place him on board that vessel previous to the arrival of the steamer, or that those who have gone down in the steamer will succeed in arresting him in the name of the Committee, and will deliver him to that body on his arrival in this city. Of course, all these remarks are based on the supposition that McGowan has been taken, which is by no means a certainty.—*S. F. Bulletin, July 14th* [*11th*].

Spanish. The description of my person was very bad, though it must be confessed I was not in a situation to be remarkably cleanly or neat in my apparel. Among other things, the placards set forth that I chewed tobacco, and did it in a filthy manner. I have never chewed a piece of tobacco in my life. In my age, too, they made a mistake of seven years. I tried very hard, afterwards, to get one of the original copies, but could not succeed. Mr. Hartnell informed me that the name of Wm. T. Coleman, president of the Vigilance Committee, was appended to them. The following is a copy of one of them, which was published in the Santa Bárbara *Gazette*: —

300 DOLLARS REWARD!!

It being rumored that one EDWARD McGOWAN, a fugitive from justice, on the charge of murder, from San Francisco County, who was last seen in Santa Bárbara, has been murdered for a sum of money known to have been in his possession, the above reward will be paid for the recovery of his body, or for information that will lead to his discovery, by applying to the office of Russell Heath, sheriff of Santa Bárbara County.   July 14, 1856.

DESCRIPCION DE McGOWAN. — Su estatura es de cinco pies y nuevo pulgados; bastante grueso, su peso sera como ciento setenta libros; mas de cicuenta años; acostumbra mascar tabaco en estremo; ojos aguiteños, pintando en canas, y sucio en su persona.

The following is a translation of the passage: —

DESCRIPTION OF McGOWAN. — He is about five feet nine inches tall; tolerably stout; his weight about a hundred and seventy pounds; somewhat more than fifty years of age; and accustomed to chew tobacco to excess. He has gray eyes and hair, and is very dirty in his person.

I remained concealed in my hiding-place, making an occasional call on the family at the house, until Saturday, the twenty-sixth day of July. Things were so quiet, and so few persons visited the Arroyo, that I began to think a storm must be brewing, and became uneasy. On that day I made an arrangement with the señora to send her to Santa Bárbara with a note to General Covarrubias, and she was also to make a careful reconnoissance, and pick up any information she could with regard to the movements of the enemy. Accordingly, she cooked me a chicken stuffed with eggs, etc., and gave me enough food to last four or five days. I gave her twenty dollars, and some money to *Chino* to spend in town for himself and buy me a bottle of brandy. She had five horses saddled, and took all of her children with her. After giving me strict instructions, on no account to come near the house for fear of a surprise, she rode off. As soon as they had gone, I betook myself to my retreat on the mountain, and prepared to lie close until my good hostess should return. When night came, I hung my chicken and other food on a limb, and supposed that it would there be safe. But what was my consternation, on awakening in the morning, at finding that it had all mysteriously disappeared! Some sneaking coyote, with which that portion of the country abounds, had stolen it in the night. Here was a dilemma! I was without food, and knew that the *señora* would not return for several days, and was at a loss what to do. Finally I walked down the cañon toward old *Konoya's* hut, but had no sooner come in sight of the orchard than, to my great surprise and alarm, I espied a man, with a red shirt on, lying down, with his face to the ground. I instantly started back into the cha parral, and escaped his notice. I returned to my hiding place at once, and remained there till dark, when I again came down, and entered *Konoya's* hut. I got from the old man some jerked beef, and immediately started back to my retreat. This was on Sunday evening, the 27th of July. I had not gone far before I heard footsteps, and immediately got out of the way. I observed two men, one of whom was Pedro, go to the place where I usually hid. I followed on after them, and when they arrived at the spot, Pedro said, "*Come.*" This was the usual word to signify to me his approach. I appeared before him, wondering who could be the stranger with him. I saw that Pedro was very drunk. He told me the man lived at Las Cruces, where he had been spending the day with him, but did not give me his name. I was very angry at Pedro's conduct, for he had promised Power, when he put me in his charge, that no one should know of my place of concealment, outside of his own family. He pressed me to drink some bad brandy out of a bottle which he had with him, which I declined, and he and his companion fell into a conversation in Spanish, of which I could understand that I was the subject. The stranger apparently did not believe that I was the person that Pedro was representing me to be, but the drunken wretch assured him that I was, and spoke to him in the most imprudent manner about my friends in Santa Bárbara, telling him their names. After they had conversed some time, the stranger asked me, in Spanish, for sixty dollars. I understood him perfectly well, but pretended that I did not, and asked Pedro what he said. He replied, "He wants you to give him sixty dollars, and he will not tell any one that you are here." My first impulse was to take out my purse and give him the money, but a moment's reflection prevented my committing that act of folly. I remembered that Pedro had never seen my money, and thought it best that he should not. I told them that I had hid my purse in the mountain, but that if they would come the next day, I would give the man what he demanded. This did not appear exactly to satisfy them; nevertheless, after some further conversation, they left me.

After they had gone, I began to reflect upon my situation, and the more I did so, the more satisfied I became that new and unseen perils were gathering around me. I knew that there were others about the house; for the appearance of the red-shirted man I had seen in the orchard was as yet unaccounted for. I determined not to sleep in my usual place, and, accordingly, I moved a short distance from it, where I could see anything that might transpire, without being visible myself, and kept watch all night.

Just before daylight I saw three men coming up the canon. They were conversing in a low tone, and I could gather that it was about me. They went to the spot where I had slept the night before, and, not finding me there, again went away.

My mind was now made up that, beyond all doubt, Pedro had some hellish design on me, and I concluded that the Arroyo Hondo was no longer a safe refuge. Accordingly, as soon as it was sufficiently light, I went down to old Konoya's hut and got the only remaining piece of jerked beef he had,—and a very small piece it was,—and, leaving there a blanket the señora had loaned me, took the one that Power had sent me, and, with many a bitter imprecation as I contrasted in my mind the treachery of the scoundrel Pedro with the fidelity of his good wife, I took my way up the mountain, and became once more a friendless wanderer.

CHAPTER VI

Whence com'st thou, Dervise?"
"From the outlaw's den,
A fugitive—"
Corsair.

My determination was to go as speedily as possible to the residence of Dr. Nicholas A. Den. I had learned from Mr. Hartnell that he had no sympathy with my persecutors; and I knew that if I could but get under his protection, I had nothing to fear, at any rate from treachery, and I believed that his knowledge of the country and its inhabitants, together with his high standing in the community, would enable me more easily to baffle my pursuers.

After leaving the *Arroyo Hondo* on the morning of the twenty-eighth, I struck out toward Santa Bárbara, between which place and the Arroyo Dr. Den's place was situated. I did not go far, however, merely crossing the point of the hill where I had my hiding-place, and, coming to a small gulch filled with a thick growth of wild mustard, I halted by the side of a little stream which I found there, and lay concealed until nightfall. As soon as it was quite dark, I took to the sea-beach and walked to the southward about twelve miles, when I came to the ranch of *Señor Ignacio Ortega*, before mentioned as being between the Arroyo and the Doctor's residence. Here I got among some bushes, and slept soundly until day. Before it was quite light, I again took to the sea-beach, and had good walking until I arrived at the Doctor's house. As I approached I saw no one but a few of the Doctor's people, mostly Indians. The family were not yet stirring.

My appearance seemed to cause them much astonishment. They eyed me very closely as I went boldly toward the house and inquired for Doctor Den. With difficulty they made me understand that the Doctor was absent from home, on a visit to Santa Inés. They also informed me that his lady, whom they called Dona Rosa, had not yet risen. I sat down on the tongue of a wagon near the house, and, keeping a good lookout, determined to wait until the family were moving. While I sat here I was very unpleasantly scrutinized by a tall, gray-haired old Spaniard, who, I afterward learned, belonged to Monterey. I sat for about an hour, and was becoming quite uneasy under the stare of the old man, when the door of the house opened, and a very gentle and amiable looking lady appeared. Her complexion was much fairer than that of the generality of California ladies, and she had a remarkably sweet expression of countenance. I at once decided in my mind that she was the wife of my friend the Doctor. I addressed her in English, but discovered that she did not speak the language. I then tried French, and was equally unsuccessful. Directly, however, she said to me, "*Poco tiempo,*" and, entering the house, she presently returned with a beautiful little child, who proved to be her daughter. I took her to be about ten years of age, though I afterward ascertained that she was exactly twelve. There was something about the child which made her appear to my eyes like an angel of mercy as she fearlessly approached me, and said to me, in silvery tones and in perfect English, "What is your will, sir?" I replied to her, "My dear, I am very hungry, and want something to eat, and then, if you can get it for me, I want a pen, ink, and paper to write a note to General Covarrubias."

As soon as I mentioned *Covarrubias*, Dona Rosa hastily beckoned to me to come at once into the house. I saw at a glance that she had heard of my persecution and suspected who I was. She appeared to be in the greatest trepidation, and I at once entered the house and informed her who I was. Her sweet little daughter, Kate, informed me, in purer English than I could use, that the road had been lined for many days with armed horsemen, who were hunting me, and that her mother was fearful I would yet be captured, unless I was very careful. Doña Rosa at once set her servants to work to prepare a breakfast for me, and informed me, through her little interpreter, that her husband, the Doctor, had gone to the college farm, at Santa Inés, to attend to some business for the Archbishop, and would not be at home for four or five days. She expressed her fears that it would be unsafe for me to remain there, because, although she could be responsible for her own people, she feared that the old Californian who had eyed me só, and who, she informed me, was from Monterey, would betray me. Her own family consisted of herself and daughter, and a very handsome young lady, whom she introduced to me as her sister, Miss Hill. There were also some twenty to twenty-five farm and house servants about the place, with their children. They were mostly Indians. Doña Rosa told me that there was nothing to be apprehended from any of these, but that the old Californian suspected who I was, and had just said to her, when she had stepped out a moment before, that she had enough persons about the place to arrest me, if she felt disposed to do so. I agreed with my kind hostess that I ought to leave as soon as possible, and determined, as soon as I had eaten breakfast, which was now ready, to do so.

At this time I had not shaved for two months; my beard was perfectly white and untrimmed, my clothes in a very dilapidated condition, and altogether I must have presented a most wretched appearance. I suppose I looked, with my long, white beard, at least sixty years old, and what with that and my torn and travel-stained garments, the Vigilante description of me, as regarded my age and dirty personal appearance, was not so far out of the way, after all. While I sat enjoying my excellent breakfast and hot coffee, Doña Rosa kept watching me, and giving expression to her sympathy, frequently murmuring to herself, "¡Pobrecito!" and other words of her own language, expressive of her feeling for my misfortunes. Everything that could be done to accommodate me was done by the kind lady. Although it is not, I believe, customary for the native Californians to eat meat at their breakfasts, still an abundance of it was cooked and placed upon the table for me. I observed that the servants seemed to wonder "what manner of man" I was, to be seated, in that garb, with ladies at the table, and treated with such respect. After breakfast, I asked permission of Dona Rosa to give a piece of money to her daughter, little Kate, but she nobly replied, that no money was taken in her house for food given to any one, and particularly to the unfortunate. I begged to be permitted to give the child a small piece, only to keep as a memento of a forlorn stranger, and, after a great deal of hesitation, Doña Rosa, merely to please me, consented. Little Kate now brought me writing materials, and I indited the following note to my friend General Covarrubias:—

My dear Gen'l:—
Circumstances over which I had no control have forced me to again become a wanderer, "houseless and helpless." I am writing this from the Doctor's, and will endeavor to be in this vicinity next Sunday. Try to see me. Your friend,
Le Juge.

To General Covarrubias,
    Santa Bárbara City.
Tuesday Morning,
    July 29th, 1856.

Having given this in charge of my hostess, to be delivered to the General by a sure hand, I again prepared to betake myself to the mountains. Doña Rosa provided me with an extra blanket, a bottle of water, a beef-tongue, and some bread, and then, bidding me Godspeed, saw me depart from her hospitable door. I at once bent my steps to the cañon back of the dwelling, but had not proceeded far when one of the servants, whom they called *Santiago*, thinking that I wanted to go to Santa Bárbara and had mistaken the road, ran after me to set me right. His mistress had seen no necessity of telling him who I was, and, although I of course knew where I was going, in order to avoid exciting his suspicion, I said to him, "*Gracias*," and came down into the main road, and proceeded along it about a mile and a half, when I came to another cañon and at once followed it up into the mountains.

The day was very warm, and my journey up the mountain extremely fatiguing. I penetrated into the thickets, I should judge, some four or five miles, frequently being obliged to cut my way through the chaparral with my knife. Toward dark I reached a point where, I knew, no horse or mule could ever come, and where I doubt whether any human being had ever been before, and, feeling perfectly sure that no one would pursue me that far on foot, I resolved there to halt. After drinking all the water that remained in the bottle, I lay me down to sleep. So high was my elevation, that, notwithstanding my blankets, I was for a long time too cold to sleep. At length the fatigues of the day overcame the coldness of the atmosphere, and I fell asleep and did not awake till morning.

As soon as I had risen, a desire for water reminded me that I had exhausted my supply of that necessary the evening before, and my first and only task for the day must be to travel until I found more. Accordingly, I ate nothing, lest it should increase my thirst before I came to water, which might not be for hours, or even the whole day. There was an *arroyo* that came down from the mountains back of Dr. Den's house, from which his crops were irrigated. In my desire to avoid arousing the suspicions of the man who followed me from the house, I had foolishly wandered away from this stream, taking it for granted that, as heretofore, I should find no difficulty in getting plenty of water almost anywhere in the mountains. I commenced my search, and continued it for some hours without being able to find a drop, or any signs that might lead me to dig for it. The fatigue of making my way through the chaparral, and the heat of a July sun, had now increased my thirst till it had become almost insufferable. The thought, too, that I might wander in those mountains, without finding water, until I became lost, and had to lie down and die a death of torture, almost distracted me. I wandered on until, to my horror, I discovered that I had already got turned around and lost my way. I could not tell, from the confused mass of hills around me, which way to go to get out of them. I was hemmed in by a dense thicket of chaparral, and had scarcely strength to extricate myself. I now sat down on my blankets and began to think seriously of death. I had no means of knowing whether every step I took was not plunging me deeper into the lonely wilds of those vast mountains, and no reason to hope that a journey of days among them, supposing that I could have held out, would have at all bettered my condition. I was indeed in a dreadful strait. I looked imploringly to Heaven for mercy. I knew that I had been, at times, a great sinner against the commandments of God, and asked for forgiveness. I could not, however, bring to my mind a single instance where I had wickedly injured any of my fellow-creatures, or where I had injured any one at all, except in retaliation for injuries done to me, and I thought my punishment was more than I deserved, if it was the intention of Heaven to let me perish there from the tortures of thirst, a lonely maniac, with no eye, save my Maker's, and the beasts and vultures, to look upon my corpse, and no tongue to tell the dreadful story to my fellow-men. I felt that, though it might be the will of Providence that I should not ultimately escape the toils of my pursuers, my sins had not been so black and many that He should have reserved me for this frightful death, and I took heart. I had a burning fever, and all kinds of wild fantasies filled my brain. I thought of the story of Aaron [Moses] smiting the rock in the wilderness for the children of Israel, and actually wondered whether I might not hope for some such miraculous interposition for me. While I sat here too exhausted to move, night came on, and I then discovered, what I did not know before, that thirst is never half so intense at night as it is in the daytime. As the night advanced, although each hour lengthened the time of my privation, still each hour refreshed me. Finally, I fell asleep. When I awoke in the morning, I felt much fresher than when I had halted on the preceding day, but still suffering dreadfully from thirst. I at once summoned all my courage, and pressed forward again, whither I knew not, in search of relief. As the sun rose higher, my agony, of course, increased, but, nerved by despair, I pressed on, eagerly looking round me for any sign of water. I thought of the clear, sparkling spring where I had bathed at the Arroyo Hondo, and the aqueduct of the Mission of Santa Bárbara, and a dozen places where I had seen water clearest and coldest and freshest, and I thought the vision would madden me. At length, after walking an hour or two, just as I had become convinced that I could hold out under the increasing heat but a little while longer, I espied some leaves on the side of a rock, which looked damp. I put my hands on them, and, to my unspeakable joy, I discovered that they were quite wet. I knew there must be water near them, and tried to trace them up to the source, but they became dry again, only a little way up the rock, and I commenced to dig with my knife among them. At first I could not discover where the water was weeping from. After a little while, however, I discovered a small aperture in the rock, shaped something like a bake-oven. The rock was very soft, being decomposed, and I could work on it almost as easily as clay. I dug away at it, and presently drops of water began to fall out of it into a little basin at the bottom of the oven. This basin I cleaned out so that it would hold more, and, after working at it more than an hour, I was enabled, by inserting a reed, which I cut for the purpose, into the basin, to suck up a few drops of water. I think I must have drank all that fell into the basin for an hour and a half before I quenched my thirst. I then ate heartily of my bread and beef-tongue, for I was very hungry, having abstained from eating lest it should increase my thirst. When night came, I made a soft, comfortable bed by spreading my blanket on the leaves, and, throwing myself upon it, I fervently thanked God for his kindness to me in my wretchedness, and enjoyed a sweet and untroubled sleep until morning. When I awoke, I found that my labor of yesterday had been rewarded by a beautiful little spring, which, during the night, had become full of clear, cold water. I took a delicious draft of it, and then washed myself, and sat down to eat the slim remnants of my beef-tongue and bread. I now bethought me that a desperate attempt must be made to get out of the mountains, otherwise, my provisions being exhausted, I should have only escaped death by thirst to perish by starvation.

Accordingly, I cut two long, slim poles with my knife, and, tying them across each other firmly with a piece of my handkerchief, I made a cross, and hung it on a small, leafless tree that stood near the spot, so that, in the event any other poor, hunted fugitive should find himself lost and dying in those mountains, he might see, by the cross, that

I cut the initials of my name on the tree on which I had hung the cross, christened the place "St. Peter's Spring," and commenced my doubtful attempts to get out of the mountain.— *Page 129.*

some one had been there, and find the water. I well knew that none but the persecuted and pursued would ever have business in those grim solitudes. I cut the initials of my name on the tree on which I had hung the cross, christened the place "St. Peter's Spring," and commenced my doubtful attempt to get out of the mountain. After partly walking and partly crawling on my hands and knees through the chaparral for nearly two hours, I heard a distant sound like the falling of water. I immediately turned in the direction from which the sound came, and in about twenty minutes more, during which I was continually descending into a cañon, I came to a large mountain stream. I looked up it, and the scene was very picturesque. It came roaring and dashing on for some distance above me, between two bold and rugged walls of rock, leaping from crag to crag in a succession of beautiful cascades, keeping continually wet with their glittering spray the leaves of the bushes that overhung them. My heart bounded sympathetically with the glad rush of the free waters, and with a heart elated with hope I followed the course of the stream, knowing full well that it must lead me to the valley. I began to suspect that this must be the arroyo that irrigated Doctor Den's estate, and the same from which I had foolishly wandered the previous morning.

It was very hot weather, and as I walked along in the stream, supporting myself on the slippery rocks by means of a pole, I felt very much refreshed. I frequently drank of the water, and toward noon I stopped and took a delightful bath. I here caught a little turtle, which I killed, and found eggs in it. These I ate, and relished them exceedingly. I kept the meat, thinking that perhaps I might want it. At length I came to a little clear place on the bank of the stream, and observed a narrow trail leading out of the brushwood down to the water. I at first thought that this trail was made by the cattle coming to the water to drink. In this I was mistaken, as there are no cattle in those mountains.

It was toward sundown, and I stopped here to rest for the night. I soon discovered what had made the trail. Hearing a rustling in the bushes, I looked up, and on the other side of the stream I saw a beautiful deer. It was looking at me, and occasionally it would stand up on its hind legs, and then paw the earth with its little flinty hoof, like an impatient racer. I was not thirty yards from it, and it remained in the same spot nearly twenty minutes. I had seen plenty of deer before, in my wanderings, for that section of the state abounds in them, but they had always fled at the sight of me. This one had probably never seen a human being before. It seemed to pity me. Its intelligent, bright eye seemed to say to me that it knew from my wretched and weary appearance that I had neither the heart nor the power to harm it. I would not have harmed a hair of its body for the world. It was a comfort to me to look into its face and fancy that I could there read sympathy for my distress, and when, at length, it turned lightly away and vanished in the bushes, I felt as though I had lost a companion. Shortly after my forest visitor had gone, I spread my blankets, and, stretching my weary limbs upon them, I was soon wrapped in a deep sleep.

The next day, Friday, the first of August, I was awake betimes, and continued my journey down the stream. I had not proceeded far before I became convinced that my conjecture as to this being the arroyo that ran through Dr. Den's farm, was correct. I saw the residence of my friend, and once more felt that I was restored to communication with my species. I did not go near the house, not knowing who might be about the premises, but crept stealthily down to the seashore and gathered a quantity of mussels, which I put into my shirt and carried back to the mountains. I also stopped and got over the fence into the Doctor's garden and pulled up some potatoes, which I carried with me, thinking that I might by some chance get fire and cook them. In the hurry of my departure, I had forgotten to ask Doña Rosa for some matches. On my return to the mountain, I laid down my load by the side of the stream and prepared to make my breakfast. I had heard of the Indians making fire by rubbing two dry sticks together, and I tried the experiment. I labored at it about two hours, but was at length obliged to give it up without succeeding. I afterwards learned from one of Dr. Den's servants how to do it, but it was at a time when I did not need the knowledge, and it availed me nothing. He had

It was a comfort to me to look into its face and fancy that I could there read sympathy for my distress.—*Page 131.*

two sticks, one round and the other flat. In the end of the flat one a hole was bored exactly to fit the diameter of the round one. Into this hole he inserted one end of the round stick, and then rolled it back and forth between his hands until the friction produced fire. The sticks have to be of a peculiar kind of wood, which he pointed out to me. I tried the experiment, and succeeded.

I contented myself with breakfasting upon the mussels raw, and enjoyed them pretty well. The tide not being far enough out when I visited the shore, I had not been able to gather many of them, and ate all that I had for breakfast. Toward the middle of the day, I again felt hungry, and resolved to try the raw turtle-meat, which I had put into the stream, in my shirt, to keep it fresh. I found, however, that it was too unpalatable. I was not quite hungry enough to get it down. Knowing, however, that if it once got into my stomach, it would be nutritious and strengthening to me, I tried an experiment, which succeeded. I peeled one of the potatoes, and then scraped it all away with my knife. These scrapings I mixed with water, and made of them little balls, into which I put small pieces of the meat, and thus swallowed it without any unpleasant taste. In this way I managed to eat a raw potato and the turtle.

I laid down supperless that night, determined to get to the beach the next morning earlier, in order to be there at low tide, when the mussels were more plenty. Accordingly, before it was quite light, I again started to the beach, and this time secured a bountiful supply. I returned, and, after breakfasting heartily, had plenty of them left for dinner. I was beginning, however, to get very tired of them. They were exceedingly bitter, and, besides, acted on my system as purgatives. They did me one good service, however: they contributed to relieve me of my obesity. Several of my fat friends have told me, since my return, that they would willingly go through my pilgrimage to be relieved of their surplus flesh. I trust they may never have occasion to know how dreadful a remedy they are willing to try. I would not again go through with the miseries of that hunt to escape from all the bloodhounds that San Francisco could put upon my track. I would far rather turn and die at bay. Indeed, I very much doubt whether many men, accustomed to ease and luxury, *could* endure the privation and suffering to which I was subjected. No man knows, however, what he can do until he tries. To a stout and resolute heart there is no such word as "fail."

I remained in the mountains until the next morning, Sunday, the third of August, when I again descended to the seaside for my usual supply of mussels, and returned to eat them. I began to think now that it was almost time to hear something from my friends at Santa Bárbara, unless my letter to Gen. Covarrubias had miscarried. Accordingly, after my breakfast I again descended, and cautiously approached the Doctor's garden. Before I reached it, I saw a man coming up the cañon, leading a horse. He was a Californian, and one whom I had never seen before. I also heard the voice of some one singing. I immediately retraced my steps and concealed myself. I did not again venture to approach the Doctor's house in that direction, but remained most of the day in the mountains, making my way northward so as to come down into the road above the ranch, toward San Luis Obispo, thinking it much safer than to enter it between the Doctor's and Santa Bárbara. After cautiously reconnoitering, I went over the point of a low hill just ahead of me, and stepped down into the road. I had not more than reached it before a Spaniard came directly upon me from the direction of the house, and, appearing to know all about me, at once gave me to understand that Gen. Covarrubias was at the house, and desired me to come quickly. I went with him at once, and, on reaching the garden, I was met by the Doctor, his wife, little Kate, Gen. Covarrubias, and eight or ten servants. The Doctor, at once seizing me by the hand, and exclaiming, "It is no time to talk," hurried me through the garden and into the house. Just as we entered it, the Doctor pointed through an open window to five armed men who were riding along the road to Santa Bárbara, coming, apparently, from the Arroyo Hondo. "There they go," he exclaimed; "the rat-catchers! They dare not search my house." I had a fair view of the miserable wretches as they galloped by, and as I looked after them I pitied them,—yes, actually pitied them. For who can fall so low, and be so just an object of pity, as the human being who can pursue a fellow-man, by whom he was never wronged, *for hire ?*

The Doctor explained to me, that he had returned from Santa Inés three days after I had left his house; that his wife had kept my note until his return, preferring to send it by his hand to General Covarrubias. As soon as he had read it, he at once ordered his carriage, and, taking his lady with him to avoid suspicion, proceeded to Santa Bárbara and found the General. While there, he discovered that a party, under the lead of the White Pig (Blake), was preparing to go to the Arroyo Hondo, with great hopes of taking me. They arrived, as he had learned, at the Arroyo on Saturday, the second of August. Besides Blake, the party consisted of a deputy sheriff who had a warrant for my arrest, a Scotch blacksmith, and two others. They were all armed with guns and revolvers.

On arriving at the house, they asked the señora a great many questions about me, but she, poor soul, who was now really ignorant of my whereabouts, told them she did not know where I had gone. Although she this time spoke the truth, they did not credit her, and forthwith searched the house and old *Konoya's* hut, and then, leaving at the house the bloody-minded son of Vulcan with his great six-shooter and double-barreled shotgun to prevent the woman or her children from giving me warning in case I was lurking about the premises, the other four beat the bushes about the mountains for some hours. Meeting, however, with no success, they returned to the house, and, the next morning, Sunday, returned disappointed and crestfallen to Santa Bárbara. These were the five worthies whom Dr. Den pointed out to me from his house as they were returning from their fruitless search.

General Covarrubias then entered and embraced me. He and his son Onésimo, and a few of Dr. Den's people, had been searching the mountains high and low with provisions for me, and would have given me up for dead but that a California woman named *María Jesus*, who lived with her husband in the garden, had seen me go to the beach for mussels on Friday. He told me he had been roaming through the mountains, singing, "Covarrubias,

Covarrubias! No Instructions!"* in order to attract my attention and let me know who and where he was. I told him I had heard the singing, and explained to him that I did not recognize his words or his voice, and therefore did not reply. The Doctor brought out some fine English ale, and I consumed three small bottles of it before I quenched my thirst. It was the first thing in the shape of stimulus I had tasted for many days, and, after the fatigues I had lately gone through, it revived me wonderfully.

In the mean while Doña Rosa set her servants to work preparing me a nice chicken, and then invited me to come into the parlor and seat myself by her on the sofa. She kept gazing at me, wretched and forlorn as I was, and murmuring "¡Pobre viejo!" etc.

I felt that I must have cut but a sorry figure in my ragged clothes, and, but for the heartfelt kindness with which I was treated, and which placed me quite at my ease, I should have felt very awkward at finding myself in such a condition in the presence of ladies.

After enjoying a fine supper and passing a delightful evening with that good and deservedly happy family, about nine o'clock it was thought advisable for me to leave the house. Doña Rosa provided me with a pillow and some blankets, and then, accompanied by the General, the Doctor, and a few of his people, I entered a corn-field adjacent

---

* In order that the reader may understand the meaning of his song, it is necessary to relate an anecdote which is familiar to many of the politicians of the state. In the convention which nominated Governor Bigler for his second gubernatorial term, General Covarrubias and Don Pedro Carrillo, now surveyor of the port of Santa Bárbara, were delegates. I also was a member. Don Pedro was of opinion that he and his colleague had been instructed by the Democracy of Santa Bárbara to vote against John Bigler for governor. The General thought differently, and when Santa Bárbara was called, Don Pedro immediately sprang to his feet and informed the convention that his colleague was voting against the instructions of his constituents. To which the General immediately replied, in broken English, "Mr. Chairman, no instructions for Covarrubias! People have confidence in him. They instruct Carrillo." This threw the convention into a laugh, and completely turned the tables on Don Pedro. The story got abroad, and the General was afterwards known among politicians as "No Instructions." Knowing that I would recognize the words, he adopted them as the burden of his song.

to the house, and in the center of it made my camp. This was destined to be my hiding-place for six weeks. The Doctor gave directions to the woman *María Jesus* and her husband, who lived in the garden, to watch over me and provide me with food until further orders. He then gave me a double-barreled gun, and told me that in the morning he would go to town and make arrangements to thwart, if possible, the getting up of any further expeditions against me, or, at any rate, get the earliest intimation of them from his friends. He cautioned me against letting any one see me but those who belonged to his own rancho, and assured me I need have no apprehensions as to their fidelity and discretion. He and the General then bid me good night and left me. When they had gone, I laid down on my blankets and felt happy. I poured out my spirit in thankfulness to Heaven, that I had, after wandering for thirty days through the wilds of Santa Bárbara, unsheltered and unfriended, save by strangers, whose good feeling to me had been rendered useless by treachery, at length found a haven of rest, and a protector and friend on whom I knew I could rely. I fell into a sound and untroubled sleep, for I knew that I was guarded by the *honor* of a hospitable gentleman.

CHAPTER VII

The truly brave,
When they behold their kind oppress'd with odds,
Are touch'd with a desire to shield and save.
Byron.

WHEN I awoke on the morning of the fourth of August, the sun was some hours high. My frequent potations of the Doctor's ale on the previous evening, together with an unaccustomed sense of security, had made my sleep more than usually sound. I found one of the Doctor's servants, *Santiago*, the husband of *Maria Jesus*, who lived in the garden, standing by me with a good breakfast and some hot coffee. He informed me as well as he could that *Don Nicholas*, as he called the Doctor, and General Covarrubias had started early for the city. I had a slight headache when I awoke, but a drop of good brandy before breakfast, and the hot coffee, made me all right. I found my place of refuge very comfortable. The corn was so tall, that I was continually shaded from the sun, except at midday, when I made myself an awning by fastening the corners of a sheet to four stout corn-stalks. I had cleared out a place sufficiently large to enable me to move about comfortably, and, all things considered, I was very snugly lodged.

During the day, I was visited by *Maria Jesus*, accompanied by the Doctor's little son, *Alfonso*. He was a bright-eyed, curly-headed little fellow of about three years of age. The Californian who had notified me the day before that General Covarrubias was waiting to see me at the house, also paid me a visit. Of course we made but a poor attempt at conversation, neither of us speaking the other's language. I ascertained, however, that he was the *mayordomo* of the establishment, and that his name was *Juan*. I made him understand that I would christen him *Juan de Dios* (John of God), inasmuch as he was the one who had informed me that friends awaited me at the house, where I had arrived at such a timely moment. The name pleased him very much, and he and I were warm friends during my entire stay on his hospitable master's premises. In the evening, I came out of the corn-field and visited Santiago's little willow house in the garden. Here I made the acquaintance of *Jacobo*, the cook for the *casa grande*, as they called the family dwelling, and his wife, *Refugia*. As it appeared to be the general rendezvous of the servants and laborers after working-hours, I met with quite a number of them. It was a great *desideratum* with me to put myself on as friendly a footing as possible with these people, on whose discretion my life was to depend during my sojourn with their kind-hearted master, and, accordingly, I made the acquaintance of all of them, particularly informing myself of their various names and occupations, and evincing as well as I could, in my ignorance of their language, a sympathy with them in all their little matters, and gratitude for their kindness in keeping my secret. Besides *Jacobo* and his wife, I made the acquaintance of his brother-in-law, also named *Santiago*, who was about twenty years of age, and a farm-servant; also of *Pedro*, an old Indian who worked in the garden. Among the females, there were *Maria los Angeles*, a kind of lady's maid to Dona Rosa; *Nicolosa*, an Indian girl about twelve years old, whose duty it was to attend the Doctor's youngest child, yet an infant; and *Simona*, an Indian woman who washed for the household. There were many others about the place, with their children, mostly Indians, whose names I cannot remember. They appeared very much pleased with the apparent interest I took in them, and we became warm friends. They were all faithful and discreet to the last, and when they ascertained that I was a Roman Catholic, in which faith they had, of course, been reared, I doubt whether all the gold in California's mines could have induced one of them to betray me. They used to say, in speaking of me, *Paisano es bueno Católico.* Would that I were! I will here remark, that, during my sojourn at Doctor Den's, among the books which he loaned me wherewith to beguile the time, were some on the religion to which I had been brought up, which I conned over with great interest, and became more thoroughly convinced than ever I supposed I would be of the efficacy of religion, and especially that of the Church of Rome.

Before I returned to my bed in the corn-field that night, I observed a white man, a hired laborer of the Doctor's, and, being fearful of him, I kept out of his sight, not knowing but that it might be unsafe to trust to his discretion. I afterwards learned, however, that he was a Prussian, named Frederick Staurer. He was a very intelligent and well educated man. He had formerly been a professor of music, but, becoming reduced, was now working for his livelihood as a day-laborer. He spoke English very well, and, after I became acquainted with him, his companionship was very agreeable to me during my long and somewhat monotonous sojourn in the corn-field. Nothing of interest occurred during my first week in my new hiding-place. Almost all of the people of the ranch visited me, to each of whom I presented a small piece of money, and in a few days my mind became perfectly easy as to their fidelity. The Doctor remained the entire week in the city, and I lost the pleasure of his occasional company. Doña Rosa, however, sent me, every day, a bottle of claret or ale, and I lived more luxuriously than I had done since my departure from San Francisco.

On Sunday, Doña Rosa, accompanied by her sweet little children, paid me a visit, and inquired, through little Kate, after my health and comfort. The Doctor did not accompany her, for, when absent in the city of a Sunday, he never returned till evening, always waiting to attend church. I replied to the kind lady, that I was very comfortable, and after a very agreeable visit she returned to the house. That evening the Doctor returned, and came out to the corn-field to see me. I learned from him that the hunt after me appeared to be rather flagging. None of the San Francisco *Vigilantes* were in Santa Bárbara, nor had he heard of their being in the vicinity. Jack Power had started off in as suspicious a manner as he could, in company with an old Spaniard disguised as me, taking the road to Los Angeles, and had been hotly pursued by the dauntless and zealous Curtis and Gough, and eight or ten lunch-eaters. The Doctor brought me a two weeks' file of the San Francisco *Herald*, besides a number of other papers, and I was abundantly supplied with the news. I here learned of another surmise as to my whereabouts. They had doubtless come to the conclusion, at San Francisco, that I could not possibly be in the state and have escaped my indefatigable pursuers, and, on looking round for some other place to locate me, had lit upon my native city.* I also had the pleasure of reading, in the San Diego *Herald* of the twenty-sixth of July, the following flattering notice of my movements, from the pen of my

---

* NED MCGOWAN.—It is stated that letters have been received in this city, from Philadelphia, stating that Ned McGowan was at his own house in that city. Such a report may prove correct.—*Town Talk, July 31st.*

ANOTHER MCGOWAN IN THE FIELD. — This wonderful genius, this "Jack-o'-the-lantern" politician with the white hat, this apocryphal hero of the Jack Ketch Committee, has again made his appearance upon the stage, lifted his white beaver, and exclaimed, "Here I am, Mr. Merryman." As a traveler, he has thrown Humboldt and Mungo Park entirely into the shade. At one time we hear of him enjoying the laborious acting of "that eminent American tragedian" at the Metropolitan, and in the same breath he arrives in Santa Bárbara, is recognized, retires into the tules, has a magnificent reward offered for him, is pursued by an enthusiastic deputation of the One-Eyed Committee, who return in disgust—when, presto! change, the Hon. Judge Edward McGowan has arrived in the City of Brotherly Love, and is quietly installed in his family mansion. If Shakespeare lived in the nineteenth century, McGowan would be his beau ideal of an Ariel. When Eugene Sue writes another "Wandering Jew," the ex-Commissioner of Emigrants will be his model. McGowan is a remarkable man; he has made his mark on the dial-plate of time, and, whether the Committee have the hanging of him or not by way of dessert in the banquet of horrors they are now feasting on, the name of the Knight of the White Hat will be a prolific theme for the future pen of the historian.

P. S. — Since writing the above, we have just heard the rumor that a telegraphic dispatch has been received from the Feegee Islands, announcing the arrival of the Hon. Edward McGowan. Quære— Where is Ned McGowan?—*San Francisco Herald, July 31st.*

soi-disant FRIEND, J. Judson Ames, Esq., publisher of that sheet: —

GOSSIP ABOUT NED MCGOWAN. — This notorious individual is probably by this time in the state of Sonora. He was seen at Cariso Creek, on the desert, in the early part of this week, by the express-rider from Camp Yuma, who conversed with him, and by whom Ned sent his respects to Major Harvey, telling him that Col. Baker had arrived thus far safe, if an opportunity should offer of forwarding the message. He stated that he was going to Sonora. The expressman says that Ned had "a very poor horse, but some mighty good brandy!" If they know at Camp Yuma that he has been indicted in San Francisco, there is some chance that the ballot-box stuffer may yet swing at the end of a hempen cord.

This fellow, after penning the above, had the impudence to approach me in Sacramento (since my unexpected return) and extend both of his hands, expressing his most heartfelt delight at seeing me once more safe and in good health. My reply to him on that occasion is not at all pertinent to this narrative, but I desire that he will call it to mind, and then be assured that it was mild and gentle in comparison with the sketch of his history, dating from the days of President Tyler to the present hour, which I have promised myself the pleasure of drawing at some future time. When I open my proposed portrait-gallery of the most distinguished of our "*Purest and Best*," he may feel assured that, on looking around the walls, he will not miss his own intelligent countenance.

After Dr. Den had returned to the house, I laid down on my pallet and thought over an idea that had suggested itself to me on reading the San Diego paper. Since the belief was general that I was in Sonora, why might I not confirm it by writing to San Francisco a letter dated on the plains near Sonora, and thus slacken the hunt after me where I was? There was some danger of the letter, in case of miscarriage, affording a clew to my whereabouts, but I thought if I could but get a trusty messenger who would either destroy or deliver the letter safely, I might benefit myself by writing it. After thinking it over *pro* and *con*, I determined to say nothing about it to any one, and in the morning to do it, and then fell asleep.

After breakfast the following morning, I requested Santiago to get me from the house some writing materials. He went after them, but returned to say to me that there was no ink, except a little dried up in the bottle, and very little paper. I then sent him to town to purchase me what I wanted, and added to my list a bottle of whisky. In a few hours he returned with everything except the ink. He had broken the bottle which contained it on the road. I had nothing for it then but to mix some gunpowder with water, and having thus manufactured a tolerably good substitute for ink, I indited the following epistle to John Nugent, Esq., editor of the San Francisco *Herald*, and a fort night afterward had the pleasure of reading it in his paper in the following form: —

LETTER FROM NED McGOWAN.

The Political Mountain of the Nineteenth Century Speaks to the Sea — The White Hat "Turns Up" Again — Remarkable Adventures of a Political Philosopher of the Modern School, Pursued by Puritanical Bloodhounds.

We have the pleasure of laying before our readers this morning one of the most remarkable documents in the history of literature. It was a mooted point for some time, and even is to this late day, who was the author of the Junius papers; very few men have ever been able to make up their minds in locating the identical individual that struck Billy Patterson, Esq.; whole demijohns of ink have been shed in proving we had a Bourbon among us; and a small invoice was wasted in discussing the fact as to whether saltpeter would or would not explode. The "Mark Meddle" press in the hireling pay of the Saints have chased the ubiquitous Napoleon of primary elections from pillar to whipping-post, — they have had him comfortably corraled every where throughout the geographical limits of this extended area of freedom, except in their own clutches, — and at last the "old joker" turns up, and pleasantly and convivially speaks of his "hairbreadth 'scapes" as coolly as if he was on his old stamping-ground — Montgomery Street — and had an admiring audience of drinking friends, hoisting in his original and peculiar fund of small talk.

The remarkable correspondence which follows is written in gunpowder and water, the old fellow not having a bottle of "Maynard & Noyes" handy, but our readers may rest assured it is a genuine production; and if any person having a knowledge of the learned Judge's handwriting is inquisitive enough to doubt, he can be accommodated with a sight of the McGowan autograph by calling at this office.

STATE OF CALIFORNIA, August 8, 1856.

EDITOR OF THE SAN FRANCISCO HERALD: — I desire to reply to a query in the *Herald*, dated about the 1st of July, in which the writer, after indulging in a pleasant bit of satire at the expense of the "Sour Flour and Salt Pork Committee," in reference to their juvenile attempts at capturing that "old patent back-acting politician" with the immortal white hat, asks the very pertinent question, "Where is Ned McGowan?" In the words of the immortal Squibob and the somewhat well-known Mr. Webster of Marshfield, "I still live!" and claim the reward for my body *(when they catch me!)*. Upon mature reflection, I do not think I came so near drinking at "death's fountain" as the godlike Daniel did when he gave utterance to his celebrated and classical remark above quoted, although, for the past few months, I have played the "game of life" very "low down," but have always kept the deck in my own hands. I will not say I have stocked the cards on the "purest and best," or that I have held more than four aces in my sleeves at any one time, but in this last deal my native talent has been brought out in bold relief, and by a little dexterous shuffling of the papers I have thus far managed to win every trick. I acknowledge it was a very tight game at Santa Bárbara,— six and six on the last game, and I turned up *Jack*,— mighty good pun, if understood. If the Vigilance Committee are still holding on in the expectation of catching me, they might as well disband, for it is not in the *cards*, and I think they are themselves pretty well satisfied of that, for they have expended time and money enough in the experiment. I have, at last, thank God, a *deal* of good luck, and, being a Catholic (bad a one as I am), I am safely arrived at the "other side of Jordan," and a hard road to travel it was, you had better believe.

On some future occasion, when I have more time and facility for writing, it will afford me the most eminent satisfaction to give you a faithful daguerreotype of my "will-o'-the-wisp" existence in the city of "higher law" previous to my departure for a more congenial clime. It will be one of the most delightful romances ever written. Truth is stranger than fiction; and when I deem it expedient to "let the cat out of the bag," what a field there will be for an American Dickens; and when the pious Committee are posted in regard to some of those who were the most instrumental in my salvation from undergoing an ordeal of their "celebrated breakneck act," what a rattling there will be among the dry bones of some of their own members. I think I "know a hawk from a hand-saw," and it never for one moment entered my head to form a source of amusement for the Sacramento Street gentlemen. I am easily pleased, and am perfectly willing to die in bed, although I sympathize heartily with the bloodthirsty Committee in their mortifying and defeated efforts to elevate me to "a high position."

After some wandering, I entered the county of Santa Bárbara on the third day of July, and if I were to tell you what I accomplished up to the time I left,— how many narrow and hairbreadth escapes I had,— you would scarcely credit it, but set it down as an imagination drawn from the fertile brain of some Munchausen romance. Whilst my horse is feeding, and the person who has promised to mail this for me waits, I will write, and am actually writing, with *gunpowder mixed with water*. Necessity is truly the mother of invention, (although I can't think just now who the father of it was,) and the law of it compelled me to stretch my genius to its utmost. On the one hand, I saw death staring me in the face, to be perpetrated by the hands of hired assassins sent to take me, dead or alive (certainly not alive); on the other hand, I had the triumphant thought of one day setting myself right before the world, and repelling the assaults made by these fiends in human form who have so savagely persecuted me, and of having the satisfaction of showing who some of the "best and purest citizens" are, or were originally, who have hunted me "bloodhound" like, even in this section of the country, almost to the death; but, thank God, I have so far escaped them. The knowledge of what I have already gone through in this unholy crusade against me has almost nerved me into a second youthful manhood, and added much vigor to my declining strength, and endows me with patience to endure suffering which, under any other circumstances, I would have shrunk from as a task being too difficult for one who had lived a life of luxurious ease for the past twenty years. No one knows how much he can perform till driven to it. *There is no such word as "fail."* The remembrance of a quotation from Lord Byron's *Mazeppa*,—

> For time at last sets all things even;
> And if we do but watch the hour,
> There never yet was human power
> Which could evade, if unforgiven,
> The patient search and vigil long
> Of him who treasures up a wrong,—

has been of great consolation to me, and I do hope that it may be verified in my case, for I certainly treasure up a great wrong, and the thoughts of some day getting "even" was that which gave me strength to walk many, many miles in the mountains, with blistered and bleeding feet, almost without shoes, and nearly worn out, body and soul; to sleep among the rocks, without blanket or other covering, or flannel, o' cold nights (I threw away my flannel the first day, it was so excessively hot); and to crawl out of the mountains before daylight to the sea-beach to dig mussels from the rocks for my breakfast, and always after breakfast *dining next day.* I did have dinner one day,—I found a small turtle in a mountain-stream, and I ate it raw, and it really tasted almost as good as that I used to eat at Ned's, so deliciously served up. The mussels certainly tasted better than any I had ever eaten at the Nightingale, although they were always washed down with champagne. For several weeks the county of Santa Bárbara, and two or three adjoining counties, and even along the Colorado, was filled with these lunch-eaters, or five-dollars-a-day men, hired to assassinate, under the command of Capt. T. D. Johns. Some of them were armed with guns, and all of them with six-shooters, over twenty-five in all; brave fellows, and each man determined to make a hero of himself by catching or killing one *poor old man*, who they themselves denominate, in their handbills, as being fifty years of age. Now, that 's a little too bad,—that 's almost as bad as Pat Hull's likeness of me,—they have got the figures too high by *ten years.* I would sooner be shot than be that old. If I live to be that old, I will get more than "even." It was curious, and sometimes even laughable, how I dodged them. On the eventful sixth of July, I was rolled up in forty yards of carpeting, which, from the smell, I thought was used as a flea-hive on the "Beau Hickman" plan, for it contained, at a rough guess,—I did not count them,—ten thousand fleas, one hundred and eighty-two pounds of what I at that time thought was flesh and blood, and all around the city the tules on fire, trying to burn me out. This was truly a delightful situation for a gentleman to be placed in, a hot July afternoon in Santa Bárbara, with no chance to get a drink for more than three hours. There was no necessity for my wishing, as some one did in a Shakespeare reading on Gov. Bigler, "O, that this too too solid flesh would melt"; mine was actually running away from me like melting lard. I only, at this writing, weigh one hundred and forty pounds, but now I *know it is flesh.*

At another time, a fellow with red whiskers and large eyes, with shot-gun (double-barrel) and six-shooter, and a keeper of the lighthouse, called "Mitch," also with six-shooter, searched a ranch *sans cérémonie,* and then the Indian huts in the vicinity. I had just left to wash myself, preparatory to taking breakfast, when a woman, the lady of the house, who knew my secret, sent her son to tell me to "vamos," while her husband kept them in conversation a few moments. These people were poor and had a large family of children, and these braves—a part of Captain T. D. Johns' gang who came down in the schooner—offered Pedro's wife $3,000 if they could find me or tell where I was. Pedro spoke English, and the fellow from the lighthouse Spanish; but their offer was of no avail: they had promised to keep my secret, and they faithfully kept their word. Subsequently, the fellow who was watching the ranch saw one of the boys carry me food in the mountains, and gave information to a busybody in Santa Bárbara, acting blood-hunter for his San Francisco brethren, called by the native Californians "*Cochi Guero,*" which, translated, means "White Pig," for he is constantly meddling with and poking his nose into other people's business. This chap was originally a runner in Santa Bárbara, but, having married into a very respectable native family, he has now the should-be honorable title of "merchant," and he, no doubt, is, big a loafer as he is consid ered at home, equally as honorable and distinguished as many of his cotemporaries residing in San Francisco. Well, the "White Pig" was a made man; he was sure to take me; he had a dead thing· told every one he met, but he explained in the presence of Judge Fernald, "Won't my name go up when I capture him!" The Judge, who is a highly honorable gentleman, looked at him with contempt, but made no reply. When the Pig left, he said to a gentleman present, who told me, "This is the first time I have ever heard any one exulting over the baseness of being a public informer; people bad enough to do such acts for pay, generally want it hid." Comment is unnecessary. These few words, spoken· by the learned Judge, give the fellow's character in full, and he is richly entitled to the cognomen he bears from his neighbors, of the "White Pig." His Pigship, a native Californian, and three others, Dutch Jews, five in all, started on their grand hunt on Saturday, the second of August, armed with guns, pistols, etc., to the Arroyo Hondo. They reconnoitered the ground, and sent one of their party to the house; the balance of them searched the immediate vicinity. They remained at this place all night, and hunted for me for many miles around in the mountains, but did not find me, simply because I had received information of their intended visit, and, not knowing how they got their knowledge of my whereabouts, I thought it was time to travel, and left, a few days before their arrival, without giving notice to any one of my intended departure; which leaves my anxious friend, the suckling, in the position I first saw him on the eventful sixth of July. I have suffered too much in this affair to allow him ever to become a full-grown hog at my expense.

I was kept well posted in all the movements both of the imported bloodhounds and of the very few who had a location in Santa Bárbara County, and from what I experienced and heard from others, I can safely say there is not a high-toned native Californian or a respectable American in the place who were in favor of the Vigilance Committee. It was the reward that made the lower orders in Santa Bárbara hunt me. The distinguished gentleman who holds the position as senator from this county, it is true, gave an entertainment to a few of the aristocracy of the Committee,—not the hired "lunch-eaters" of the Executive,—given as strangers, not as blood-hunters,—at which my little friend "Woody" and pioneer Shanghae coat Thompson figured very conspicuously, and the "White Pig" was "rooting around" the kitchen somewhere. There was music and dancing, and the entertainments of the evening were concluded by the servants playing on a "tin trumpet" and "penny whistle," and singing in Spanish, which I have since had translated into English, the following couplet:—

> " For things of use and things of sport,
> The gay and curious here resort."

Did you get my letter of the twenty-second of June, from Carson Valley? I made a big ride from San Luis Obispo to within a few miles of Santa Bárbara on the third of July. Some persons I met on the road wanted to spend the Fourth there, and we made the trip and crossed the mountain (and, great God, what a mountain!) at Santa Ynez that evening. When I told the Californians about this, they shook their heads and looked at me rather cunningly, and said it was forty leagues. Yes; and I did it without getting out of the saddle except to change horses once, and without eating, and once thirty miles without a drink, and in one of the hottest days I ever experienced; but it had to be done, if I wanted to keep company with those I had fallen in with.

Tell the boys I will see some of them at the inauguration of "Old Buck" on the fourth of March. He will walk over the course; there is really no contest in this fight. I wonder what state I shall vote in at the coming election; I suppose in my present state—desperation. Well, if I should happen to miss one election, according to my friend Bailie Peyton's views when he introduced to the meeting the double-headed ballot-box, "the harp of a thousand strings," and named me as one of the harpers, I have done enough voting to be excused for one election. I voted to send "Old Buck" to the Senate in 1843, and also voted to instruct the delegates from California to vote for him in the Cincinnati convention, and was also in the glorious state convention that nominated him for the Presidency in 1845.

With ordinary luck I will be in Sonora in four or five days, and will write you again. I remain yours, &c.,

EDWARD McGOWAN.

I had written the above in the corn-field, without the knowledge of a single individual, and a trusty Indian had mailed it for me at Santa Bárbara.

Nothing occurred during the next week, of any interest, and indeed my life, during the whole six weeks that I remained in the corn-field, was pretty much as I have described the first few days. I would sometimes venture out onto the mountain with my gun, and shoot quails, which were very plenty, always taking care to send the best of them to my good hostess. I was daily visited by the people of the ranch, and occasionally by some members of the family. I enjoyed a great deal of agreeable and instructive conversation with the good Doctor, who was a close observer of nature, and told me many wonderful stories of the instinct of birds and animals.

Among others, he told me that, on one occasion, he and his father-in-law had actually watched the *trial* of a culprit crow by his peers! They had a regular jury, and every day, for three successive days, they came to the same spot upon a hillside, bringing with them the defendant crow, who was continually guarded by a kind of bailiff. After keeping up a chatter all day over his case, they would adjourn at night, and return the next day and resume the trial. Finally, on the third day they appeared to have come to a verdict of "guilty," for they all pounced upon the prisoner and killed him on the spot. They then flew away, and returned no more. Whether or not the defendant had the benefit of counsel, it was impossible in the general chatter to ascertain. I fear, though, from the Doctor's account, that the poor bird's trial was but a one-sided, Vigilance Committee kind of arrangement, after all. This the Doctor assured me upon his word he had actually witnessed. None who know him personally will need any other guaranty of the truth of his assertion.

When the *Herald*, containing my letter to Mr. Nugent, arrived in Santa Bárbara, the Doctor happened to be in town. On his return, he informed me that speculation was rife as to my whereabouts. Many, who before believed that I had gone south, were strengthened in their conviction by the letter; but some of the shrewd ones, and among them one S. B. Brinkerhoff, suspected that I was, after all, still concealed in the county.*· This man Brinkerhoff, as I have been informed, some years ago acted in the capacity of coachman to Don Abel Stearns (one of the old Spanish families in Los Angeles). However, he turned physician, *pulling teeth*, and, by dint of quackery, effrontery, and parsimony, has managed to drift into a position of apparent respectability and affluence. His chief occupation now is loaning out money to his neighbors, at usurious rates of interest; and by his close attention to that honorable calling, he has earned for himself the appellation of "Old Cent-per-Cent Brinkerhoff."

As before stated, this fellow still suspected that I was lurking in the county, and, on reading my letter to Mr. Nugent, was, as the Doctor informed me, almost suffocated with rage at my assurance in daring to pen anything against the best citizens of Santa Bárbara County, and particularly his friend Mr. Harvey Benjamin Blake, *alias* the "White Pig." Poor Harvey! Perhaps it *was* cruel and unjust to write impolite things about him, merely because he had subjected me to the trifling annoyance of being hunted for my blood for days and weeks like a wild coyote, but, smarting as I was under the lash of misfortune, I could not, perhaps, when I wrote the letter, look upon the matter in the

---

* NED MCGOWAN AGAIN.—We learn from a gentleman, recently from Santa Bárbara, that, in all probability, McGowan is really in that vicinity yet, notwithstanding the rumors of his arrival in Philadelphia. Our informant is one of those who saw him and talked with him face to face. He had shaved off that old white mustache, and was letting his beard grow all over his face, which, considering the color of his beard, gave him a hideous appearance. Is is thought by the residents of that locality that the Californians, who have manifested quite an antipathy to the Vigilance Committee, have him in charge, and will succeed in screening him from the detection of the officers, or any persons who shall search for him. Our informant is confident that he is not thirty miles from Santa Bárbara this moment. —*S. F. Bulletin*.

same charitable spirit of Christian kindness that "Old Cent-per-Cent" himself did when he instigated the mob to burn me alive, and proposed to one of my friends the treachery of offering me protection, and then delivering me over to him. As I grow older, however, I shall *perhaps* grow milder.

Boiling over with virtuous indignation, old "Shylock," as he is also called by some of his most ardent admirers, forthwith proceeded to institute another crusade against me. He had gone so far as to engage the horses and men with which to scour the county, when a friend of mine, who had much influence with the livery-stable keeper of the town, suggested to him the wisdom of getting his money before he let his horses go. Accordingly, when all things were in readiness to start, and the amiable gentlemen connected with the laudable enterprise already saw me, in fancy, dangling at the end of a rope, the party, on inquiring for the horses, were met with the demand for their hire. Here arose a struggle, in the bosom of the virtuous Brinkerhoff, between the love of gold and the thirst for blood. He at length hit upon an expedient by which he fondly hoped to avoid the dilemma. He told the stable-keeper ("Old Adonis," as he was called by his familiars) that the sheriff was then absent from town, but that on his return he would settle the bill, whatever it was, that functionary being authorized by the puissant and immaculate Committee of Vigilance of San Francisco to inundate the county of Santa Bárbara with money, if necessary, so that he but delivered the "*ubiquitous*" safely into their clutches. The arrangement, however, did not appear to be satisfactory to the stable-keeper, who, I fear, was ungodly and *impure* enough to have some slight misgivings as to the propriety of a mob's hanging their fellow-creature like a dog, and he accordingly again insisted on his money in advance, and thus again threw "Cent-per-Cent" between the horns of his dilemma. What was to be done? The struggle was fearful in the bosom of the "pure" and "good" Brinkerhoff. To let that audacious wretch of the "white hat" bask with impunity in the very glare of the "Hog's Eye,"[*] until that insulted

---

[*] To those of my readers, either here or elsewhere, who may not have known that the Vigilance Committee used, for a *vignette*, on all

optic fairly shed tears of baffled rage, was horrible to contemplate. But, on the other hand, to be mulcted out of his hard earnings, in a sum exceeding perhaps the monthly interest on one hundred dollars at ten per cent, was not to be thought of. Direful and dread was the mighty struggle which heaved that patriotic breast. At length, however, it terminated, as all things must, and with a long-drawn sigh of bitterness he reluctantly came to the conclusion that the frightful sacrifice demanded of him, in his penury and want, was greater than even the glorious cause in which he was embarked had a right to exact, and, turning sorrowfully away from the heathenish proprietor of the horse-flesh, the splendid campaign which he had projected "fell through."

Had this expedition started, due notice would, of course, have been sent to me by my friends, and I could soon have placed myself where neither horses could have reached me or men found me. In consideration of that state of things, I am now disposed to regret that the struggle in "Cent-per-Cent's" bosom terminated as it did. I confess that I am no more exempt from the desire of vengeance for a wrong than other men, and as I believe from what I can learn of this man's character, confirmed as it is by my own experience, that neither the upbraidings of one whom he has oppressed, nor the merited scorn of his species, can so much afflict him as the loss of a little gold, I am sorry that he did not invest the paltry amount of that horse-hire. I can assure him that it would have afforded me the liveliest satisfaction to know that he had been so keenly stung in his most vital part. I beg, however, that for this natural expression of feeling I may not be charged with the offense laid to my door, by old "Cent-per-Cent," in the case of his friend Blake, viz., that of impudently writing against the *best* citizens of Santa Bárbara.

Shortly after this demonstration, my friends became of opinion that the persecution of me by my enemies in Santa

---

documents emanating from them, a representation of an open eye, which they somewhat blasphemously called the "All-Seeing Eye," I will state that such was the fact. The "Law and Order" men, partly to relieve the conceit of its wickedness, and partly in derision, vulgarly termed it the "Hog's Eye"; hence I have used that designation in the text.

Bárbara had about ceased. I now began to be more free from alarm than I had been since the commencement of my pilgrimage. I not only had the friendship and protection of Dr. Den and all his people, but also the sympathy of all the respectable portion of the inhabitants of the county. Indeed, so freely had Dr. Den expressed his abhorrence of the persecution I had suffered, that few of those who had taken part in it cared to come about his premises. Besides, about a month after I had entered the corn-field, those of my pursuers who belonged to San Francisco became generally convinced that I was in Sonora.* Thus circumstanced, I began to be very comfortable in mind, and the first ray of hope that my troubles were drawing to a close began to dawn upon me.

Early in September, I received a visit from my friend the Hon. Pablo De la Guerra. It was the first time I had seen him since my arrival in the county, though I was by no means ignorant of his many good offices to me during my adversity. I was, as may be supposed, delighted to see him, and his visit, though short, was very agreeable. He was on his way to San Luis Obispo, on some private business, and had taken the opportunity to call on me.

A few days afterward, I was visited by the gallant and chivalric Captain Thomas Moore. This gentleman is the

---

* NED MCGOWAN.—The *Herald* of the 16th says, speaking of confounding Col. Baker with McGowan:—

"We have since received information which corroborates the statement of the expressman. Mr. Lloyd, who has been stationed at Sackett's Wells, in charge of Dr. R. C. Matthewson's provision depot, arrived in town on Tuesday evening last, and has stated to us that Ned McGowan spent a night at his camp, subsequent to his having been seen by the expressman at Cariso Creek. Mr. Lloyd assures us there can be no mistake in the matter of identity, as he knows McGowan, and that his German traveling companion addressed him as Judge, and more familiarly as Ned. With due deference to the opinion of our correspondent, we cannot but conclude that the 'Col. Baker' of the expressman and the 'Judge' of Mr. Lloyd are one and the same person,—Ned McGowan.["]

MORE ABOUT MCGOWAN.— *El Clamor Público*, of the 23d, says that a person lately arrived from Sonora has informed them that he saw Ned McGowan cross the river Colorado. He was armed with a rifle, two Colt's pistols, and a long knife. Alfred Shelby, of Los Angeles, was in company with him.—*Town Talk*, August 30.

son of a post-captain in the British navy, and an Irishman by birth. He had adopted the sea for a profession, and he it was who secreted in his ship the Irish patriot D'Arcy McGee, when the British authorities were in pursuit of him, and brought him safely to America. He had been a great traveler, and the chances and changes of a sailor's life had thrown him, in 1851, on the shores of California. He had married a young and beautiful California lady, and was located, as a permanent citizen of Santa Bárbara, on a rancho called "*Sal si Puedes*," about forty miles distant from the residence of Doctor Den. I was very much pleased at making his acquaintance, and found him a most worthy gentleman and agreeable companion. He had recently been to San Francisco, and informed me that one of the Executive Committee of Vigilance had declared, in his hearing, that if they could but get me back there, they would spare my life just long enough to erect a gallows on which to hang me, and no longer. He informed me that himself and some friends had been endeavoring to procure a schooner for him to command, and safely run me into some port in Mexico, but had failed in the enterprise. After a very long and agreeable visit, he departed, having first cordially invited me to visit him at his house, which I promised to do as soon as it could be considered safe.

About the middle of September, Doctor Den started for San Francisco. His little daughter, Kate, had been for the past two years under the care of the Sisters of *Notre Dame* at San José, and it was now past the time when she should have returned to her studies. She had learned to speak and write English fluently and grammatically. Her Spanish, too, I was told, was pure Castilian. She told me she disliked French, but I told her all young ladies ought to learn it, and without it she would not be accomplished. She promised me she would pay more attention to it the coming year. I sent several messages by the Doctor to certain friends in San Francisco, and, wishing me comfort and safety while he was gone, he and his little daughter departed.

A few days after this, as things appeared pretty quiet, it occurred to me that I would avail myself of Captain

Moore's invitation and visit him at his ranch. Accordingly, on the morning of the twentieth of September I told *Santiago* that I intended to take a trip to *Sal si Puedes*, and asked him to accompany me as guide. He was delighted at the idea of a holiday, and, saddling two of the finest horses on the place, he reported himself ready for the journey. The *Sal si Puedes* is situated on a wagon-road that runs from Santa Bárbara to San Luis Obispo, through what is called the *Gaviota* Pass, avoiding the mountain of *Santa Ynez*, which is, of course, impassable for wagons. As we did not get off until late in the morning, we did not arrive at our destination until just before nightfall.

The road lay, for the first twenty-three miles after leaving the *Dos Pueblos* (Doctor Den's place), along the coast, passing Señor Ignacio Ortega's ranch and the *Arroyo Hondo*. It then suddenly turns into a very deep and narrow mountain-gorge running eastward from the coast. This is the *Gaviota* Pass, and a more wild and lonely spot one would not wish to see. It seemed as if formed by nature for purposes of ambuscade. After traversing this pass for about three miles and a half, we came suddenly to the rancho of *Las Cruces*, the residence, it will be remembered, of my Spanish friend whom Power had deceived as to my destination when he took me to the Arroyo Hondo. As may be supposed, I had no particular desire to see any one here, or to be seen. We therefore rode on without halting, seeing only one man on the road, a Californian, from whom we got some grapes. The country now became more open and level, and, after riding about seven miles farther, we came to the rancho of *San Julian*. This is one of the De la Guerra estates, and is an extensive and valuable piece of property. About eight miles farther brought us to *Sal si Puedes*, the residence of my friend Captain Moore. We had left the road, shortly before getting there, to take a near bridle-path over the hills. As *Santiago* had not been there before for three years, he remembered this path but indistinctly, and the consequence was, that it took us some time to find the place. At length, however, we stumbled directly upon it. Turning the foot of a low hill, who should we see but the Captain, who, on seeing us, welcomed us very cordially and guided us to the house. I could not help telling the Captain that *Sal si Puedes* (get out if you can) was a good name for his place. I saw that he kept a store there, and told him that he reminded me of the fool in Philadelphia, who said, if all the world were dead he would open a house on the "Ridge Road," not stopping to think where his customers were to come from. He told me to come into the house, and to-morrow he would show me where his customers came from. I then entered with my kind host, and he introduced me to his young bride. He had been married but three months. The señora is a daughter of Captain James W. Burke, an Irish gentleman who has resided in Santa Bárbara for thirty years, having married a California lady shortly after his arrival. The wife of the Captain, whose name is Madelina, speaks no English as yet, and is very pretty, ladylike, and hospitable. I had by this time picked up enough Spanish to understand most that was said, and generally make myself understood, and, though it was a little awkward, I managed, with the aid of Captain Tom, to get on in the conversation pretty well. I enjoyed an excellent supper at my friend's hospitable board, and, after passing a very pleasant evening, we retired for the night. My friend seemed very apprehensive that I had come from my hiding-place in the corn too soon, and, lest any one should have observed me on the road, he placed me in the room adjoining his own, so that he could be on hand to assist in case of a demonstration against me. I enjoyed a sound sleep, however, without molestation of any kind, and in the morning took a delightful bath in a hot spring adjacent to the Captain's house. I then sat down to a pleasant breakfast, and was made to feel quite at home by my hospitable host and hostess.

It being Sunday, we were visited by a great number of Californians and Indians, who came to purchase all descriptions of goods at the store. Some of them had ridden fifteen and twenty miles out of their way to get the Captain's whisky, which was a pure article, and only fifty cents a bottle, while at the Mission of Santa Inés, and other places of the sort, the article was miserable and the price a dollar. I told the Captain I wanted to purchase a dress for *María Jesus*, the wife of *Santiago*, whereupon he directed her husband to select one that pleased him, and then presented it to him. I could not induce him to let me pay him for it. In vain I expostulated. He only replied, "You have probably use for what money you have; another time you can pay me." And I had to submit.

I remained with my hospitable friend till the next day (Monday), at four o'clock, P. M. He would not permit me to start earlier, lest some one of the people who had been at the store should have identified me, and, in order to secure the reward that had been offered for me, lie in wait at *Las Cruces* or in the *Gaviota* Pass, with the expectation of my passing in the daytime.

All things being in readiness, the Captain gave us a bottle of his best whisky, and particularly impressed *Santiago* with the necessity of great care and watchfulness in going through the *Gaviota* Pass. Santiago promised faithfully to obey his instructions, and, bidding farewell to the good Captain and his lady, we started. My visit to the *Sal si Puedes* had gratified the Captain and been most agreeable to me. I felt as though I had another true friend in case of need, and I began to look upon myself as less of an outcast, and more nearly approaching, every day, my former position among my fellow-creatures. Indeed, the Captain had told me, before I left him, that, in case of any unforeseen circumstance compelling me to leave my asylum at the good Doctor's, I must unhesitatingly make my way at once to him, and, as long as he had life, I should have protection.

Santiago and I rode on without anything of interest occurring till shortly after we had passed the San Julian Ranch, when we saw a couple of grizzlies playing on the side of a mountain not far from us. There were a great many cattle in the vicinity, and they were running in every direction, frightened at the grim intruders on their domain. I felt alarmed, and drew my pistol, anticipating an attack. *Santiago*, however, gave me to understand that there was no cause for apprehension, and the horses we were riding, having often been used for lassoing these animals, cantered on without exhibiting any signs of fear. Santiago told me that at that particular ranch these beasts are very destructive of the stock, killing a cow or a bullock almost every night. The Californians hunt them with the lasso, on horses trained for the purpose. Notwithstanding we rode at a brisk gait, it was after night when we arrived in the neighborhood of *Las Cruces.* Here we dismounted and tightened our saddle-girths. *Santiago* laid his ear to the ground and listened for the sound of horse-hoofs, but, hearing none, we again mounted, and rode silently past *Las Cruces* and through the *Gaviota* Pass without molestation. Having struck the coast, we rode the remaining twenty three miles at a round gallop, and alighted at Dr. Den's at two o'clock in the morning. Of course no one was stirring about the premises, and, betaking myself to the corn field, I slept till daylight. The day after my return from *Sal si Puedes*, Doña Rosa told me that, if I thought it perfectly safe, a room was at my disposal in the house, where I would be more comfortable than in the corn-field. All things taken into consideration, I concluded that by this time I could safely accept the offer of my kind hostess, and accordingly a room was prepared for me, and I was from that time, until my departure from Santa Bárbara, domiciled under the hospitable roof of the good Doctor.

I was now very comfortable, and almost began to forget my sorrows. One thing, however, I could not banish from my remembrance, and that was, that an indictment for murder, found by a grand jury of my countrymen, was hanging over me. My original intention, as has been stated, was to proceed to Philadelphia, but it was only to escape the mob that was hunting me, not to shirk the indictment. I had preserved, through every vicissitude of fortune, the determination to one day stand my trial before a legally constituted tribunal, unjust as I knew the finding of the bill to be. Conscious of my own innocence, I had nothing to fear from an impartial jury, and was anxious honorably to wipe out that indictment from my record. The circumstances which have been detailed had thwarted my project of going to Philadelphia, and there was now some prospect of men's minds once more returning into the channel of reason. Hence my every wish and hope was for the arrival of the hour when I could deliver myself up to the officers of the law, without the danger of being murdered by the mob, and I anxiously awaited the tidings the Doctor should bring from San Francisco as to the disbanding of the Vigilance Committee.

I was supplied, every two weeks, with all the papers, and knew all that was going on at San Francisco and in other parts of the state. I felt very confident that Mr. Buchanan would be elected to the Presidency, but, as I saw but few of the Eastern papers, I had no idea that Colonel Frémont could possibly carry the number of states that he did. I was thunderstruck when I heard the result, and, seeing how nearly an anti-national party had caught us napping, I became a stronger Democrat, if possible, than ever.

About a fortnight after I had commenced sleeping in the house, an accident occurred, which subjected my good friend the Doctor to a serious loss, and as I was partly the cause of it, it grieved me not a little. A man whom the people at the ranch called *Señor Benito* came to the *Dos Pueblos* for the purpose of hunting deer. The first day of his arrival, he went out with his rifle and killed five, bringing home with him nothing but the skins. He said it was too much trouble to pack the meat, and besides, it was out of season. It struck me that it was a pity to kill the beautiful animals merely for their skins, which were only worth half a dollar apiece; so I proposed to accompany him in his next day's hunt, agreeing to bring home the meat myself. Accordingly, we started the next morning, and had not been long on the hunting-ground before *Benito* killed a fine buck. We skinned him, and I hung half of the meat on a tree for my friend " Fred " (the Prussian), who was cutting poles for the garden some distance up the moun tain, and packed the other half on my horse to the house. That night *Maria Jesus* cooked the meat in the garden, and, notwithstanding its being a little out of season, every one about the place seemed to enjoy it very much. The next day, I proposed to Fred a *picnic* in the mountains, on the spot where he was cutting poles. This he agreed to, and accordingly we provided ourselves with bread, potatoes, Chile peppers, etc., and rode to the place where I had hung up the other half of the deer, and, putting it on one of the horses, proceeded up the mountain. As he was paid by the thousand for his poles, I agreed, both for my own amusement and in order that he should lose none of his time, to cook the dinner myself, which I managed to do quite to the satisfaction of both of us, and we enjoyed our feast heartily. As a full half of what we had was left uncooked, Fred proposed to let the fire continue to burn until the next day, when he would cook the remainder for his dinner. I suggested to him that there might be danger in leaving the fire, on account of the dryness of the weather, but he thought not, and, accordingly, placed a large log on it, and we left the spot. We had not more than got down to the plain when the sea-breeze began to blow very fresh, and presently we observed that the mountain was on fire, and the flames rapidly spreading in every direction. So long as it confined itself to the mountain, no great damage was to be apprehended, and I tried to comfort myself with the hope that such would be the case when I first saw the spreading of the flames. I was doomed, however, to disappointment, for, as the night wore on, it increased until everything for miles around was wrapped in conflagration, and before morning it had passed the Doctor's house, and, it being the driest season of the year, not a drop of rain having fallen for six months, everything burned before it like tinder. The cattle, deer, and all sorts of game, were driven in frightened throngs to the valleys, and as for rabbits and hares, basketfuls of them might have been picked up. Doña Rosa's brothers and several of the neighbors came to her relief, and I think I never worked so hard in my life as I did in assisting to put it out. At night it was the most awful, and yet the most magnificent, sight I ever beheld. Notwithstanding my sorrow and vexation, I could not but admire the fearful splendor of the scene. The mountain-side seemed one vast nest of hellish serpents as the hissing flames coiled around the stunted trees, licking away with their fiery tongues the dry twigs and branches. Ever and anon they would get into some hollow trunk and roar through it like a forge-chimney, while dazzling spouts of fire shot through the knot-holes in its sides, giving it the appearance of a tree with branches of flame. They reminded me of the side-lights in a brilliant theatre scene; but the background was a thousand-fold more terrible and grand. At length, when it had got into the plain, with nothing but the short grass to feed it, we managed to get it under, but not until it had destroyed a vast quantity of pasture.

The Doctor's loss from the grass which had been destroyed amounted afterward to nearly a hundred head of stock by starvation. As may be supposed, I felt very wretched about this affair, and the fact that I had expostulated with Fred against leaving the fire burning was but small consolation to me. I had suggested the miserable idea of the *picnic*, and I ought to have insisted on the fire being put out. Notwithstanding the Doctor's severe loss, after that amiable gentleman had returned from San Francisco, and I was upbraiding myself to him for my carelessness, he simply replied, "*Mac, if I had n't had them, I could n't have lost them.*" He said, that, owing to his superior pasture-land, his neighbors yearly lost twice as many cattle as himself from drought, and it was but reasonable he should sometimes have a little bad luck. As for "Fred," five hundred dollars of wages was due him, every cent of which he was paid without a word of reproach, and further employment procured for him through the influence of the Doctor.

On the second day of November, the Doctor arrived from San Francisco. He brought me several letters and messages from my friends, and all the newspapers. I ascertained by the latter that it was now pretty generally conceded, on all hands, that I was in Sonora. In the *Town Talk* of October 30th, I read the following:—

NED McGOWAN.—From a gentleman who came passenger on the Senator the last trip, and who has been residing in Sonora for the last two or three years, we learn that Judge Ned McGowan is at the present time residing in Sonora. Our informant stopped at the same house with Ned, while the latter was *en route* for Sonora, at a place below Warner's ranch, and, although he has no acquaintance with him, has no doubt of its being the genuine Ned. In fact, it is, he says, notorious to every one there that he is in Sonora.

The Doctor also brought me a kind message and a couple of bottles of excellent brandy from my good friend B. F. Johnson, Esq., the well-known and popular proprietor of the Magnolia Hotel, in Sacramento. On the day of the election, while the Doctor and his people had gone to the Mission of Santa Bárbara to vote, it struck me that I would

As the night wore on, it increased until everything for miles around was wrapped in conflagration.— *Page 158.*

write to my friend "Baldy." I did so, and afterward saw published, on the 19th of November, in the *Democratic State Journal*, the following extracts therefrom:—

LETTER FROM NED MCGOWAN.—A day or two ago, a letter was received in this city from the ubiquitous Ned McGowan, of Vigilance Committee memory. We have been permitted to read it, and we assure the reader that it is a genuine document. Notwithstanding the letters from Philadelphia, telling us that Ned is rusticating in that locality, and other reports that he is dying of the bowel complaint in Utah, Ned is still resident within the bounds of California,—"was never in the enjoyment of better health." It will be seen, from the extracts we publish below, that Ned, as usual, is disposed to laugh at his own troubles. He thinks, with Mrs. Gamp, that "them as lives in a walley must take the consequences of sich a sitivation," and he is resolved to make the most of the few creature comforts left him. The story of his escape from San Francisco, and his wanderings, would make an interesting book, and, since Ned is of a literary turn of mind, we have no doubt that he will put himself in print one of these days.

The letter is dated at "Hidden Diggins, Sky County, California." He says:—

"DEAR 'OLD BALDY':—Your 'Elixir of Life' reached me in due season, by the hands of the best of men, and not a member of the 'purest and best,' either, but a high-toned, honest, and intelligent son of the Emerald Isle, who has the good fortune to be well off in this world's goods. You have my thanks, for it has been a long time since I swallowed anything in the liquor line half so delicious, and under any other circumstances it would give me infinite pleasure to recommend your dark brandy to the drinking fraternity of this peaceful and glorious land of liberty!!! But, 'situated as I am,' I can only thank you by letter, and not in the customary manner, through the free, independent, and untrammeled press at the Bay; and further I will say to you, that to those who, like myself, can enjoy a bumper in *solitude*, having, for a season, gone into retirement, and quitted this gay and heartless world, auspiciously and wisely, it will prove an invaluable medicine."

It is evident that Ned found a great solace in his "Elixir of Life."

"I still like to hear something of you poor fellows who are forced by circumstances to remain in it (the gay and heartless world)—and particularly when the news is made the more welcome accompanied by such precious stuff—stuff! that's very significant, is it not? I wonder how I chanced to write that obsolete phrase—stuff, stuffer, stuffing! I was about writing you an apology for this *lapsus penquæ*, when '*Chino*,' who was looking over my shoulder, said that it was not quite blotted out of existence, being still extant in turkeys and chickens for Christmas, and besides, that, in this election for President, the Democrats will be at their old tricks again, and stuff the ballot-boxes from San Diego to Shasta.

"I am now studying the Castilian tongue *à la française*. My system of learning Spanish is far superior to Ollendorff's mode, particularly when the teacher is young and innocent. I will give you a small specimen of my improvement. Imagine me in a cañon adjacent to steep and rugged mountains, where I daily retire for my devotions. A little boy runs up the cañon, seeking me.

"Boy.— ¡Don Edwardo, Don Edwardo!
"McGowan.— ¡Aquí, aqui, mi bueno muchacho!
"Boy.— ¡Arriba, arriba! ¡vamos!
"McGowan.— ¿Porque, mi bonito pájaro?
"Boy.—Bastante hombres en el casa. ¡Mucho malo! ¡Vigilantes!

"I heard enough, and quietly, but not slowly, walked to the top of the mountain to catch the cooling breeze — that's all.

"I have often thought of the paragraph little Bartlett (Jules) wrote about me last winter. I like a good thing, even at my own expense,— anything but strangling,— say what they please; but hands off. After saying something about my acquaintance with a French lady, playing draw-poker, &c., he concluded by prophecying 'that my political career, like my amours, would end in a blow-up.' It was lucky, some folks think, it was not a 'hang-up.'

"'From mock to earnest, even into tones
Of tragic, and with less and less of jest,
To such a serious end.'

"Resp'y your friend,
"Edward McGowan."

The Doctor had promised me that on election-day I should go to the Mission of Santa Inés, an out-of-the-way place, and vote. On reflection, however, he thought it would be unsafe, and I was reluctantly compelled to forgo the pleasure of casting my vote for Mr. Buchanan. Doctor Den, although a good and true Democrat in every other particular, has a strong personal attachment for Colonel Frémont. During the war, he saw much of the Colonel, and entertained him at his house, and he felt himself constrained, by considerations of personal friendship, to give him his support, which he did, but not, by any means, from sympathy with the political party of which he was the nominee. I had cut several copies of the Democratic ticket from the head of the *San Francisco Herald*, intending to electioneer them at *Santa Inés*, but was prevented by the caution of my good friend the Doctor. General Covarrubias had sent a quantity of the Democratic tickets to the Mission, but not one of them were voted or seen during the day. Colonel Frémont received the entire vote of the precinct, which gave him the county by a majority of four. As several Democrats did not vote at that precinct at all, for want of tickets, I am satisfied that had I been there with my *Herald* tickets, Santa Bárbara would have gone Democratic. However, it resulted very happily. My kind host, the Doctor, had the satisfaction of doing his utmost for his friend, and Mr. Buchanan carried the state.

The Doctor's news, as regarded the Vigilance Committee and my chances for a safe return, were very discouraging. All of my friends who had written me cautioned me by all means to remain where I was till things looked better; consequently I had nothing for it but to stay quietly where I was, which I did till Christmas had come and gone. My life was pretty much the same every day as I have described it. Occasionally I would quietly ride over to Señor Ignacio Ortega's to purchase whisky for the Indians, especially on Saturdays, when they would say to me, in Spanish, "To-morrow is Sunday: there will be no work, and we'll drink whisky with *Paisano*." I amused myself very often by hunting. The country abounds in game of all sorts. A party, of which the husband of María los Angeles was one, killed no less than one hundred and thirty deer in one month. Geese, too, and ducks, were very plentiful, and could be got by going only a short distance from the house.

A great field-sport of the Californians in the dull winter months, and by no means a contemptible one in point of excitement and danger, is *lassoing* grizzly bears. I saw several of them captured in this way. Both the horses, which are trained for the purpose, and the men exhibit great quickness and skill in this dangerous sport. Relying on the activity and sagacity of their horses to keep out of the monster's reach, the horsemen soon have a lasso around one foot of the bear, and as quickly as possible each of his other feet is similarly secured, and the horses hold all four of the legs stretched out in opposite directions while he is dispatched with a knife. One party, which started out from Santa Bárbara, succeeded in thus killing ten bears in one day. They are very numerous, and exceedingly destructive of the cattle.

Now and then an incident would occur to remind me that I was not yet safe from pursuit myself. For example, one day the sheriff of Santa Bárbara, Mr. Heath, and his lady came to visit the Doctor, and remained all night. The Doctor and I were just seating ourselves at the dinner-table as the visitors arrived. I had barely time to get up and go into my room without being observed. I did not feel quite sure that, even had he seen me, he would have attempted to arrest me then, but I thought it prudent to take no chances. María los Angeles brought my dinner around the house to the window of my room, where I remained until night, and then, taking a pair of blankets and my gun, I stepped quietly out and slept in the garden.

Not far from the house, there was a kind of lagoon on the sea-beach, where always might be found, early in the morning, great quantities of ducks and geese. When I awoke in the morning, I determined to go to this place and shoot a brace of ducks for breakfast. Accordingly, I took my gun and proceeded down the cañon which led to the shore. On arriving there, who should I see but the Sheriff! He, too, had a gun, and was there, I suppose, for the same purpose that I was. He said nothing to me, however, although I thought at the time he must have known me, and I quickly walked down the coast, and so by a circuitous route back again to the garden, leaving him in undisputed possession of all the ducks in the pond. I thought, as he was a stranger at the *Dos Pueblos*, it was a courtesy to which he was entitled. After he had gone, the Doctor told me that he had related to him the circumstance, and told him that I was perfectly safe from arrest by him, as he knew full well that I was only awaiting an opportunity to go to San Francisco in safety and stand my trial.

About this time a queer old Indian came to live with the Doctor, who used to amuse me very much. He must have been at least eighty years of age, and, according to the old chroniclers of the county, he had been baptized sixty years ago. He was employed to look after the sheep and protect them from the coyotes. The Indians about the place called him *El Pastor* (shepherd). He used to keep his account of the number of the young lambs with notches on a stick. He could do very well until he got up to forty, but beyond that number he never could mark. Forty-one notches on the stick would have so confused his account that he could make nothing out of it. Any combination of numbers exceeding the aggregate of forty was, to him, all the books of *Euclid* condensed into one problem. When asked how old he was, he would reply, "¿*Quien sabe?*—about forty," and that had probably been his answer to the question for at least forty years.

I used frequently to take my gun and roam up into the mountains where he was herding the sheep, and try to talk to him. Sometimes I would be quite low-spirited, and he would say to me, "Why are you sad, old man?" I would shrug my shoulders and say, "I don't know." He would then say, "Is there not brandy at the house?" I would tell him there was, and he would ask, "Why, then, are you sad?" He considered it unreasonable that I should wish for a greater share of earthly happiness than a bottle of brandy afforded. I beguiled many a weary hour in trying to study out the thoughts and machinery of that poor, old, benighted Indian's mind.

At length the legislature met, and I began seriously to prepare my plans to return once more to the companionship of my fellow-citizens.

CHAPTER VIII

<blockquote>The day at last has broken:
What a night
Hath ushered it!
Sardanapalus.</blockquote>

ABOUT the twenty-second of January, an Indian brought me, from Santa Bárbara, a box containing some clothing and several bottles of good wine and brandy, which had been kindly sent me from San Francisco by my good friend James W. Stillman, Esq. This box was found in Santa Bárbara, together with several letters for me, by the Doctor, who immediately sent it to me, but put the letters in his pocket, intending to bring them himself.

On opening the box, I found several of the late papers, and, as I was glancing over one of them, my eye fell on the words, "now that Mr. Broderick is elected to the United States Senate." I read no farther. Forthwith I opened the brandy and circulated it around among all the people of the ranch. I shouted and danced, and made the Indians do the same, and absolutely went wild with delight. I presented Doña Rosa with a bottle of sweet wine, and begged her to drink the health of my friend the Senator, which she did. The Indians did not know what to make of my antics, and I could only shout to them, "*Bueno para mi amigo.*" They knew that I had received some good news, and were not at all backward in doing their share of the drinking. I believe I fuddled every Indian about the place, and became sufficiently elevated myself.

The next day the Doctor came home, and we exchanged congratulations on the good news. He is, himself, a very warm admirer of Mr. Broderick, and had been making a night of it in town with some others of the Senator's friends.

I found, among the letters which he brought, one from a friend, informing me that preparations were being made for my return, in order that I might stand my trial. Daylight had at last broken on the night of my misfortunes, and I anxiously looked forward to the hour when I might go back and mingle once more with my fellow-citizens. At last that hour arrived.

On Wednesday, the tenth day of February, as we were sitting at the supper-table, I heard a voice, which sounded familiarly to me, inquiring at the garden gate, *"Is this Doctor Den's place?"* The Doctor went out, and Dona Rosa and I followed him. It was at seven o'clock in the evening, and quite dark. It did not take me long, however, to recognize in the visitor my friend Captain J. Martin Reese, of San Francisco, and formerly of Philadelphia. He had just dismounted from his horse, which he had given in charge of a servant, and as I rushed forward to embrace him, the Doctor and Doña Rosa saw by my conduct that he was a friend. I introduced him to my good host and his lady, and we all entered the house. The Captain was the first San Francisco friend that I had seen since I had left Dennison on that dreadful sixth of July, in Santa Bárbara, and I could scarcely control my joy. Supper was immediately prepared for him, and I soon became absorbed in the contents of the letters he had brought me. Among them was the following, from the Hon. E. T. Beatty, then speaker of the house of assembly: —

SACRAMENTO CITY, Jan'y 27th, 1857.
JUDGE EDWARD MCGOWAN: —

DEAR SIR, — I have had much conversation with Capt. Reese and others in regard to the practicability of having a special act passed by the present legislature, granting you a change of venue from San Francisco without the necessity of your personal appearance in that county, and am of opinion that there will be no difficulty in accomplishing it. It is so notorious that your person would be in danger of mob violence were you to go back there, to say nothing of the absolute impossibility of your procuring a fair trial in that community, that I cannot conceive of any honest man's opposition to a law so obviously just and necessary. I would therefore recommend to you by all means to come as quietly and quickly as you can to Sacramento, where you certainly will be at least safe from personal violence.

       Very truly your friend
(Signed)   E. T. BEATTY.

 This, together with some other letters which I received from friends in San Francisco, at once resolved me as to my course. I determined to go to Sacramento at all hazards, and trust to the sense of justice of the members of the legislature to be put in a condition honorably to stand my trial without the danger of falling a victim to the fanaticism of the San Francisco mob.

 My friend Reese had a plan to purchase or charter a schooner at San Francisco, and take her, with me in her, directly from Santa Bárbara to Sacramento. This arrangement, however, was not satisfactory, for the reason that everything depended on my arriving at the capital before the legislature adjourned, and the time necessary to procure the vessel and send her down the coast and make the passage back with her to Sacramento, making due allowance for calms and head winds, was likely to exceed the time which the legislature would probably be in session, the senate having already resolved to adjourn on the fourth of March. Accordingly, after consultation with the Doctor, I made up my mind to start immediately for Sacramento by land, avoiding San Francisco, and going by the "*Pacheco Pass*" to Stockton, and thence to the capital. The Doctor and Reese and myself sat up late that night, talking over the events of the past ten months in San Francisco and discussing my future plans of action, occasionally indulging in potations of my host's good brandy; and when I retired that night I felt really a sense of sadness that with the termination of my misfortunes would also terminate my delightful intercourse with my generous friend and his family. So kind had the Doctor and Doña Rosa been to me, that I felt somewhat of the regret of the "Prisoner of Chillon" when the hour of his release from captivity approached. Not, however, like him, from excess of despair and long familiarity with misery, but from the reflection that my return to the haunts of my fellow-men, earnestly as I longed for it, was bought at the sacrifice of those delightful pleasures which only he can know who has been the recipient, in the hour of his adversity, of the spontaneous and heart-gushing benevolence of one of nature's noblemen.

My friend the Captain, on being apprised of my determination to return north by land, instantly declared his intention of accompanying me. This proof of his friendship, though not unexpected, was greater than I was willing to accept. I expostulated with him on his folly in incurring the dangers and discomforts of such a trip at that season of the year, assuring him that I could make my way through alone; but all to no purpose. He only replied, that he had come to me to help me out of my misfortunes, and did not intend to leave me until he had seen me safely through. Accordingly, it was arranged that we should start together, and the next morning the Doctor, sending Reese's hired horse back by an Indian, drove him to town in his buggy, where it was necessary he should go, in order to provide himself with equipments for his journey. I gave him a note to an Irish gentleman of the name of F. J. Maguire, Esq., who I thought would be a proper person to assist him in making his arrangements.

I forgot to mention that I had made the acquaintance of this gentleman during my stay at the *Dos Pueblos*. He was a frequent visitor there, and a very clever and intelligent man. He was one of the patriots who were driven from Ireland by the tyranny of their rulers, and is very respectably connected at home. His brother is a member of the British Parliament, and editor of the *Cork Examiner*, one of the ablest presses of the kingdom. Although for a year past he has been at perfect liberty to return to his native land under shelter of the bill of amnesty passed by Parliament in behalf of the expatriated Irishmen, he prefers to remain under the wings of our Eagle, and has permanently located upon the soil, having married a California lady, a sister of the wife of Captain Thomas Moore, of *Sal si Puedes*. He was originally educated to the bar, but has abandoned his profession, preferring to engage in mercantile pursuits. He is a gentleman of fine attainments, and will doubtless ere long take a distinguished position among the citizens of his county. To this gentleman, who keeps a store in Santa Bárbara, I commended my friend Reese.

The Captain was received very kindly, not only by Mr. Maguire, but also many others of my friends in Santa Bárbara. He was introduced to the mayor, Don Antonio María De la Guerra, who gave him a letter to one of his brothers at *Los Álamos*, a place we were to pass on our journey north; also one to a nephew of his at *San Luis Obispo*. In short, the Captain was so kindly treated, and liked Santa Bárbara so well, that he did not get back to the *Dos Pueblos* until Thursday night.

Being a little superstitious about starting on a Friday, it was arranged that on Saturday morning we should bid adieu to the hospitable roof of my protector. I was not sorry for this respite, for I knew I should feel many a pang at parting with the Doctor's little children, who were very much attached to *Paisano*, as they called me, and I really loved them, particularly my little favorite, *Alfonso*. I knew that he would miss me, for I was always the confidant of his little childish sorrows, and he would have no one to go with him into the mountains, and carry him over the brooks, and make little boats and shoot quail for him. Then, too, there was smiling little *Nicolas, Guillermo*, and *Alfredo*, who used to run to *Paisano* every morning to get him to help them hunt the new-laid eggs. Poor little innocents! May they never be scathed by the *sirocco* breath which first introduced them to their wandering friend.

At length the hour of parting came. On Saturday morning, the 14th day of February, everything was got in readiness for the start. It was a wild and wintry day, but time was everything to me, and start I must. Two of the Doctor's finest horses, for our relays, had been in some time, resting for the journey, and a guide had been provided, whose name was *José Lopez*. He was to accompany us the first three hundred miles. In case of trouble from arrest on the road, I was provided by the Doctor with a letter to the district judge, Don Joaquin Carrillo, who was then in San Luis Obispo, which would, as far as his authority was concerned, have insured me, at least, fair play. We were also to be accompanied, on our first day's journey, to the Mission of Santa Inés, by the Rev. Father F. C. Rubio, who was chief in control at the Mission, and was at that time on a visit to Doctor Den. The good Padre made a short prayer for our safe return to our friends and my speedy deliverance from all my troubles, and we were then ready.

I kissed each of the little children, and shook Doña Rosa warmly by the hand. I then shook hands with all the servants, and presented to *"Juan de Dios"* a little mare which was unfit for the journey. I had bought her some three months before, from a German, for the sake of the saddle and bridle that were on her. The Doctor and I then walked to the gate, and I must confess that I could not keep back the tears which were streaming down my face. The rest of the party had started, and, as I was about to mount, I desired to express to Doctor Den my appreciation of his great goodness and the everlasting debt of gratitude I owed him, but my heart was too full, and the words stuck in my throat. All that was in me of my mother gained the ascendency, and I could not articulate. The Doctor bade me desist, and told me he wanted no thanks. He then, in a few words, gave me some good advice about my future course in life, and, murmuring "God bless you!" I waved my hand to him and his and rode after my companions, who were already some hundreds of yards on the road.

The Father Rubio appeared to have taken quite a liking to my friend Reese. He had ascertained that he was a Catholic, and, being himself from old Spain, he thought it was a rare thing to find one of his own religion among the Americans. We cantered on as comfortably as we could in such weather, smoking our cigars and chatting with the old Padre, and, without anything of interest occurring, commenced, about twelve o'clock, M., to cross the mountain of Santa Ynez. It was raining very hard, and the trail, bad enough in the dry season, was now rendered very slippery, and in some places dangerous. The crossing occupied about two hours, and was very trying to our animals. The Father and myself rode the entire distance, but no gibes nor coaxing could induce the Captain to venture it. And indeed I do not blame him. To any one unaccustomed to such traveling, it seemed foolhardy in the extreme to risk one's neck on such a road. I had ridden it once before, at night, and considering that I ought, after that, to be willing to try it by daylight, I would not dismount, though, I confess, at times I felt by no means certain of safely reaching the other side. Reese frequently walked, and led his horse, until we reached the plain on the other side. We arrived at the Mission of Santa Inés, at the foot of the mountain, about two o'clock, P. M. We had ridden twenty-two miles.

Father Rubio had a good dinner provided for us while we dried ourselves by a roaring fire, and we soon were making ourselves very comfortable over the Padre's excellent California wine. As the weather was very tempestuous, and our guide wanted to procure an extra horse at the college farm, distant about three miles, we determined to remain where we were till the next day. Every thing about this Mission, except the old church building, is in a state of sad decay. There are still there, however, the vestiges of fine improvements built by the Indians in the palmy days of the Church in California; and I observed, among other things, the ruins of what was once a splendid aqueduct built of brick, and the shattered remnants of an extensive grist-mill. At a distance, however, the general appearance of the Mission of Santa Inés is still imposing, and it is only upon a nearer approach that the marks of ruin become painfully apparent. There is still a splendid domain, containing many leagues of land, connected with the Mission. It is the property of the Church, and under the supervision of Archbishop Alemany, whose agent is Doctor Nicholas A. Den.

There is also a school here, for boys, under the management of a Mr. Campbell, formerly of Philadelphia. There were but twelve scholars in it, however, at the time of our visit. Three of them were nephews of the Hon. Pablo De la Guerra, and three of them sons of the Mrs. Robbins from whom, it will be remembered, I obtained food when starving back of Santa Bárbara. The boys all spoke English with but slight Spanish accent, and when the little fellows discovered that I was the wanderer of whom they had heard, they were untiring in their efforts to please me.

On Sunday, the fifteenth, after the Padre had finished the morning services in the chapel, he gave me a letter to the Mission of San Juan, in Monterey County, in case I should need assistance when I got there, and after dinner we departed for "Los Álamos." A great part of the road was very bad, and it rained hard the entire distance. Just as night set in, we arrived, very cold and wet, at our destination. Alighting, we sent in, by the guide, the letter with which Don Antonio De la Guerra had furnished Captain Reese, and presently we were ushered into a very comfortable apartment, where a bright fire was blazing, and were introduced to the family, which, including children and grandchildren, numbered some twenty-six persons. At this place we were treated very hospitably. After supper, one of the family played and sung for us, and when we were shown to our room, we discovered that the lady of the house had surrendered her own to us, as being pro bably the most comfortable she had. Several Americans were about the place, and, partly on this account, and because we wished to make San Luis Obispo in one ride, distance about fifty miles, we left the next morning without stopping to take coffee. We breakfasted as we rode along, on *pinole* and California cheese, a supply of which the guide appeared to have had ever since he left the college farm at Santa Inés.

About noon we stopped at a place called the Guadalupe Ranch, and dined on jerked beef, without bread or salt. We rested about an hour, and again took the road. Owing to the misfortune of being led the wrong road by our guide, we did not reach San Luis Obispo that night, but were compelled to stop some ten miles short of that place, long after dark, hungry, wet, and weary, at the ranch of a gentleman of the name of John Price, Esq. This gentleman has been in the country some thirty years. Owing to the lateness of the hour, and our being strangers to him, it was some time before he would consent to accommodate us for the night. Finally, by dint of persuasion, and telling over the names of my friends among the old Californians, with whom he was acquainted, I succeeded in opening his heart, and he admitted us. He gave us some excellent whisky, good beds, and plenty of grain for our horses. He was quite inquisitive as to our business in the lower country, and in reply to his questions we told him that we had come down from San Francisco in the steamer to attend to some business in connection with the sale of some land, but that, being detained till after the steamer had started, we were making the best of our way back by land, having important matters to attend to at Sacramento before the fourth of March; which latter part of the story was literally true. After a comfortable night's rest, we partook of an excellent breakfast, and, on offering to pay our host for his accommodation, he declined taking recompense for anything, except the barley our horses had eaten. Bidding Mr. Price good by, we resumed our journey, but, owing to rather a late start, did not reach San Luis Obispo until about ten o'clock, A. M.

Remembering that I had been identified in that place on my journey down the country, I did not care to pass through it, and so endeavored to go around by a very rough and hilly road. Observing that our movements were watched, in the outset, by persons about town, we thought it was best that the Captain should ride at once into the place and purchase some cigars, sardines, etc., and in the event of any one identifying him, to say that we were looking for a lost horse. Accordingly, he rode through the town, stopping to make his purchases, and, on joining me on the other side, he said he had been recognized by a man, to whom he had told the story agreed upon, and had no further trouble. We rode on about two miles farther, when we stopped and turned our horses out to graze, while we sat down on our blankets and enjoyed a luncheon and a smoke. After resting about an hour, we again took the road, and, with nothing further occurring, about the middle of the afternoon reached the rancho of Santa Margarita, distant but twelve miles from San Luis Obispo, where we concluded to stop for the night. This rancho is the property of Señor *Joaquin Estrada*. It has been a Mission, but the old building is now used as a sort of restaurant. One of the brothers of our host had married into the De la Guerra family, and, on discovering that we were acquainted with Don Pablo, he treated us with marked hospitality. We had an excellent supper and good beds. At this place

I found an Irishman who had seen Reese in Santa Bárbara, and I judged from the way he looked at me that he knew me. He talked a great deal about McGowan and his persecutors. Being pretty well posted on that subject, I joined freely in the conversation, and finally told him that I had seen McGowan at the house of Dr. Den, at which place I understood he had been since leaving Santa Bárbara. This appeared to satisfy him that I was not the "ubiquitous." Whether he knew me or not was of very little moment, for I felt sure from his conversation that he was an out-and-out *anti-Vigilante*. He finished the conversation by saying that McGowan could not be the monster he had been represented, or Doctor Den would not have sheltered him so long as he had done. In this opinion I of course acquiesced, and shortly afterward we all retired for the night.

The next morning, after breakfast, we again took up our line of travel, and rode on without stopping until we came to the hot spring mentioned in my journey down the country. Here we halted and took a pleasant bath and luncheon. We let our horses feed a short time, while we rested and smoked our cigars, and then rode on as far as the Mission of San Miguel, where we halted for the night. Notwithstanding the Mexican who keeps the place had informed us, before alighting, that there was feed for the horses, when we had unsaddled them we discovered that there was not a particle for them to eat about the premises. Here was a quandary. To turn them loose to graze was out of the question, as the place was infested with a parcel of Indians, who had a trick of *stampeding* the horses of travelers, for the purpose of getting the reward usually offered for their recovery. It was at this place, I remembered, that young Castro had lost a horse in this manner, on the downward journey. I had the horses securely locked up, and then set about trying to buy some corn for them from the Indians. I managed, after hard work, to induce an old Indian to sell me a dollar's worth, by bribing him with a drink of brandy. This was but short allowance for four tired horses, but we were compelled to be contented with it.

The fellow who kept this place was a surly brute, and

evidently mistook us for robbers. When we first alighted, the members of the household, including several *señoritas*, were assembled in the main building, but, on seeing us, he drove them at once out of sight. Having distributed their scanty allowance among the horses, we entered the house and sat down to a miserable supper, which we attempted to wash down with some villainous claret. After supper, we were shown to a kind of cell in the old building, where, on dirty beds, we passed a most uncomfortable night. As soon as it was light, I arose and went out with the guide among the Indians, to endeavor to procure some more corn for the horses. For some time my efforts were unsuccessful. I showed them money, but they said they did not care for any of it; they had no corn to sell. I had a bottle of good brandy left, and, traveling at that season of the year, I would not have parted with it for five dollars. Neverthe less, if money would not do, the brandy had to go, rather than the horses should go unfed. My eye fell on a good-looking young Indian leaning against a door-post, and list lessly looking at us. I asked him, in Spanish, if he would not like a drink of *cognac*. He replied, "Very much", whereupon I told him if he would get me the corn I would give him the bottle, and pay him besides. He entered the house, and, after a noisy altercation with an old hag, returned with a *serape* half-filled with corn and acorns. I gave him the bottle and some silver, and he and an old Indian, who appeared to be his father, finished the liquor in two drinks. We then bought some sardines from the Mexican who kept the place, and left it in extreme disgust. I cannot conscientiously advise any one who may travel that road to stop at the rancho of San Miguel. The cross-grained varlet who keeps it is but a poor specimen of a California Boniface. He not only charges three prices for all that he sells, but treats his guests all the time as if by so doing he was conferring an immense favor on them.

After riding some eight or ten miles, we came to a small stream, which, in order to cross, we were obliged to swim. Here we found several parties encamped on both sides of the stream. They had wagons, and among them were several women. They had arrived, respectively, from the north and south the previous night, and had waited until morning, in the hope that some one would come along and show them the best crossing-place. I told the guide, supposing that he was most accustomed to that sort of thing, to go in first, but, being a very timid man, he hesitated. Presently, however, to cut the matter short, Captain Reese plunged in with his horse, and the guide and I following, we all reached the other side in safety. The wagons then followed, but the mules became entangled in the harness in the middle of the stream, and a young Spaniard, who afterwards told me he was from Martinez, on his way to Los Angeles, went to the rescue of the women, and crossed them over safely, one by one, on a fine little mare he had with him. I gave this young fellow a box of sardines and some of our claret, in return for which he treated us to some hot coffee some of his Indians had just made. We unsaddled our horses, and let them feed while we breakfasted and took a smoke. After an hour's rest, we resumed our journey, and traveled without stopping until we reached the rancho of *San Benito.* We had been told at *Santa Margarita* that we should find good entertainment at this place, and we were not disappointed.

The proprietor is Mr. Thomas Watson, an American gentleman who has resided in Monterey County some thirty years, and has a large family of sons and daughters, one of the latter of whom is the wife of E. L. Williams, Esq., county clerk of Monterey. We did not have the pleasure of seeing the proprietor himself, but his son, Thomas Watson, Jr., entertained us very handsomely. Shortly after we entered the house, I saw a gentleman who I ascertained, was a deputy sheriff of Santa Cruz County, and had been at the ranch several days. Not caring to be much in his company, for reasons which will be understood, and besides, being very weary, I retired early. I had not been asleep long when I was awakened by two men entering the room. One of them, whom I recognized as the Sheriff, had his face blacked. This circumstance puzzled and somewhat alarmed me. At the same time, I heard him remark, "It would be funny if they were to steal my horses, and I am to leave to-morrow." Presently he washed his face, and he and his companion again went out. I lay awake for some time, wondering what the blacking of

H*

his face could mean, but finally coming to the conclusion that it probably had no connection with me, yet still very curious as to the mystery, I fell asleep.

After breakfast the next morning, we were informed that the Sheriff, who was on his way to Santa Cruz, two days' journey on the road we were traveling, would embrace the opportunity of having company and ride with us. I did not like the idea much, as the face-blacking of the previous night was still unexplained. I was fearful that he was on the lookout for me, but had as yet failed to identify me. I knew that a letter had been very foolishly written from Santa Bárbara to San Francisco, to an indiscreet friend there, apprising him of my intended journey to the capital, and I feared that he would inform every one of the fact, and thus, perhaps, unintentionally have me intercepted. Indeed, I afterward discovered that he had circulated the news far and wide, but, fortunately, those who ought not to have known it did not believe it, a statement having appeared about that time, in the *San Francisco Herald*, that a passenger, recently arrived in a ship from Canton, had seen me in that place. I presumed, if the Committee contemplated capturing me, that between this point and Stockton would be the most likely place they would undertake it. Therefore, considering everything, I felt by no means pleased at this addition to our company. There was nothing for it, however, but to ride off boldly with the Sheriff, which we did.

Happily, however, we had not gone far before my apprehensions were relieved. The Sheriff, who proved to be a very pleasant, companionable man, accounted for the mystery of the previous night by telling me he had been engaged with the young ladies in a game called "smut," and having been beaten, had submitted to the penalty and had his face blacked. This gentleman's name is Charles Williams, Esq., and he is a brother of the above-mentioned county clerk. We had, that day, a very pleasant ride, and arrived early in the afternoon at the Misión Soledad, where we halted for the night. I recognized the keeper of this place, whom I had not seen on my way down. His name was Harris, and he was formerly bartender at the "Willows," a resort well known to San Franciscans. He did not know me, however, I was so much altered, having lost forty pounds of flesh since he had last seen me. He desired us to register our names in his book, and I wrote mine as "Samuel Chapman." I procured from him writing materials, and addressed a letter to a gentleman at Monterey, named Charles Harron, Esq., an old Philadelphia friend, informing him of my journey to the capital. I knew that he was discreet, and my only object in writing was to have the pleasure of once more communicating with an old friend.

We were very comfortably quartered at the Soledad, and the next morning, after breakfast, prepared to renew our journey. We were told, before starting, that, a few miles from the Mission, we should come to a stream which, at that season, was impassable, owing to the quicksands, unless we were fortunate enough to find an old Indian who lived about there, and induce him to show us the firm footing. Both the Sheriff and Harris were of the opinion that we had better go another road, which was thirty miles longer, the chances being against our finding the Indian. As thirty miles, however, was a great item to tired horses, I thought it was best to go on to the stream and take the chance of finding the Indian. After some consultation, this plan was adopted, and we started for the stream, where we were fortunate enough to find the Indian, and at last, by dint of silver and coaxing, and, above all, some whisky, we were safely landed on the opposite bank.

Here we found a party of travelers with wagons, waiting for some one to guide them across the river. Some horsemen were riding in front of the wagons, armed with rifles, and for a moment I fancied that they might be my old friends the *Vigilantes*, and prepared for an attack. I soon saw, however, that one of the wagons contained a woman, and was reassured as to the character of the party. The Sheriff was acquainted with one of them, and stopped a moment to converse, while I rode on. I learned, when he rejoined us, that they were on their way to the lower country to purchase brood-mares, intending to take them through Mexico to Texas, and that they hoped to accomplish the trip in one hundred days. The animals can be procured at very low prices on this side, and, if safely got through the journey, command a handsome profit. At noon we stopped to eat something and let our horses graze. As we were now within thirty miles of San Juan, in the *Salinas Plains*, up to which point the Sheriff knew the road well, and beyond it we did not need a guide, I determined here to dispatch *José* back to Doctor Den. Accordingly, I gave him a letter for the Doctor, letting him know how we got on, and, taking with him two of the horses, the guide started back.

After he had gone, the Sheriff loaned me one of his fresh horses, and we galloped on our journey. We stopped at one or two places to get water, one of which was the ranch of the Mexican who had been so near being shot for a deserter, at whose house, it will be remembered, I passed a night on my journey from San Francisco. His wife recognized me, but he did not till he saw her smile at me, and then he, too, remembered me. He asked me many questions, and I told him that since he had seen me I had been in Mexico. I doubted, however, from his looks, whether he believed the story. It mattered little, however, for, of course, he was ignorant of my name, and we stayed but a few moments at his door. After riding a few miles farther, we came to a place called the *Cañada Verde*, where, to oblige the Sheriff, we stopped a little while to give him an opportunity to see a friend on business. This gentleman was the judge of the plains, and I knew him the moment I saw him. It was Don Manuel A. Castro. He had represented San Luis Obispo, the previous year, in the legislature, and it was at the capital I had seen him. As he did not recognize me, however, I did not accost him.

A few miles farther on, we came to the store of Mr. Johnstone, where we halted for the night. This gentleman came to California during the war, as a member of Colonel Stevenson's regiment. I had known him before, when he was employed in the office of P. K. Woodside, Esq., at that time clerk of the supreme court. He did not appear to recognize me, however, and I did not, that night, make myself known to him, although I knew he was a Democrat of the right stripe, and had no fears as to his discretion.

We were very comfortably accommodated at this place, and in the morning, as we were about to start, I paid all the bill, including the Sheriff's, who had so kindly loaned me his horse, and who I knew, having been some time absent from home, had paid away his last dollar at the Soledad. Here the Sheriff was to part from us, he being within a few miles of his home, and our roads lying from this point in different directions. Accordingly, we bid him Godspeed and saw him off. As I was about mounting, I observed Johnstone eyeing me very closely. He seemed to know me, and yet was in uncertainty where he had seen me. He had a bottle of whisky in his hand, which I suspected he wanted to give me. Knowing that it would be perfectly safe, I at length asked him if he did not know me. He said he knew me very well, but could not for his life say who I was. I told him, and he seized my hand and pressed it very hard. He asked me why I had not stopped at his place on my way down the coast. Dennison, with whom I then was, had been a fellow-soldier with him, and had stopped at his door, where I took a drink, but did not dismount, and hence he had not recognized me. He gave me the bottle of whisky, and, wishing me a safe journey, saw me off.

It was Sunday morning, and, as we approached the town of San Juan, we thought it safer, as many persons would probably be there from the country, not to pass through the place. So we avoided it by a mountain-road to the right, and sent the letter which the Father Rubio had given us, to the priest at the Mission, by a man whom we found cutting wood, and who told us he knew him. A few miles farther brought us to the *Pacheco Pass*, through which we were to strike into the interior, and shape our course in a northeasterly direction for Stockton. At the foot of the mountain, we saw a small ranch, and, on being informed by some women, whom we saw gathering mushrooms, that we could get quarters for ourselves and horses for the night, we concluded to finish here our day's ride.

The person who kept this place looked familiar to me, and I soon identified him as a stage-driver I had known on the road between San Francisco and San José, named Harper. He and his partner had each married a Frenchwoman, and settled down in this romantic spot, where they were farming and raising a few stock. We had a good supper and comfortable lodging, and started early the next morning, before breakfast, to cross the mountain by the Pacheco Pass. It is seven miles over the pass, and the road is perfectly good and passable for wagons at all seasons of the year. It was constructed by a Mr. Firebaugh, under a franchise granted him, for a term of years, by the legislature, for that purpose. He has the privilege of keeping a toll-gate, which is situated at his house on the summit. About a mile and a half from the gate, we met Mr. Firebaugh in company with a workman, superintending some repairs in the road. We paid him our toll, and asked him if we could be accommodated with breakfast at the house. He told us that his wife would prepare some for us, and accordingly, on reaching the summit, we stopped. Here we saw Mrs. Firebaugh with her little son. She had apparently just arisen, and the Captain and I were both struck with her singular beauty and ladylike deportment. I could not help wondering how a lady so charming could content herself in so wild and out-of-the-way a place as the Pacheco Pass. I should infer, however, from what little I observed of her, that she is one of those rare and precious gifts, in the shape of woman, whose happiness is in her husband and whose paradise is his home. We informed her of what her husband had said about the breakfast, but at the same time declined to trouble her. The fire was not yet made, and before she should have put herself to the trouble of making it for me, I would have dispensed with breakfast every day for a week. She set before us a bottle of excellent whisky, of which we partook, but she declined receiving any pay. I gave her little son a small piece of money, and, bidding her good morning, we resumed our journey. After riding about twelve miles, we came to a large unfinished frame house. The people about this place appeared to be a mixture of French and Spaniards. I identified one of them as a San Francisco Frenchman, but he did not know me. I imagine he was but a visitor there. Here we took breakfast, and, again mounting, rode on until we came to Hill's Ferry, on the San Joaquin River, where we found a very good hotel, and stopped for the night. At this place we fell in with a tall, cadaverous-looking old fellow, who I judged, from his conversation, to be a squatter. He was accompanied by a young lad, and he told me they were looking out for a place to "locate." He said he had lived in the valley of San José. They were traveling on foot, with one pack-animal. He had been a lawyer, he told me, and I should judge by his appearance and sanctified *twang* he had been a preacher too. After conversing with us some time, he and the lad made their bed on the floor, and we retired to our room. After an early breakfast the next morning, we resumed our journey, intending, if possible, to reach the city of Stockton that night, but forty miles distant. It rained and stormed dreadfully, however, and, after riding about twenty miles, we were fain to ask shelter at a neat little cottage we espied on the roadside. This house was kept by a young Welshman and his wife, who lived very comfortably, and were surrounded by a family of pretty little children. The gentleman's name is Griffith. We were hospitably welcomed, and a large fire was soon made for us, at which we dried our clothes and blankets. We found here an old gentleman named Major James Martin Lewis, familiarly known in that neighborhood as "Uncle Jemmy Lewis." He is a brother of Colonel Joel Lewis, so well and favorably known to the citizens of Sacramento. This old gentleman, I have since learned, has lived seventy years, and had served as a sergeant under General Jackson during the Creek War. He was gazetted by that veteran for his gallantry in being the first man on the enemy's ramparts at the famous battle of the *Horseshoe*. He knew me, though I did not recognize him. I suppose he called me to mind from the circumstance of my having once acted as the friend of his nephew, Doctor Dickson, of Mississippi, in an unfortunate affair of honor, in which that gentleman fell. I did not know, until after starting the next day, that the old gentleman had recognized me. I entered freely into conversation with Mrs. Griffith, and found her very intelligent, and not a little inquisitive. She asked me why I had not stopped at a large hotel we had passed after leaving Hill's Ferry. I replied, that I always preferred to stop where there was a lady, because I invariably found the accommodations better and neater. She looked very knowingly at me, and told me that my dress and language did not correspond, and that for some reason I was traveling in disguise. I thought this was very strange, not knowing at the time that "Uncle Jemmy" had told them who I was, and, making some joking reply, I changed the conversation. I also met at this place a gentleman of the name of Judge Seneca Dean. He is an uncle of Mrs. Julia Dean Hayne, the actress. At the table, the conversation turned upon the "ubiquitous" Judge McGowan. Judge Dean stated that McGowan had been pointed out to him once in San Francisco. At this I observed a sly smile on the face of mischievous Mrs. Griffith. I, however, looked them full in the face, and continued my dinner as though McGowan was a personage in whom I felt no interest whatever. I told Judge Dean that I had business with the legislature, and he gave me a letter to the member from Stanislaus, in which county we then were. In this letter he mentioned no name, but simply commended the bearer to the gentleman to whom it was written.

It rained incessantly all that day and night, and the next day, at twelve o'clock, we started for Stockton. I saw two persons approaching the house after I had mounted, and rode off first, to avoid observation. Presently I was overtaken by Captain Reese, who told me that, just as he was leaving, Uncle Jemmy had said to him, "Young man, that is Judge McGowan. I know it is. Don't tell me any lies about it. I am his friend, and if danger threatens him, let him come back here. I've a good double-barreled shotgun, and *we'll protect him!*"

Reese laughed, and, bidding the gallant old fellow good by, rode away. I now understood the remarks of good Mrs. Griffith and Judge Dean.

Stockton was now but twenty-two miles off, and, notwithstanding the roads were very bad, and it was raining very hard, we determined, if possible, to reach it that night. We pushed on without stopping until we got to French Camp. Up to this point we had been enabled to travel at a pretty fair rate, but in traversing the five miles which intervened between it and Stockton, so wretched was the road that we were occupied full three hours. At length, some time after dark, wet, weary, and cold, we rode into the good city of Stockton, and I felt, after nine months of pilgrimage and banishment, that I was once more really mingling with my fellow-men.

CHAPTER IX

<blockquote>
Once more to view those old familiar haunts,
Round which, in memory, I have lingered,
Were a joy, and yet a joy not all untinged with grief.
Old Play.
</blockquote>

ON entering the town, Reese met a person with whom he was acquainted, and I requested him to inquire for the residence of Samuel Brooks, Esq., the county treasurer of San Joaquin County. I had not the pleasure of an intimate personal acquaintance with Mr. Brooks, but I knew enough of his character to believe that, under the circumstances which then surrounded me, I might safely trust my life in his keeping. He was, however, spared the annoyance of my visit, for Reese was informed that he was absent in San Francisco.

My next inquiry was for Col. John O'Neal, the county clerk. That gentleman soon appeared, and, after congratulating me on my safe return, conducted us to a good place to stable our horses. He then accompanied us to the room of one of his friends, and very kindly sent out and had a warm supper prepared and brought to us, which was very acceptable, as we had eaten but one meal that day. Many of my friends who resided in Stockton were now informed of my arrival, and before we retired for the night I was visited by several of them. I cannot convey any idea of the gratification I felt at finding myself congratulated and sympathized with by some of the first men of the state, notwithstanding the continuous stream of vilification and slander that had been poured over my name during my voluntary exile. It was to me a harbinger of happier days, and an assurance that not only my individual troubles were about ending, but that there still existed in the minds of the true men of the state sufficient respect for the constitution and our laws to render their supremacy in the land once more *certain*, and that at no distant day.

The next morning, I was visited by the Hon. Charles M. Creaner, district judge of that judicial district. He was very glad to see me safely returned to stand my trial, and when, in the course of our conversation, I asked him if he was not afraid, on account of his position, that he might be compromised by visiting me under such peculiar circumstances, "Sir," said he, "if I am to be compromised by extending the hand of sympathy to one who has been barbarously hunted by bloodhounds, the sooner the better." Such a sentiment, fervently expressed by such a man, infused new life into me. Personally, I was a comparative stranger to Judge Creaner. Although both of us were members of the same political party, we had sympathized and acted with opposite wings of that party, and there was very little more in common between us politically than, from our slight acquaintance, there had been personally. When, therefore, I contrasted this language of the high toned Judge with the pitiful cowardice, meanness, and ingratitude of some of my *friends*, into whose nostrils I had blown the breath of political life, I could not but painfully learn and bitterly digest the lesson I was thus taught in human nature. The Judge, on learning my intention to proceed to Sacramento for the purpose of endeavoring to procure the passage of a law by which I might be safely and fairly tried under my indictment, very kindly furnished me with a letter to the Hon. A. R. Meloney, the senator from that district, and, after a most agreeable visit, took his leave.

I remained in Stockton the whole of that day, and, before leaving the next morning (Friday, the 27th of February), I mailed a letter to the *San Francisco Herald*. Knowing that my arrival in Stockton would certainly be known and published in San Francisco, I thought, by way of an item of news, I might as well let my friends of the *Herald* have it in advance. Indeed, the day after I left Stockton, the following notice of my arrival in that city was published in the *San Joaquin Republican:* —

On Wednesday evening last, Edward McGowan arrived in this city from Santa Bárbara, overland, by the way of San Joaquin Valley, and left again yesterday morning. From a gentleman who conversed with him, we learn that he is in excellent health and spirits, although not so fleshy as formerly. He narrated at length his hairbreadth escapes from the Vigilantes, and stated that he frequently found himself hard pressed by the enemy, and was often compelled to change his hiding-places, in the vicinity of Santa Bárbara, from which city he had not been distant, during his seclusion from the public gaze, more than thirty or forty miles.

He also stated that the letter written with gunpowder, and published in the San Francisco *Herald*, was a genuine document. He sent a Californian into Santa Bárbara — distance seventeen miles from his rendezvous — for a bottle of ink; on the way back, the messenger broke the bottle, compelling him to use gunpowder and water as a substitute. Ned was much chagrined because of his inability to vote for Buchanan and Breckinridge at the last Presidential election. He had cut the ticket out of a stray copy of a Democratic paper, but, owing to circumstances over which he had no control, he was prevented from depositing it in the ballot-box. He still wears — and always has worn — the famous mustache, by which he is easily recognized; the white hat, however, has been laid aside for a black one. We have received the above information from a gentleman of well-known veracity.

My letter to the *Herald*, as will be perceived, was nothing more than an outburst of fun, suggested by the high spirits I was in on account of the kindness of my friends in Stockton. The following is a copy: —

STOCKTON, Feb. 27th, 1857,
Five o'clock, A. M.

Editor San Francisco Herald: —

SIR, — I arrived at this place the day before yesterday, from the "*Celestial Empire*," by the overland route — *via:* the Sandwich Islands, Santa Bárbara City, Santa Ynez, Pacheco's Pass, &c. Had rather a pleasant passage, only it rained all the way — swimming a few rivers, &c. I made this trip in the short space of twelve days. During my sojourn in this city, I have been the guest of the *élite* of [the] place — had a public dinner, and the freedom of the city tendered to me, all of which I was forced most respectfully to decline, as prior engagements at the " CAPITAL" precluded the possibility of my accepting them.

I have been invited by the legislature to deliver a series of lectures before them, previous to their final adjournment. The subjects —

"Higher Law," "Soft Pork," "Sour Flour," and the morality of the CHIEFS OF THE "CHOKERS" generally.

I contemplate holding a *levee* at the "MAGNOLIA HOTEL" on Sunday, the first of March next, at ten, A. M., and if any of the "purest and best" in your "city of blood" and "solvent (?) merchants" still have a curiosity to see the "white hat" which covers the head of the "ubiquitous" undersigned, they can be gratified by appearing, at the time and place above mentioned.

Respectfully yours,
EDWARD MCGOWAN.

After dispatching the above, we bid our friends good by, and turned our horses' heads in the direction of Sacramento. For the first six miles, the road lay through a lake of water, formed by the recent heavy rains, and in many places it came up to the horses' flanks. We saw no one until we had got through this, but, on striking the dry road again, we met a woman on horseback, and alone. She inquired as to the condition of the road, and I explained it to her, advising her, at the same time, to turn back, as it was very doubtful whether she could find it, covered as it was with water. She replied, that she was obliged to go to Stockton at all hazards, and see a magistrate, and thereupon unbosomed herself of her sorrows to me. It appeared that she was a victim of the "green-eyed monster," and some recent pranks of her faithless lord had resolved her to seek redress of some sort at law. I endeavored to comfort her, but in vain, and, heedless of my information as to the road, she pushed resolutely on toward Stockton.

After riding but a short distance farther, we came to Wood's Ferry, where we stopped to feed our horses and dine. I related the incident of the poor woman to the lady of the house, who knew her, and gave me some additional particulars as to her case. We had a hearty laugh at the expense of the poor, neglected lady, though, as is too often the case, that which was a source of merriment to us was doubtless a sore grievance to her.

At this place we met Mr. John Hodges, a partner of Judge Terry in the proprietorship of "Terry and Hodges' Mills," which, as many will remember, were burned down while Judge Terry was imprisoned by the Vigilance Committee. After dinner he pressed us to accompany him to his home and pass the night. As we did not care to reach

Sacramento till Saturday night, we accepted his kind invitation, and accordingly set out for the mill, which is some ten miles off the road, and situated on the Mokelumne River. On arriving at the crossing-place near the mill, we found that the water had risen so much that it was idle to attempt to ford the river, and so remained on the side where we were, and found lodgings with some young friends of Mr. Hodges, who treated us very kindly, refusing any compensation for their hospitality.

In the morning we mounted our horses, and, bidding farewell to our hosts, commenced the last day's ride of our weary pilgrimage. We rode on without stopping or meeting with anything of interest until we came to the ranch of Mr. Thomas Harrigan, the proprietor of the Centerville Race-course, a few miles from Sacramento. Here we concluded that it was advisable to halt and get some information as to how matters stood before venturing into the city. We found everything all right, however; for my friend Harrigan, who was delighted to see me, informed us that friends were prepared for our arrival, having been expecting it for several days. Accordingly, after partaking of a hearty supper, we again mounted, and, shortly after night, rode into the capital. We put up our horses at a livery-stable, and repaired at once to the Magnolia Hotel. I immediately sent for Mr. Charles T. Botts, a lawyer of eminence in Sacramento, and engaged his professional services. A writ of *habeas corpus* was prepared, to be sued out in case the sheriff of San Francisco, hearing of my arrival, should be compelled, in the discharge of his duty, to come to Sacramento to arrest me, and preparations were made to draft such a bill, to be introduced into the legislature, as would meet the circumstances of my case.

These steps being taken, about eleven o'clock I went with some friends to the bar of the Magnolia to drink, and, though I saw dozens of familiar faces around me, I was not recognized by one. Every one took me for a ragged old miner just come in from "the diggings." It was soon known, however, that I had arrived, and I was visited by swarms of friends. I did not get to bed that night until three o'clock. I arose early in the morning, and, placing myself in charge of my good friend William Williamson,

Esq., I proceeded at once to a clothing-store, and dressed myself in a full suit of decent apparel, and in the course of the morning a friend sent me a present of a very stylish WHITE HAT, which I immediately donned, and felt that "*Richard was himself again.*"

It was thought advisable that on that day (Sunday) I should see as many of my friends as possible, and make the acquaintance of those new members whom I did not know, in order that I might tell them my story, and my reasons for asking the passage of the law which was being prepared. Accordingly, I remained in my room, holding a sort of *levee* and my friends must have brought nearly a thousand persons to see me. I stated my case to those on whose power I was compelled to rely, and had every reason to believe that my application would not be made to the legislature in vain. That night, I thought it prudent to leave the hotel, lest the officers of San Francisco should arrive late, and a hearing of the writ (it being Sunday) could not be obtained. Accordingly, I went with a friend to a retired part of the city, letting but few know the place of my retreat. On awaking the next morning, I inquired for the San Francisco papers, being desirous of seeing how my return to the upper regions suited my *Vigilante* friends, and one of the first things that met my eye was the following, from the *Town Talk* of Sunday, March 1st:—

> NED MCGOWAN REDIVIVUS!—The ubiquitous Ned McGowan turned up yesterday as a topic of conversation, a rumor having gained currency that he had arrived in Sacramento. The report was received with considerable misgiving by the public, and we hesitated to announce it on the bulletin-board until we could ascertain its source.
>
> The rumor was promulgated by a gentleman who arrived from Stockton yesterday morning, stating he saw Ned off for Sacramento from the former city, where he had been residing the past month. The latter portion of the information staggered us—so we sought for more proof. A member of the bar of this city, however, confirmed the report, stating a letter had been received from Ned, giving the motives of his return. This statement has been further confirmed to us by a gentleman who said he read the same, but refused to disclose the recipient's name. A week or so ago, it was currently reported that Ned was on his way to the capital from the southern country, but it was discredited.
>
> To add to the mystery which surrounds the movements of a man who is said to be in China, at Santa Bárbara, in Sonora, on the Plains, and in Philadelphia at one and the same time, we have been

assured that a well-known gentleman of this city, famous for his enterprise, who has been on Ned's track ever since his rumored flight, has indubitable proof that Ned has not been out of the city since, except two weeks, during the Vigilance excitement, and a month since! His custodian is said to have been a lady of this city, whose friendship for Ned has dated from early childhood.

The following also appeared in the *Democratic State Journal*, of Sacramento: —

THE UBIQUITOUS. — Mr. Edward McGowan, a personage somewhat known to fame and the San Francisco Vigilance Committee, arrived in this city last evening, from Stockton. He has, for some nine months, been sojourning in the counties in the southern portion of this state, the assertion that he has been seen, "by persons who knew him well," in Philadelphia, China, and a few other out-of-the-way places, to the contrary notwithstanding. By advice of counsel, he has come to this city, and intends to ask of the legislature the passage of an act to secure to him the rights of a trial by jury in some county where he can have a reasonable chance of obtaining justice, and where the laws are respected. As no confidence can be placed in San Francisco in this respect, an armed mob having entire control of that city, he will not go to that place. We learn that he has been treated with great consideration by those persons who learned the object of his visit to the capital, and no attempt has been made to arrest him. Mr. McGowan is in good health and spirits, though he is much thinner than he was previous to his leaving San Francisco, and his dress is decidedly *outré*. We have no doubt but that the legislature will grant him the constitutional rights that he asks. McGowan has been most of the time in Santa Bárbara County. There have been many absurd rumors in reference to the action of the San Francisco Vigilance Committee in this matter, but we place no confidence in them.

In the mean while, my friend, the San Francisco *Bulletin*, true to its antecedents, and with its usual decency and good sense, thus uncourteously held forth to the good citizens of Sacramento: —

Ned McGowan, the ubiquitous, has actually arrived in Sacramento. This time there is no humbug about it. He puts up at the "Magnolia" Hotel, where, during all of yesterday, he was the center of a large circle of admirers, with the like of whom this city swarms at present. Sacramento at this time resembles one of the old Jewish "cities of refuge," where murderers and other criminals could flee for shelter from the avengers of blood. How long this state of things shall continue depends entirely upon the inhabitants themselves, and of course is no business of the San Franciscans.

The next day, my counsel, Mr. Botts, set about the drafting of a proper bill for my relief, to be introduced into the legislature. It was thought, however, on reflection, that a copy of my indictment had better first be procured, in order that the bill might be made to hold water at all points, and exactly meet my case, without the possibility of its object being defeated by any "afterclaps" in the way of technical quibbles. Accordingly, a telegraphic dispatch was sent to a friend in San Francisco, requesting him to go to the office of the county clerk and procure a copy and send it up at once. Lo and behold! however, it was ascertained, on application, that, notwithstanding the indictment had been found ten months previously, there had been filed no such document in the clerk's office of the court in which I was to be tried! After much diligent inquiry, it was found that the exceedingly scrupulous and careful district attorney of that county, Mr. H. H. Byrne, had actually *deposited it in bank*, lest, I suppose, some of my friends, in their anxiety for my safety, might steal it from the county clerk, and thus expose his precious carcass to the wrath of his great "bugbear," the Vigilance Committee, of which institution, doubtless for sufficient reasons of his own, he stood in mortal dread. He probably would have spared himself this precaution had he known that, attributing my indictment more to his base and selfish cowardice and ingratitude than to a conviction, on the part of the grand jury, that I was guilty, I always intended, conscious of my own innocence, to return and be tried whenever I could safely do so.

After some trouble, the copy was procured and sent up to Sacramento; and the bill being prepared, on the third day of March it was placed in the hands of Gen. Jefferson Hunt, of San Bernardino County, one of the most influential members of the assembly, to be by him introduced into that body. The bill provided for a change of *venue*, in my particular case, from the San Francisco to the Sacramento, or sixth, judicial district. On the reading of its title, its introduction was objected to by the entire San Francisco delegation of nine, composed of members of the Vigilance Committee, most of them being Black Republicans, and all of them elected in the *furor* of the mob ascendency in that city. They were seconded in their objections by *all of the Black Republicans* on the floor every one of whom was a sympathizer with the Vigilance Committee. The question then became, under the rules, "Shall the bill be rejected?"—upon which the "ayes and noes" were demanded, and it was found that the Democracy, who were largely in the majority in the house, with a few exceptions* voted in mass in the negative, while every Black Republican voted the other way. Thus, notwithstanding many of my friends were absent, the rejection of the bill was negatived by a handsome majority. Prior to the putting of the question, the Hon. Gaven D. Hall, member for El Dorado County, and chairman of the judiciary committee, made one of the most able and effective arguments in my behalf that had been heard that session, and I cannot refrain from here returning him my thanks for the same.

Another, though much lesser light in the legislature, Mr. Patrick, of Tuolumne County, though calling himself a Democrat, made some severe remarks against me, and afterwards put himself to the trouble of having a most scurrilous speech against me published as having been delivered by him. Those who heard him, however, have only to read the speech to know that he never delivered it.

---

* The *Democratic State Journal*, in commenting upon the proceedings the next day, held the following language:—

EDWARD McGOWAN.—A bill was introduced in the assembly yesterday, the effect of which would be to grant Edward McGowan a trial in some county out of San Francisco. There is no doubt that if McGowan were taken to San Francisco he would be seized by the mob and hung, without judge or jury; or, were he to be regularly tried there, no jury could be obtained that would not be prejudiced on one side or the other. He desires that his case should be investigated by an impartial jury, and his request ought to be granted. We pity the man who has so little sensibility, or sense of justice, as to vote against the granting of such a reasonable favor. The bitterest fate that could be desired for him would be that he himself should, by some accidental circumstance, be left to the tender mercies of a mob jury.

We were sorry to see law-and-order Democrats vote against the measure, influenced thereto, probably, by the fear expressed, that its passage would do injury to their party. Pshaw! It has long been a household word among us, that "Democracy oppresses no weakness," and was never ashamed to associate with mercy. Besides, it ought not to be considered a party measure, but one which every man, of whatsoever party, ought eagerly to approve.

The scurrility of it is the only thing about it that bears his mark. The grammar and diction are far superior to anything that was ever heard from him by his fellow-members.

What induced this member to put himself out of the way to appear as my especial oppressor, I do not know. I know that I never wronged him in my life. Indeed, I never knew him until I saw him as my enemy, when I was pleading to the legislature for protection from a blood thirsty mob. I suppose there is only one way to account for his course, and that is, by giving him credit for a most inordinate passion for *"buncombe."* Indeed, his desire to be on the popular side of every question must be very strong, if I am correctly informed; for I understand that when the rebellion first broke out in San Francisco, as the feeling was rather in favor of law and order in his county, he joined a military company called the "Sonora Greys," and also carried his son to their armory, professing his willingness to hold himself and his family in readiness to respond to the call of the governor, and shed his blood, if necessary, in support of the laws. The feeling altered, however, in Tuolumne, and when, through the influence of the Vigilance press, the public mind in that section became poisoned, and law and order was no longer popular, the views of Mr. Patrick underwent a sudden change, and he became one of the members from his county in the legislature. I am deeply pained to learn that he was defeated, the other day, in Tuolumne County, for the Democratic nomination for sheriff. When such consistent and reliable citizens are willing to enter the public service (which is rarely), the people should by all means improve the opportunity to secure their efficient aid in the administration of the laws, particularly in the high and responsible office of sheriff.

After this signal defeat of the "reformers," the bill was referred to the judiciary committee of the house. Two days afterward, it was reported back, with an amendment making it a general law, giving to all other citizens the same privilege of moving for a change of *venue* without personally appearing in court, but leaving with the judges the selection of the districts where their cases were to be tried. This, of course, contemplated fully as much fairness and justice as my case required, and the opponents of my petition being, I suppose, by this time, ashamed of their narrow-mindedness and injustice, took this for an excuse to withdraw their opposition to the bill, and it passed the house without a dissenting voice, as amended by the judiciary committee. On the next day the bill was reported to the senate, and the day following a motion was made in that body to suspend the rules and consider it at once. As I desire to state the facts in this narrative *as they were*, and to do full justice to all, I will here record that Senators Woodworth and Sullivan, both from San Francisco, and elected by the Vigilance Committee, voted with the majority in favor of the motion. So manifest was the necessity and justice of the measure, that they, bitterly as they were prejudiced against me, could not oppose it. Notwithstanding a majority voted in the affirmative, it was not sufficient, it requiring, by the senate rules, a two-thirds vote to suspend a rule. It being toward the close of the session, and other business pressing, that vote could not be obtained. Accordingly, on motion of Mr. Coffroth, the bill was referred to the judiciary committee, with instructions to report it back the next day. In accordance with these instructions, the committee reported it on the eighth of March, recommending its passage, with an amendment to the effect that the judge of a court to whom application might be made for a change of *venue* in accordance with the provisions of the bill, should have the power to grant or refuse the order, in his discretion. In this shape it passed the senate unanimously, but the house refused to concur in the senate's amendment, not knowing what influences might possibly defeat the merciful intent of the bill, in my case, in San Francisco. Accordingly, it went back to the senate, which body receded from their amendment, and on the ninth day of March, the bill having unanimously passed both houses as originally recommended by the judiciary committee of the assembly, it received the signature of the Governor and became a law.

As may be supposed, this simple act of justice enraged my enemies at San Francisco not a little. Anything that savored so much of mercy to me, necessarily gave mortal offense to that portion of the press which had been so industriously instigating my fellow-citizens to hunt me for my blood for the past ten months.* Their howlings annoyed me, however, but little, and, so soon as my counsel could obtain a copy of the law, the proper affidavits were filed in the fourth district court at San Francisco, and Judge Hagar, who occupied that bench, made the order for the change of *venue*, making Napa County the place of trial.

Having now secured the certainty of an impartial trial, I patiently awaited the bench-warrant of the Hon. E. W. McKinstry, judge of the seventh judicial district, to which my case had been transferred. I kept very quiet, being visited by my friends, and occasionally amusing myself by listening to the debates at the Capitol. In this connection I cannot but relate an incident which, while it sets forth in its true colors the inexpressible meanness which

---

*The editor of that delectable sheet, the *Bulletin*, supremely disgusted that a sense of right and decency should have induced those sworn to support the laws and constitution, to differ with him in his insane fanaticism, published the following silly and bombastic threat:—

LET THEM BEWARE THE FUTURE. — We understand from good authority that J. Martin Reese, one of the parties arrested at the time of the capture of Judge Terry, and who was released from the rooms of the Vigilance Committee on his parole of honor (which he afterwards broke), was engaged, some time since, in collecting, by subscription, among the law-and-murder sympathizers, a sufficient fund to carry the notorious McGowan to Sacramento. These factionists were actually deceived by Estell's pompous assertion, that a reaction had taken place in the feelings of the people, and, calculating on the great chances of the Young Men's Democratic Club succeeding in the election of their candidate to succeed Frank Tilford as senator, thought it would be the most favorable opportunity to return with McGowan and produce a collision with the friends of reform. This crowd of lawless men seem determined, now that they find sympathizers in the legislature, to force the Vigilance Committee to commit some overt act.

We tell these men frankly, that the Vigilance Committee, and their friends throughout the state, are alive to all their schemes, and will not foolishly or rashly be drawn into their meshes. But, should they deem it essential for their own protection, or in vindication of law and justice, again to take the reins of government in their own hands, there will be no child's play, nor will San Francisco be alone in the general cleaning out that will most assuredly follow. Los Angeles is now engaged in the work. The mountains will soon follow.

characterized the impotent rage of the poor wretch who edits the *San Francisco Bulletin*, at the same time shows the bold and manly scorn in which his littleness was held by a gentleman occupying the second highest position in the state government.

I went one day, by invitation, into the assembly hall, and was seated within the bar, at the table of the member who had invited me, when the reporter of the *Bulletin* espied me. I had not been there five minutes before a dispatch was telegraphed to that paper, stating the fact of my being there, together with the name of the member who had invited me. In that evening's issue of the *Bulletin*, a scurrilous article appeared, commenting not only on me, but very severely on the gentleman who had taken the liberty of introducing me within the bar. It was, of course, a source of no annoyance to my friend, who had often shown, in his legislative course, how little he heeded shots coming from that quarter, nor should I probably have remembered it now, but for the fact that the Hon. R. M. Anderson, lieutenant-governor of the state and president of the senate, on reading the article the next day, tendered me a standing invitation to enter within the bar of the senate chamber whenever I felt disposed, adding at the same time, that "such pitiful persecution could never fail, among decent men, to make for the victim of it friends. even among strangers."

While awaiting the action of the court at Napa, a gentleman, who I *knew* to be my friend, called on me and informed me that he had every reason to know that important testimony would be adduced against me on the trial, which had not been given either before the coroner who held the inquest on Mr. King or before the grand jury. I listened attentively to the gentleman, for I knew him to be my friend, and then told him that it was all a fabrication which had been told him to induce him to persuade me, if possible, to leave the country. I may as well here state that I understood it all, and that this was no shot from the Vigilance Committee, but was a *ruse* of certain gentlemen nearer home, whose treatment of me had left them no cause of congratulation on my unexpected return from exile. I said nothing of this, however, to my friend, for I knew that he was actuated by the kindest of motives, and simply told him that I had come many hundreds of miles to stand my trial, and meant to do so.

The interview had one good effect, however: it awakened me to vigilance as to the machinations of the Committee, who, it struck me for the first time, might be endeavoring to suborn witnesses to insure my conviction, and, as the sequel will show, this suspicion was not entirely groundless, and the defeat of their schemes was, in a great degree, owing to my watchfulness.

For some time after my case had been certified to the court at Napa, I waited in Sacramento, expecting every day that the sheriff of that county would arrive with a bench-warrant and take me into custody. During this period, nothing of interest occurred to me, except that, from time to time, my presence in the city, unconfined within a jail, elicited a howl of baffled rage from the "mob organ" of San Francisco, which, to my great amusement, was invariably taken up and re-echoed in the feeble yelp of such *poodles* of the press as the *Sacramento Age*, and other twopenny sheets which have sprung into an ephemeral existence under the benign influence of sedition, even as mosquitoes are engendered by the exhalations from a pestilential swamp. Their bite is but a trifle, but their *hum* is an insufferable nuisance.

At length, on the 14th day of May (which happened to be the anniversary of the shooting of James King of Wm.) a bench-warrant was sent from Napa to Sheriff White of Sacramento County, under which I was immediately arrested by one of the deputies of that officer, and remained in his custody, at the "Magnolia," until Sunday, the 17th, when Mr. Charles Clark of Napa, who had been specially deputed by the sheriff of his county for that purpose, arrived in Sacramento, and on the same day I accompanied him, by way of Benicia, to Napa City.

CHAPTER X

Now the play is done:
All is well ended, if this suit be won.
All's Well That Ends Well.

ON arriving at Napa City, though still in charge of the sheriff, I was permitted to put up at the Napa Hotel, and was at liberty to go about the streets of the town, accompanied by an officer, until Tuesday, the 19th of May, when I was arraigned before Judge McKinstry, and plead "not guilty" to the indictment. I was then remanded to the county jail, where I remained until Friday, the 22d of May. To the credit of the citizens of Napa County be it said, I found myself the only occupant of the jail. I was permitted to go about the entire building, and was under no other restraint than my confinement to the house. I was treated with kindness and made very comfortable by Sheriff Stark and his deputy, William Towns, Esq. Mr. Charles Clark, who had been sent to Sacramento for me, also visited me frequently, and by many acts of kindness rendered my captivity less disagreeable than it would otherwise have been. To all of these gentlemen I beg now to repeat my many thanks for their consideration and kindness. On Friday, the day fixed for my trial, I again appeared in court, and, as will be seen by the following report of the proceedings, taken from the *San Francisco Herald*, the prosecution was allowed a postponement of the case for another week.

[*First Day.*]

NAPA CITY, May 19, 1857.

The trial of Edward McGowan commenced this morning in the seventh district court, Judge E. [W.] McKinstry presiding. Messrs.

Edgerton and Heslep appeared for the state, and Messrs. Botts and Coffroth for the defense.

On the opening of the court, the District Attorney (Henry Edgerton) read an affidavit setting forth that the testimony of Dr. D. H. Toland was necessary to the prosecution of the case, and asking that an attachment be issued to compel his attendance.

The District Attorney then asked for an attachment for the body of John Butts, an important witness, who is now in the city prison of San Francisco.

The Court said an affidavit would be necessary, showing that Butts was an important witness, and was in prison.

Pending the above motion, the clerk proceeded to call the names of the jurors impaneled in the case,—forty-two in number.

Mr. Lafayette M. Byrne then appeared and made the affidavit required by the Court, setting forth that Butts "is said to be a material witness."

The Court ordered the process to issue.

The District Attorney then moved a continuance of the case till Monday, on the ground of the absence of Dr. Toland and the man Butts. He offered an affidavit stating that the testimony of Messrs. Toland, Stillman, and Butts was absolutely necessary to the prosecution; without it they cannot proceed; and that by Monday their attendance can be secured.

Mr. Botts objected to the affidavit, on the ground that it does not show that due diligence has been used to secure such absent testimony. The District Attorney ought to show the exact means he had used to secure the same. All the witnesses, he understood, had been ordered to appear on Tuesday last, and if they were not here then, it was the duty of the state to have asked for attachments to compel their attendance at this time. He would undertake to say, if the postponement now asked for was granted, that this case would not be through in a year. Every time it came up, a continuance would be moved, on the ground of the absence of a material witness.

The District Attorney said that this indictment was only received from San Francisco on the 8th of last month. The subpœnas had been promptly issued and returned. On Tuesday, the subpœna for Dr. Toland had not been returned. He thought that this fact, alone, showed that there had been no *laches*.

The Court intimated that the rights of the defense would be jeopardized by the continuance.

Mr. Botts asked, as a favor, that the continuance be extended to next Friday, which was agreed to by the District Attorney.

The jury was then discharged till that day, and the witnesses told to be present on that day also.

So the case was postponed as agreed upon.

Immediately upon the order of continuance, I was recommitted to the jail, where I remained until the next Friday, the 29th of May. This postponement of the case on motion of the prosecution, who had professed to be only waiting for a chance to try me for nearly a year, not only disappointed me, but many others who had journeyed to Napa for the purpose of witnessing the trial.* However, it rather helped than prejudiced my cause, and I passed my week in jail very comfortably, being visited by scores of friends. To John B. Milliken, Esq., J. M. Dudley, of Wells, Fargo, & Co.'s Express, and Edward J. Gage, Esq., I am under many obligations for unremitting kindness and attention during my imprisonment. I also met here an old Philadelphia friend, of the name of Frank Whitticar, one of the proprietors of a circus then at Napa, who offered me, if I needed it, the use of his purse. I beg him again to accept my thanks for his good feeling toward me. Indeed, with few exceptions, the entire population of Napa City and the surrounding country treated me with marked sympathy and kindness. Many persons rode to Napa on no other business than to gratify their curiosity to see me. From the woodcuts they had seen of me in the mob papers, and the stories they had read of me, they expected, doubtless, to behold, at least, a moral if not a physical monster.

While in prison, fearing that a scurrilous and lying article, which just then appeared in the *San Francisco Alta California*, in relation to my antecedents in Philadelphia, written for the purpose of injuring me in the opinion of the people of the county in which I was to be tried, might have its effect, I addressed a card to the people of Napa, accompanied by the originals of some letters I had received from some of the first men of my native state.† Whether it had the effect I desired (that of keep-

---

* The town is crowded with strangers, and every hotel is crowded. Numbers will be much disappointed at the postponement of the trial of Ned McGowan.—*Napa Reporter of May 23d.*

† ED MCGOWAN'S CARD. — We publish to-day a card by Ed McGowan, who is, as our readers know, confined in our jail on a charge of being accessary to the murder of James King of Wm. The card is rather pungent, but, considering the position of the writer, it is not only moderate, but manly and dignified. Ned does not pretend to be altogether a saint, but he is evidently one "who hath sat at good men's feasts," and not the vulgar and low-bred ruffian which some have described him to be. He is visited by crowds daily, and

ing the people unprejudiced), I do not know; but I here take occasion to assure the citizens of Napa that nothing should have induced me either to annoy them or honor the mob press by a newspaper rejoinder to their scurrility, short of an absolute conviction that, under the circumstances, silence would have further imperiled me.

I was pleased, while lying in prison, to experience an instance of gratitude in my fellow-men. A Frenchman named Sanderson, who keeps a restaurant in the town, daily sent me the best of his viands, wines, cigars, etc., and, on offering to pay him my bill, I discovered that I owed him, according to his account, nothing. It turned out that, long ago, in San Francisco, I had the good fortune to do him a slight service, which I had entirely forgotten, (and, indeed, I had not seen him since,) but which he gratefully remembered, and took this time and manner of evincing his gratitude. I was touched by this proof of his goodness of heart, and would have gladly paid him for his articles, assuring him that I was not in pecuniary distress, but he positively refused to accept a dollar. The proprietor of the Napa Hotel, who had also treated me with great kindness, in like manner refused to accept any recompense. Indeed, on leaving the city after my trial, all I could get the good people of Napa to accept for their courtesy was my *white hat*, which they insisted on having, and provided me, in return, with a black one.

I cannot refrain from here recounting the singular manner in which quite a distinguished citizen of California (Gov. Henry S. Foote) became (when, from circumstances I am now about to detail, I least expected it) my bitterest persecutor. He who had *volunteered* to *"serve the people"* as associate counsel with the district attorney was A. M. Heslep. So much of infamy has already been heaped upon

---

bears himself most cheerfully in his confinement. His long-sufferings have excited the sympathies of all classes, and, from the tone of popular sentiment here, we should consider his ultimate chances of becoming governor of the state a hundred to one better than of being hanged. We paid Ned a visit last night, and found him looking well and in fine spirits. As to the letters annexed to his card, there is not a doubt of their authenticity. They were set up from the originals, which are still in our possession. — *Napa Reporter*, May 23d, 1857.

this man, — such wonderful and incredible crimes have already been charged to him, — that I am loath to sully the pages of this book by more than a bare allusion to what has already shocked the moral sense of California, loose and reckless as that moral sense may, by some, be esteemed. Had the conduct of my prosecution, so far as volunteer counsel are concerned, been confined to him, I should, for the reason given, have had nothing to say with regard to it. I prefer to reserve his history for a future book, wherein I propose to forgo the pleasure of endeavoring simply to interest, amuse, and instruct, as is the object of this volume, and bend myself to the unwelcome task of tearing the veil from hypocrisy, and showing forth, in all its hideousness, the depth of infamy which the human soul *may* explore, while setting itself up as a monitor over the actions of its fellows. Unfortunately, however, he was not the only one who, in my case, placed himself in the unenviable position of public prosecutor. Governor Foote, with the consistency so characteristic of his career in California, said to this poor wretch Heslep, when he understood he had volunteered to assist the gentlemanly district attorney of Napa, whose official duty it was to prosecute me, "Sir, you will gain nothing by this ruthless persecution of an old man! It is a disgrace, sir, to the profession! Nothing good can come of it!" This he said in presence of Mr. Coffroth, one of my counsel, Mr. William Towns, a deputy sheriff of Napa, and others, at the Napa Hotel, while I was awaiting my trial, in prison! This would have been all very gallant and chivalrous in the old gentleman had he acted in accordance with his expressed sentiment. Unhappily, however, he did not. All the *gentlemen* in Napa County, residents of the place and visitors, took occasion to express their disgust at the conduct of Heslep. So loudly did they do this, that Governor Foote himself saw, however strong might be his desire for my conviction, that the probability of it was very remote with Heslep acting as prosecutor.

Here, then, was an opportunity not only to make a fee, but at the same time, what to him was of inestimably more value, *buncombe* with the strong side in San Francisco. Accordingly, he repaired to the city of the "purest and best," and informed them of the desperate strait the prosecution were in to carry their case. Utterly ignoring the views he had expressed to poor Heslep, he received a fee of five hundred dollars, *and undertook the conduct of a case he had himself declared to be such an one as should entail disgrace on the prosecutor and on the profession!* However, if I may be pardoned the paradox, even in his *inconsistency* he was *consistent*. They who have watched the political course of the venerable gentleman since he has been in the state will be, doubtless, less astonished at his tergiversation in this instance, than they would have been had he scrupulously adhered to the sentiments he at first avowed. As will be seen, I publish, in the account of my trial, the report of his speech. I do this, partly that, both sides being published, this chronicle may be deemed a fair one, and partly that his old law-abiding and constitution-loving friends in Mississippi may see how steadfastly and zealously he has studied the peace and perpetuity of that glorious *Union*, to preserve which he has made so many weary pilgrimages, and, according to his own account, fought so many intellectual battles side by side with Clay, Webster, Calhoun, Cass, Dickinson, and others.

I also give to the reader the speech of my own counsel, Mr. Botts. To those who love our institutions and respect our laws, I commend this singularly able and bold championship of them as far more worthy of perusal than all the rest of this imperfect product of not a little labor.

Edward McGowan's Trial.
First Day's Proceedings.

NAPA CITY, May 29th, 1857.

The court was called to order at a quarter to nine o'clock.

The court called the names of the selected jurors.

The impaneling of the jury was proceeded with, and the whole of the day was consumed in impaneling it.*

---

*THE McGOWAN CASE.—This case was called in our district court yesterday morning. Some important additions have been made to counsel on both sides since the adjournment last week. Gov. Foote has been associated with counsel for the state, and Jack W. Smith, Esq., of this place, with the defense. All of yesterday was spent in impaneling a jury. Both sides will be conducted with great ability, and no legal point will be surrendered by either side without a closely contested argument. If we may judge from appearances, the trial will be very long and very interesting.—*Napa Reporter.*

The list of jurors as sworn in is as follows: Robert C. Gillespie, Wm. Hargrave, David Hudson, George Ware, Morris Twist, Wm. H. Younger, Charles McBride, Peter D. Bailey, Ralph L. Kilburn, Harrison Hornback, James Glassford, and Charles Stillman.

The court adjourned until nine o'clock in the morning, instead of seven and a half in the evening.

Second Day's Proceedings.

NAPA CITY, May 30, 1857.

The court was called at nine o'clock, Judge McKinstry presiding, and all the jury were present and answered to their names. The indictment was read by the assistant clerk.

The clerk read the minutes of yesterday's proceedings, and, on motion of Mr. Botts, they were amended in two particulars.

Mr. Foote moved that the witnesses be put under the usual rule, and that the doctors be first "arrayed against each other, and allowed to return to their extensive practice." I suppose it is well to move for the ordinary rule in capital cases at this stage of the proceedings, because we are not desirous of having them hear any portion even of our few general opening remarks.

The list was called, the rule given by the Court, and the witnesses retired, when Governor Foote made his opening speech.

Testimony.

Lafayette M. Byrne, called and sworn.

Examination by the prosecution.

Reside in San Francisco; was deputy sheriff last May; was in San Francisco after five o'clock, in the vicinity of Montgomery and Merchant streets; usually dined at five o'clock; had not seen Casey prior to the time mentioned.

Mr. Heslep asked the witness if he had seen Casey that day.

Mr. Botts objected to the question, on the ground of its irrelevancy. In order to allow the admission of such testimony, the indictment should have set forth that McGowan was an accessary in a particular mode. The statute requires a *precise* statement of the crime,—how committed, when, and where. "The indictment must descend to particulars," and they, being recited, must be *proved*. This much is required in civil cases. The object of special pleading was to eliminate every point in the case. I recollect a man charged in one case with stealing a heifer, when he stole a cow. The charge was overthrown. Although the rule has been somewhat relaxed, the existing principle is the same. The charge must be specific, and not general. You cannot charge McGowan with killing James King, and proving that charge by showing that Casey killed him. He understood that the charge is that of killing James King, and he comes here with a witness to prove that he was twenty miles off. Could there be a greater surprise than that afforded us? Here we find it is attempted to prove that he aids, abets, or advises the killing of King, not that he is literally a principal, as would appear to be set forth.

Mr. Botts read the law indicating the proper form of an indictment, as he conceived, in this case.

Unless the indictment is precise, it can be overthrown by a demurrer; if it is precise and particular, as in this indictment, it must be proved with particularity.

Examination proceeded with, and *Mr. L. Byrne* testified to his having seen Casey shoot King, and arrested him and took him to the station-house in the City Hall.

Mr. Botts asked the Judge to stop the examination, unless the counsel intended to prove that McGowan was near enough to aid in the assault. I think it is wholly irrelevant.

Mr. Foote—We expect to prove that McGowan was in a convenient distance to render assistance. We will show a confederacy between the parties; that this scene was all concocted by the parties charged. We expect to show the strongest kind of a case in this particular.

Mr. Botts contended that it must be proved that McGowan was prepared to aid in the murder, if necessary, as well as on the scene of action, in order to render the proof of a blow from a confederate relevant.

Mr. Foote said he was prepared to come up to the requisitions of the law. We shall not get through with this case in twenty days, if we keep on in this way. We expect to prove that McGowan was the chief manager of this transaction.

Examination resumed—Was not on particular friendly terms with Casey. Had no knowledge concerning his shooting propensities.

Cross-examined—Knew McGowan about five years; didn't see King's hands; his hands were under his talma; hadn't seen McGowan for two or three days previous to the murder, and did not see him until one day after the same.

James W. Stillman, called and sworn—Reside in San Francisco; was at the Bank Exchange on the 14th May, 1856, about five o'clock, P. M.; didn't see the act of shooting; heard the report; was in the street as the time; first came out at the door to go to dinner; not five minutes from five o'clock; immediately after the report, I turned; was standing with my back to the direction in which the pistol was fired; Mr. King passed me just before I heard the report, going in the direction of the express-office; spoke to me as he passed; heard the report; then I saw both King and Casey; Mr. Casey was in the act of stooping to pick up his cloak, or talma; King was in the act of walking towards the express-office; ran and took hold of him, and asked him if he was hurt; he replied, "Yes"; assisted him to the express-office, to the back part; he groaned when mounting the steps; the clerks got a mattress to lay him down on, and I then commenced unbuttoning his clothes to see where he was hurt; unbuttoned his coat, took a pistol from his pocket and handed it to a gentleman standing by; I then unbuttoned his shirt-collar, until I found the wound; told him the wound was not mortal; don't profess to be a medical man; doctors came in and examined the case; don't know what became of Casey; told King I did not know where Casey was; the crowd had broken the windows, and they were talking outside so that we could hear them; had not seen Casey for two or three hours before; then saw him on Montgomery Street; I was talking with Mayor Webb and Horace Hawes; think they were the men; it was about half-past two o'clock; I am entirely ignorant of anything else connected with the case.

Cross-examination—Found a pistol on Mr. King; on the right side, I think; it was not in a pocket, but laying loose; it was a small revolver; didn't notice whether it was cocked or not; told Mr. King not to be frightened; he appeared to be very much alarmed at the time I spoke to him; know Mr. McGowan; did not see him there.

Dr. Toland, called and sworn—Reside in San Francisco; am a graduate in medicine; about ten o'clock on May 16th [14th] (evening) saw several messages for me, requesting me to visit Mr. King at the Express Building; when arrived, found Mr. King lying on the counter, on a mattress; I did not examine the wound; saw the anterior wound, as it was exposed; I suppose twenty physicians were in the room; there were two openings; lying on his back; the posterior wound was concealed; Dr. Hammond had charge of the case,—King's family physician; Mr. King's extremities were cold; vomited everything taken; very little pulse in the right arm, and none in the left; physicians were administering stimulants for the purpose of trying to bring on a reaction; applying mustard-plasters, &c.; I remained about two hours, finding physicians enough there, and not regarding him as my patient; I left about ten o'clock; before leaving, was requested by Dr. Hammond to return at seven o'clock the next morning; I then found Drs. Hammond, Bertody, and Gray in council; reaction being partly established, we determined to have him removed to Montgomery Block; this was at seven o'clock in the morning; we met at five o'clock in the afternoon, and examined his wounds more particularly than we had before; the anterior wound was about an inch below the collar-bone, apparently over the first rib; the ball passed backward and rather inward, and escaped on the inner side, near the upper extremity of the shoulder-blade; the arm was entirely paralyzed; motion and sensation destroyed; very cold and somewhat swollen, and very slight pulsation in the artery could be distinguished; (this was in the afternoon of the 15th May;) he was still vomiting; right pulse, though more full than in the morning, was still soft and impressible; not stronger than in the morning; believing that the vein, in consequence of profuse hemorrhage (can't assert hemorrhage),—infer he lost a great deal of blood, from the length of time it took to procure reaction,—having lain twelve hours almost pulseless,—we concluded to allow a small sponge, introduced, to remain, for fear of a return of the bleeding if it was withdrawn; he lay on his back; posterior wound large, and there was a constant discharge of bloody serum escaped, which prevented any accumulation within the wound; posterior wound much larger than anterior; believing that the artery, in consequence of indistinct pulse at the wrist, although it might not be wounded, was so much injured that it might slough or yield to the pressure of the blood above, a compress, wet with the cold water, applied over the anterior, and a tourniquet arranged so as to prevent bleeding; no force applied; horseshoe tourniquet; all necessary was to turn a key. On the third day, found him much more unwell than on the previous afternoon; I suggested the propriety (for the purpose of satisfying the public) that some other physicians be called; Drury Myron attended next consultation; next morning, met to remove the sponge; Dr. Griffith opposed the removing the sponge; fourth day, opening entire armpit to allow concealed matter to escape, but none was found; portion of lint passed in to keep the incision open; fifth day, in the morning, still more unwell, pulse more rapid, expression of his countenance more anxious; I administered chloroform immediately and cautiously; object to lessen the sensibility of the wound; did n't think it necessary to bring him wholly under the influence of ether; this was about twelve o'clock, fifth day; all the physicians agreed to the action; no discharge took place from the wound, except a small amount of coagulated blood; his symptoms became gradually more unfavorable, though he had been getting worse from the fourth day; on the sixth he died, late in the afternoon; was living at one o'clock; heard he was dead at four or five; told Dr. Hammond in the morning that he had phlebitis; so two or three days before he died; suggested for consultation Dr. Hastings and others; thought the subclavian vein was injured; think that vein and the veins of the arm were injured; the subclavian vein passes from the wrist, under the collar-bone, and over the first rib; was a gunshot wound; found the ball had injured the intercostal muscle, the fleshy substance that connects the ribs; ball had not touched the vein; the wound had brought inflammation of the pleura; found over a pint of bloody matter in the chest; the post-mortem examination was made the next day after death; the nerves which supply the arm were injured; the general prostration was great,—thought he would die two hours after the receipt of the injury; after almost any serious injury, patient becomes faint, and vomiting comes on,—all caused by the loss of blood, and the shock sustained by the nervous system, and reaction comes on after an hour, sometimes two or three hours, sometimes not at all; if reaction does not come on, the patient dies; reaction in King's case was never as fully established as I desired; it is inadvisable to attempt an examination of injuries until reaction takes place, unless it be to tie a wounded vein; the hemorrhage was arrested when I first saw King,—no bleeding; found the lungs in a bad state, on a post-mortem examination,—tubercular masses as large as my thumb in the chest.

Afternoon Session.

The court was called at two and a half o'clock. All the jury answered to their names.

Dr. Toland's examination continued—Was in bad health some time before he was shot; found lungs diseased,—the left one, that is,—did not examine the right; his chance for recovery from an injury like the one received was much less than that of a healthy person; in all probability, some men would recover from such a wound; I infer that he lost an immense amount of blood; violent and protracted pain produces sometimes a prostration like that resulting from great loss of blood; a lacerated wound sometimes causes death, where there has been no loss of blood; the inflammation of King's veins extended to the heart; the result of venous inflammation is always fatal, particularly if the vessel is large; am now speaking of the subclavian vein;

compress applied with cold water, and the tourniquet placed over it, to stand in case of the artery becoming loose; there was no pressure from the instrument; nothing in the treatment that would produce venous inflammation,—all the result of the wound,—that was the immediate cause of death; I think Mr. King was treated as well as possible; have nothing to regret; I have received a good medical education; was in Paris nearly three years, attending the hospitals and lectures, after graduating in Kentucky; practiced ever since; have a large practice; have large surgical experience; I was eighteen years in Columbia, South Carolina; have been in San Francisco since 1853; Doctors Gray, Bertody, Hammond, and Griffin were in attendance on Mr. King; no other physician had control in the case.

Botts—With an admission of competency, I will ask some plain questions.

Cross-examined—Was called to see Mr. King in the express-office, on May 14th; room nearly as large as this; warm evening, I think· the evenings are generally raw and cold in May in San Francisco; examined or looked at the anterior wound; when called, the sponge was introduced and a bandage on the wound; knew the wound was plugged up; saw where the wound was; saw the bandage wet with blood, and from that knew the position of the wound; it resembled a gunshot wound; the wound was inward, and ranged rather upward; the ball entered about an inch below the collar-bone, and was one third the distance from the collar-bone to the breast-bone; ball went behind head arm-bone, and passed out near the upper side of the shoulder-blade, near the spine; the shoulder-joint was not injured; there are some portions of the body which cannot be injured without causing death; no large artery was injured in this case, but the wound of a vein is about as dangerous as an injury to an artery; a large artery is frequently wounded without causing death; the subclavian artery rests upon the first rib; lies close up to the collar-bone; the ball passed over this artery; the wound was an inch below the clavicle; this artery is as large as the little finger; the ball injured some of the sympathetic vessels; an inflammation of the vein is called phlebitis; common disease; scarcely yet known to recover; any wound may produce it; in Parisian hospitals, frequent; seen two in San Francisco die from inflammation of the veins; seen fifty die of the same disease; one in San Francisco died of a knife-wound; have a large practice; seen smaller veins inflamed, and not produce death, but it is rare; a wound of the vein by pistol-shot is a tearing of the vein; necessary to use sponge or lint in such wounds; suppuration takes place in a few days; never think of removing lint oftener than two or three days; more danger in closing the wound than keeping it open; at the time we supposed matter was formed, we opened a part under the armpit; keeping the wound close and keeping the matter in might have produced inflammation of the vein; plug size of the wound; should only be removed on the fifth day; time for the first, two or three days; after that, it was pus; incision under the arm, merely a puncture; applied a tourniquet; the hemorrhage could have been below the collar-bone; requires a long time for reaction from the prostration caused by bleeding or a nervous shock; reaction, coming on, partially prolonged Mr. King's life; otherwise he would have died next day; by reaction, I mean partial recovery; cold water was applied; can't say that an application was made on the last night; appearance was such as showed pleurisy came from pistol-shot; might have come from cold; some division of sentiment among the physicians; advised the taking out of the plug the morning after the injury; thought the artery was wounded; can tell venous blood from arterial blood; I thought the artery was wounded; the bleeding was stopped; always bloody matter expended; the sponge might have reached the artery and stopped the hole; thought the ball, in passing, might have made a small opening; in a case I saw the other day, an orifice was made in an artery by a buckshot; felt satisfied he had inflammation of the vein; small pulse usual after such an injury; Dr. Nuttall told me he dressed the wound; examined Mr. King's arm; Drs. Gray, Hammond, Bertody, and myself were selected by King's brother, wife, and friends to attend him; the armpit incision was not for the purpose of counter-irritation; every wound inflames and pains somewhat; the sponge was very soft; the reason we gave Mr. King chloroform was so as to be ready to increase his insensibility speedily; gave chloroform partly for the pain to be produced by pulling out of the plug; conceive that there is no danger in giving chloroform; think Dr. Valentine Mott has more reputation than any other doctor in the United States; think a man may be a good doctor, who has not lived in Paris or Germany.

Orlando C. Osborn—Was in San Francisco on the fourteenth of May, 1856; present at the time Casey shot King; heard report of pistol; saw Casey standing about seventy or eighty feet from him; saw him pick up a coat; had a pistol; it was a revolver; was advancing all the time, and as I advanced saw Mr. King taken into the express-office; some persons came up to Casey, and ushered him across the street in a diagonal direction; think some person then took the pistol; there was a person came up to Casey and took hold of his arm; they were going up Washington Street; saw Casey raise his arm and drop a pistol in the hands or pocket of a person on his left; saw the pistol pass; it was a small-sized pistol; about ten feet off, was a yellow-mounted pistol; positive of that; never saw it afterwards, or knew anything of its whereabouts; looked like a derringer; didn't look like a revolver.

Cross-examination—Casey was about seventy feet from the corner of Burgoyne's Building; then he dropped the pocket-pistol; taken from his left hand; I was advancing towards Casey at that moment, and was on the pavement right behind him; south side of Washington Street; couldn't describe the pistol particularly; the guard was yellow; I know that; saw butt-end and mounting of the pistol, and that was yellow; did not see the muzzle; guard and butt all I saw, and that was yellow-mounted.

Charles Burroughs—Saw McGowan on the 14th of last May, at Mr. Moses', over Pat Hunt's stable, between six and seven o'clock, on the corner of Sacramento and Kearny streets; had no particular conversation; there at dinner; whole topic of conversation about King's shooting; said nothing to me then or afterwards concerning a knowledge of Casey's assault.

Jacob Curtis—Reside in San Francisco; there last May; saw defendant on the 14th, on Montgomery Street; said "How do you do, Judge?" he replied,"Very well"; he gave me an introduction to Mr. Whiteman at the same time; this was near Dan's Saloon, between Commercial and Clay streets; Judge asked me to drink; did so; it was between four and five o'clock; Judge and I went in; said I'd take a brandy punch; Whiteman said he'd take lager-beer; Judge said he'd take a gin cocktail; before the drinks were ready, a lad came in and said,"You are wanted"; lad said he wanted White man's pistol; Whiteman drew it out and laid it on the counter; I took hold of it; says I,"It's a noble pistol"; his reply was,"Yes; it will shoot two hundred yards"; says I,"You had better be careful who you let have the pistol, or you may lose it"; young man went off; we drank our liquor off then; he asked me,"Don't you know Jimmy?" I said I knew him by reputation; lad took the pistol with him; we talked there for a few moments; told them they must excuse me, as I had to go to the post-office; then McGowan or Whiteman said,"We'll go out and see what they want of us"; then I went and put in a letter for Sacramento, but the boat had left—boats left at four o'clock; returned to Jackson Street; got opposite Burch's Hotel; heard the report of a pistol; looked up Montgomery Street and saw people running, and I ran and saw quite a crowd up the street, before the express-office; this was two or three minutes after the report; between the time of leaving McGowan and hearing the report of the pistol, there was an interval of seven or eight or ten minutes; did not see King or Casey; didn't notice which way McGowan and Whiteman went from the drinking-saloon; pistol was one of Colt's navy revolvers,—one of Colt's "first make," so said Whiteman; couldn't say which said "We will go and see what they want of us"; no other person came in, but the boy, to speak to them.

Cross-examination—Fifty-three years old; born in New Jersey; came here in '50; been in the lumber business; worked at planking roads; was a member of the *Vigilance Committee*; came to San Francisco last year, May 14th, from my men in Stockton Street. It was after four o'clock; went down Washington Street to Montgomery; post-office in Washington Street; found by the Monumental clock it was after four o'clock—two reasons by which I knew it was after four o'clock; was going up to see Mr. Perry after I found the mail was gone; no particular business with Perry; went up Montgomery till I saw the Judge; no one ever saw me drunk; generally find Perry at Biggs & Kibbe's; Dan keeps between Commercial and Clay streets; wanted to see Perry about contracts; near half a block from Dan's to Biggs & Kibbe's; got within a hundred feet of where I supposed Perry was, then turned and went to the post-office, with the intention of seeing Perry on coming back; don't know what made me alter my mind. Have known McGowan since '53 or '54; considered McGowan one of my friends; have been present with the Judge on several occasions; I first met him at the Monumental Engine House. McGowan introduced me to Whiteman; on same side with Dan's Saloon; I took a brandy punch, Whiteman took lager-beer, and McGowan took a gin cocktail; while there boy came in; did n't know the boy; never see the boy since,—sure; never told anybody who the boy was; told persons it was not Butts; boy said, "You are wanted"; after that, said Casey wanted Whiteman's pistol; Whiteman drew it and I took it; very large,—six-shooter; can tell a six-shooter from a five-shooter by looking at the size; the boy said, "Casey wants Whiteman's pistol"; I picked it from the counter. Then the boy took the pistol and went away. Then I said, "Better be careful about who he let take the pistol." Then he asked me "Don't you know Jimmy?" Whiteman took out another pistol, which Whiteman said was a six-shooter too. Could n't say as to whether it was a yellow-mounted pistol or not; then went out, McGowan and Whiteman following; they said they were going to see what Casey wanted; I did n't look back; don't know that they ever came out of the house; don't know who was in the saloon besides our party and the barkeeper, as I saw; don't know whether "Dan's" is a bit or a quarter house; never examined on this matter before· have talked about what I knew in the case; think I told you (Mr. Botts) about it once; did not say at one time that this affair took place at Dan's; told you it took place on Montgomery Street; I say upon oath that it was in Dan's Saloon; I was never before the Committee; I did not say it was at the Bank Exchange; told some persons that it might have been at the Bank Exchange, but I was certain, and I am certain, that it was at Dan's Saloon; it was not possible for this to have taken place at the Bank Exchange; told you it was on Montgomery Street; "was very careful what I said to you"; said I wished the Judge well; said he always treated me well; don't recollect who asked me about the testimony; was asked why I did not go before the grand jury; talked a little with the box-tender; went on west side of Jackson Street; did not stop on the way from Washington Street to Dan's Saloon; talked with several persons; said, How do you do? or the like of that; only a short time in the saloon; might be five minutes, more or less; from the "Clock Place" to Montgomery Street it is about two blocks; about two and a half blocks to Dan's from thence; Whiteman told me, if I came down to New World Market, I would find him; was ten or fifteen minutes talking with the Judge, outside of the saloon; know Mr. Parker of the Bank Exchange; know he is the barkeeper of the Bank saloon; first knew he was subpœnaed here last week; don't know whether Dan has been subpœnaed up here or not; don't know E. Gould Buffum; believe I talked with him of the matter, at Napa Springs, about a week ago; it is impossible I said to him that it was no use for me to be here, as Butts knew all the case; Butts said I was mistaken in the place; you 'll have Butts by and by [laughter]; Butts said this affair took place at the Bank Exchange; I said it did not; don't know that I told Buffum that Butts lied; Butts could n't know what I knew, although he tells the same story; knew of the conflict in our testimony; what Butts tells is pretty much the same story that I do, except as respects the place; did n't want to come here; don't recollect telling Buffum that Butts would give my story; was annoy d about being brought up here; think I did not tell Buffum that this affair took place at the Bank Exchange; I told Buffum the truth.

By Mr. Foote—

All that I know about Butts was what I read of his testimony before the grand jury; thought Butts's testimony was equivalent to mine; I stated to Mr. Buffum the case as I give it now.

Mr. Botts objected to the examination.

Mr. Foote contended that, in justice to the witness, who had been called a liar on the stand, and otherwise very coarsely insulted, he should be allowed to proceed.

Judged of Butts's testimony as given before the grand jury; supposed it was like my own; understood that he swore he was the lad; so, if it was, I thought I could be dispensed with.

At six o'clock the court adjourned until seven and a half in the evening.

EVENING SESSION.

The court was called at 7½ o'clock.

Mr. Andrew J. Taylor—Reside 209 Clay Street; dealer in firearms; was in San Francisco 14th May, 1856; saw McGowan that morning, in my house; loaned him a navy pistol, and a knife manufactured in my house; I loaded the pistol, and loaded him a derringer pistol; this happened on the day King was shot; Judge fetched the derringer to my house; it was a gold-mounted, plated, or galvanized. Spring at cap-box broke; did not repair the spring; in shooting order; a pistol of that kind I had sold; had not seen Casey just before that; did not see Casey that day; had not seen Casey or McGowan for a day or two before that; McGowan took the pistols and the knife with him; this was early in the morning.

Cross-examined—Dealer in guns, pistols, small guns, and divers other things in shooting-gallery; common for me to load pistols; McGowan not the only one who gets pistols loaded by me, demands being frequent for me to load pistols sometimes; didn't know Casey and McGowan were intimate friends; loaded a pistol for King that time; followed loading pistols before this; been in the pistol-loading business long time; been here since 1850; the practice of wearing arms is common in California; the leading men of San Francisco wear them; frequently persons come and discharge their pistols at my house and have them reloaded; McGowan has been in the habit of having his pistols loaded by me for the last three or four years.

John Butts—Reside in San Francisco; was in San Francisco on the 14th May; saw McGowan and Casey an hour or so before the shooting of King; saw Casey on Montgomery Street, and McGowan in the Bank Exchange; was sitting in the window of the Exchange, and Casey came and asked me to tell the man with McGowan to come out; Peter Whiteman; know Peter; went in and told Whiteman, and he asked me who was the man wanting, and I told him Casey; I then left the saloon and went out to the street; McGowan said, "You go and see what he wants"; after that no more said; Judge and Whiteman went out after that; went and talked with Hamilton Bowie; saw no more of him; saw Casey when he shot King; at the time he shot King, was talking with a boy called Geo. Winslow; saw him shoot King; told King he was going to shoot him; he then fired,—his coat falling off meanwhile; big-sized revolver; couldn't tell whether King tried to shoot or not; he was walking with his hands or arms partly folded; when Casey came up to him, he started back and received the shot; this was James King, I was told; seemed to come from the *Bulletin* office; Casey was arrested by Mr. Byrne and Peter Whiteman; took him up Washington Street; was afraid, and then fled; was first man I ever saw shot, and it made me feel very nervous [laughter]; saw him in Vigilance Committee rooms; last time I saw him, he was hanging out of the window [great laughter]; saw McGowan once in Sacramento; don't know what became of Whiteman.—"Saw him about San Francisco?"—No; O, no; not since the Vigilance Committee.

Cross-examined—After McGowan went up and spoke to Bowie, it was twenty minutes or half an hour before King was shot; the corner was a loafing-corner; I had nothing to do in those days, and I was loafing around there; had read the piece in the *Bulletin*, and awaited the result; I was never before anybody but the Vigilance Committee; have lately been in prison; sometimes out; police take us out and make us work [laughter]; 13th March first trouble, and Judge Coon let me go; have been taken up for stealing a leg of mutton and for stealing money; never did steal any money, but the last time I was up before Judge Coon he was rather excited, and so he sentenced me, I suppose [laughter].

Henry H. Byrne—Don't know as to the familiarity of McGowan and Casey; am little in the street; never knew of their political operations; know that they were acquainted, that's all.

J. M. Warner—Know McGowan well; don't know Casey; McGowan never made any declaration concerning the affray,—never said he saw Casey make his will.

The court took a recess of fifteen minutes.

Night Session.

The court reassembled at twenty minutes to 10 o'clock, when counsel proceeded with the

Testimony for the Defense.

Gen. James M. Estell—Ou the evening of May 14th, 1856, was on Montgomery Street, in front of office, on the opposite side of Pacific Express office, five or six doors to the north; office fifteen feet from Washington Street; saw King shot; was in front of my office; was detained a few minutes after business hours, which kept me there; had heard of no difficulty between King and Casey up to time I heard Casey's voice; not read the *Bulletin* of that evening; I heard Mr. Casey's voice speaking in a short and excited tone, near the door of the Metropolitan Saloon; heard his angry voice, in front of the Metropolitan Saloon, saying, "Come on; come on," sharply; looked south, and saw King about the center of the street, facing Casey,—both standing in rather a defiant attitude, as I conceived [Gov. Foote objected], looking towards Casey, with his arms folded, and his right hand inside of his left breast; the parties were 100 feet apart at that time; both had on talmas, or short cloaks; Casey approached rapidly, asking in a sharp, excited voice, "Are you armed?" immediately following, he said, "Defend yourself," or "Prepare to defend yourself"; all this took place in a few seconds; Mr. King made no reply that I heard; as Casey said "Defend yourself," he let his talma fall and raised his right arm, which held a revolver, which must have been cocked at the time cloak fell, and he immediately fired at Mr. King; whilst Mr. Casey was in the act of firing, Mr. King turned his face slightly towards the west, shoving his arm down in his vest,—rather in a defensive position; the ball struck King on the left breast and shoulder, when he cried out "O Lord!" several times, and walked to the Pacific Express office; he (King) observed Casey before the fire, but paid no attention to him whatever afterwards; on his way to the express-office, I heard him say, "Oh, my arm!" several times; judged his arm was broken; Casey, immediately after firing, threw his revolver across his knee and used both hands in cocking it; walked some steps forward in the direction of King, who was at this time passing obliquely into express-office, and behind an express-wagon; the act of passing into the express-office naturally placed King and Casey on either side of the express-wagon; when Casey saw King going towards the express-office, and in rather an opposite direction to himself, he stopped, hesitated, and, after turning half-way round and looking about him, uncocked his pistol with both hands; picked up the cloak he had dropped; about the time he reached his cloak, I saw two men approach him rapidly from the direction of the express-office, one of whom was Lafayette Byrne; the other man I had never seen before; I have never seen him since, to my knowledge; seemed to be in the act of arresting him; Casey appeared to make some little resistance to the arrest, although he submitted; taken off by these men to and up Washington Street; I have never seen him since I saw him in Committee rooms; when I first saw King and Casey, I was nearly between them; they being in the middle of the street, and I was on the sidewalk; nearly 45 feet apart when Casey fired; when Casey called out first, was 100 feet apart; advanced 55 feet; am familiar with the use of fire-arms; King had ample time to fire accurately a five-barrel pistol after Casey first called out; can't say whether Casey's first call attracted King's attention or not; don't know whether King expressed a willingness to meet an enemy in this way.

Mr. Foote objected to the examination.

"Do you know whether King publicly proclaimed his readiness for such rencounter as this?" (Ruled out.) "Was the action of Casey on this occasion that of a fair and honorable combatant?" (Ruled out.) "What is the difference in size of these two persons?" (Objected to.)

Mr. Botts contended for the propriety of the question; is it not legal to urge this question? I expect to prove that Mr. Casey was at that time smarting under an insult not improperly resented by a rencounter of this kind.

Mr. Foote contended that unless he (the defendant) proved the offensive position of King, the question was out of order. I say, so far as I am concerned, if the gentleman really wishes to show an *insult* complained of, we have no objection; I deny that Casey was ever wronged by King, or that King ever did anything but what was justly demanded of him, as an editor, by the public. Question admitted.

Casey was a small man in stature; suppose he might weigh 125 or 135 pounds; muscular for his size, and active; King was 6 feet high, I should suppose, weighing, I should judge, 190 pounds at least, with rather an uncommon degree of muscular strength and power.

Cross-examined — Did not know King was sick; would say he weighed 170 or 180 when well; don't know that Whiteman conducted Casey off; had started to the American Exchange to get a drink; recognized Mr. Andrew Hebon, a butcher; no recollection of seeing any one else until immediately after the firing; saw, after, Ex-Mayor Webb, Wm. Neely Johnson, Richard Sinton, A. M. Smith, and most of my acquaintances on Montgomery Street; think I saw Ham Bowie in the crowd — not positive.

To Mr. Botts — Know Dan's Saloon; knew it in May, '56; went in frequently to take a drink.

"Ever see lager-beer there?" Objected to.

Question allowed.

Feel no modesty; had intimate acquaintance with brandy cocktails; have seen five hundred or five thousand persons drink there; popular bar — generally full; first-class saloons never keep lager-beer.

Gov. Foote — "Was it not distinguished for a fighting-place?"

Politics made up there; judge it respectable from the number of respectable gentlemen who want to mix in. [Laughter.] McGowan drank there; don't know that lager-beer was not kept there; universally not kept in that class of saloons; there are drinking-saloons in San Francisco where lager-beer is not kept, of the highest price; cheaper than best liquor; sold sometimes aboveground.

William F. Williamson — Saw King after he had been shot on May 14, 1856; saw arms upon his person; saw a six-shooter inside of his breast-pocket — left side.

Cross-examined — Noise of the pistol carried me to the spot; was living at the Mission, and was in the habit of going out at 8 o'clock; was waiting for an omnibus at corner of Clay and Montgomery streets; expected there would be a difficulty that day; did not expect that particular contest; don't recollect positively whether I saw Casey before, that day, but I think I did; saw McGowan when I saw Casey and Tom King talking; standing conversing with Casey on some business, and King (Tom) came up and asked Casey to step aside, as he wanted to talk with him; Vi Turner was near us; was not there as the friend of Casey to overhear the conversation; McGowan wore a white hat.

Alexander Dodge — On the evening of the 14th of May, 1856, I was in the city of San Francisco; saw McGowan about five minutes to 4 o'clock; saw him at Barry and Patten's five minutes to 4 o'clock; last saw him twenty minutes to 5; was with McGowan all the time intermediate; went with him to Justice Ryan's court, N. E. corner of Kearny and Pacific; went in and sat down; Justice engaged in trial; wanted to put off a trial; went out with another, and both had a drink; came back; McGowan got up and interrupted the court, and I got my case put off; cause of absence of witness, etc.; went out and took another drink with same person; somebody in the "court" asked Ned if he had seen the *Bulletin;* said he had n't, and the gentleman passed it over to him; suppose he read it; he passed the paper back and made a remark; took another drink, and went down to Merchant Street, to Dunbar's Alley; then McGowan stopped for a moment; walked on; McGowan overtook me; went down into Montgomery Street, into Nickerson and Lovett's saloon; proposed to them to take another drink; this place is next door to the *Bulletin* office; from there he (McGowan) left me, and I told them I must go down aboard; McGowan went out before me, and I met him as I was going down the street; when I met McGowan last time, it was two nights after King was shot; case in court was to come off at four o'clock; ascertained by the saloon clock or by my watch that it was five minutes to four; was in Barry and Patten's five minutes; was five to ten minutes walking to the courtroom; was in court three minutes; went out and came back; was four or five minutes getting a drink; was in court, second time, some ten minutes; five or ten minutes in drinking-saloon; from the time I first met McGowan (five minutes to four) to the time I left him, it was forty-five minutes; before five, I parted from him; nobody walked with us; when I left Nickerson's I was going to Clay Street; McGowan was walking toward Merchant Street; McGowan was on the same side of Nickerson's saloon.

Cross-examined— Ned was half a block from Dan's Saloon when I met him last; was defendant in the case referred to; am certain I did not get to the court until after three o'clock; don't recollect whether I looked at Nickerson's clock or not,— am uncertain on that point; looked at clock or watch; feel pretty certain I looked at my watch; am as sure that I looked at my watch as I was that I looked at the clock the other day; my recollection is not confused; I started from Patten's at near four o'clock; saw McGowan in Patten's; asked him to take a drink; got him to go and put my case off; took a drink, and away we went to the court; took eight to ten minutes to go to court, two or three minutes in court, four to five minutes drinking; came back to Justice's court and stayed five or ten minutes; went back to the "corner" and stayed ten minutes or so; then went to Nickerson's, consuming ten minutes thereby; did not stop at Nickerson's; saw McGowan a few minutes thereafter,— ten minutes to five. After McGowan read the *Bulletin,* he said that Casey would take care of that; McGowan had white hat and mustache. Talked about my testimony to-day; talked with Ryan to-day; Ryan approached me; all been talking on the matter; have not talked with counsel to-day on testimony; don't recollect of talking of my testimony with the counsel since deposition was taken.

Gilbert A. Grant, called and sworn— Saw McGowan in the afternoon of May 14th, 1856, about half-past four o'clock, in Merchant Street, with another gentleman; don't recollect that it was the last witness on the stand; about half-past four on the day mentioned, Messrs. Sutherland, Chamberlain, Smith, and myself were standing on the south side of Merchant Street, west of Montgomery, immediately in front of the assay-office of Wass, Molitor, & Co., talking about an apprehended difficulty between Casey and Thomas King; while standing there thus engaged, McGowan and this other person passed down on the north side of Merchant Street, toward Montgomery; Sutherland called to McGowan to come over, saying, "Come over; something is out"; the accompanying gentleman went in the direction of Nickerson & Lovett's saloon; this might have been twenty minutes past four o'clock; in a short time after this, Casey came down from the second story of Bolton & Barron's Building, and went down to Montgomery Street; after a lapse of a little time, we heard the report of a pistol, and ran down to Montgomery Street; it was Mayor Webb who told us that King had been shot; suppose this was after five o'clock; don't know Peter Whiteman.

Cross-examined—My impression is that it was half after four when McGowan came down the street; think the shooting occurred five minutes past five; did not look at my watch; suppose it was ten or fifteen minutes before the firing that Casey passed down; McGowan had on a white hat, black mustache, green pants, and black coat; knew that Casey and McGowan did not affiliate politically; they might have been intimate, however, for aught I know.

To Juryman—Did not see McGowan at the Pacific Express office.

The court adjourned at twelve o'clock, until Monday morning, at nine o'clock.

Third Day's Proceedings.

MONDAY, JUNE 1st, 1857.

The court was called at nine o'clock.
Testimony for the defense continued.

John Nugent was called and sworn.—Was police-officer in San Francisco last 14th May, 1856; saw defendant (McGowan) on that day, about five o'clock, on Washington Street, about five doors from Kearny; wanted to see him; went across to the north side of the street to see him; was in his company about ten minutes; went to Kearny Street together; did not see Hamilton Bowie; McGowan spoke to some one who was with him; saw a buggy near to Palmer, Cook, & Co.'s; did not hear the report of a pistol; the rencounter took place whilst I was with McGowan; left McGowan on Kearny Street, fifteen steps from Washington.

Cross-examined—Am special-police officer; no person in company with McGowan when I saw him; I was standing in Dunbar's Alley when I saw him; McGowan was with Stevenson and Green; no one else with me; standing at corner of alley and Washington Street; did not look at the clock; knew the time by hearsay; McGowan was walking towards Kearny Street; accompanied him eight doors on Washington; went ten or fifteen steps down Kearny Street; heard that there was a man shot, while standing there on Kearny Street; don't know who told me that a man had been shot; Stevenson, I think, told me; he was an officer; McGowan was standing by me when the communication was given me; left McGowan in Kearny Street; can't say which way he went; I ran down to Dunbar's

Alley; judge I walked with McGowan some ten minutes; did not see any one I knew while standing with McGowan; my business with him was to get him to see a man for me; don't know how long ago it was I let McGowan know of this matter,—while he was in Sacramento; spoke of it to some of his friends in San Francisco,—to Curtis (Chief of Police), for one; have seen McGowan in prison most every day; sometimes three or four times a day; did not have any conversation with any one on board the Sophie; don't know any one by the name of Brittingham; was not with Brittingham two hours in this town, that I know of; made no statement to him (Brittingham) or any person that I could clear Ned; never; did not say to him or any person that everything was fixed to clear McGowan; am an old police-officer, since 1852; business to hunt down persons accused of crime; always a witness on those I detect; generally receive a consideration from parties, outside of my regular fees; do up-country business mostly now; did not hear the report of the pistol; don't recollect as I did; this day, was standing by Palmer, Cook, & Co.; can't say I saw H. Bowie; might have done so; was north of Washington Street, on Kearny Street; the lots are three hundred and fifty feet; was four hundred feet from the place where King was shot; if I had heard the shot, I should have run to see where it came from; left Stevenson at Dunbar's Alley; think it was Stevenson who told me of the shot; the person who gave me the information ran with me down the street; had some difficulty that day; had some trouble then; had a difficulty with North; never was broke; often in difficulty as an officer; did not know that there was likely to be a difficulty that afternoon between Casey and Tom King; did not know that such was the common talk of the afternoon; since I have been here as a witness, have not heard any testimony given here; heard old man Taylor say that he did not know anything, and he told all he knew. [Laughter.] It was four hundred and twenty feet from where I was to the place of rencounter.

To a Juror—I was about ten minutes with McGowan before the report came that a man was shot.

Samuel Stevenson, called and sworn—Was a police-officer on the 14th of May last. (The testimony of this witness was the same as that of Officer Nugent.)

James McNab—Was in San Francisco on the 14th of May, 1856; saw Casey on that day, several times; saw him in the neighborhood of "Natchez"; after four, was on corner of Kearny and Clay streets, talking with a friend; Casey came along; thought I'd watch him; Casey went into "Natchez"; stayed fifteen minutes in there; noticed, when he came out, had a pistol bulging out his coat; he went down Merchant Street; was a large pistol; Natchez has assistants in his pistol-gallery.

Cross-examined—Have seen assistants in "Natchez"; Taylor said it was not possible that Casey was in his shop; Natchez said Casey never came to his shop; Taylor told me this after the case came on; had no conversation with Taylor.

Judge—Think I told the witnesses not to talk to each other; I just contradicted Taylor; overheard Taylor at Revere House; he went on some time; he was telling stories; think all I said was, that he was mistaken; he said that Casey had never been in his house for three months; said I thought I had seen Casey go into his house the 14th May; have been intimate with Casey for a series of years; first knew him in San Francisco in '54; have been enemies; did not speak for two months; followed Casey up when I saw him go in Natchez'; expected difficulty between him and Tom King; was not my business to come here and help the defense; not present when Casey was arrested; went up to the jail that night (May 14th); went into the jail some time after; went in to guard the jail; went in voluntarily to guard; ther was a mob outside; heard it rumored that it was to be attacked· don't know who let me in; thought all in the jail were in danger; expected to see the jail torn down; can't say I went to guard Casey; believed that violence would occur on account of the King and Casey affray; thought Casey was menaced; went in to defend the jail; no special relations with Casey; did not stay in jail ten minutes; went to get arms. I was one of the proscribed of San Francisco; am the man who was engaged with Malony to get the arms.

To Mr. Botts—I was first lieutenant of a company when I went for arms; I was kept aboard the revenue cutter for eight weeks; they tried to take me and send me off; they came to my house and searched; I got out the back way; can't say whether they brought the "all-seeing eye" or not [laughter]; am living in San Francisco now; Captain Ashe sent me for arms; was resisted in the execution of that order by the Vigilance Committee; took me in San Pablo Bay.

To Mr. Foote—I got my commission from Gov. Johnson two days before Casey was arrested; had no commission before; went, under orders, to Benicia and got all the arms we wanted; was apprehended in the bay and taken to San Francisco; sympathized with the other side; got some of our arms at Benicia.

To Mr. Botts—Was robbed of those arms; looked like robbing.

E. G. Buffum—Objected to on account of his attendance during the trial. Objection withdrawn.

Saw Curtis (witness), of Napa Springs, a few days ago. Had a conversation with him in regard to the testimony he was to give; the conversation originated from his complaining of his being brought up there, away from his business; my impression is, that he said there was no necessity for his testimony, as that of Butts would testify to all he could; think he said he was with McGowan in the Bank Exchange when Butts came up.

Dr. B. Cole— Am a practicing physician; graduate; graduated at the Jefferson Medical Institute in '48; been practicing since then without interruption; was practicing in San Francisco in May, '56; saw King within seven minutes after he was shot; made an examination of his wound; knew of his (King's) medical treatment; heard Toland's testimony.

Do you think Mr. King died of his wound, or from the treatment he received?

Objected to on the ground of its too general nature.
Overruled.

In my opinion, the wound was not necessarily a mortal one. The treatment was of such a character as to make it a mortal wound, or in other words, to cause death.

Cross-examined — Studied in Washington and Philadelphia; commenced practice in Philadelphia — practiced there for seven years; been in California about five years; pursued the profession continually here; was engaged in the drug business with Little; Nott and McClelland's reputation are good; saw King's wound soon after it was inflicted; wound still bleeding; Dr. Nuttall was stooping over the patient, in the act of examining the wound; introduced my finger into the wound after Nuttall; decidedly venous blood issuing — quantity did not seem to be unusually great; the wound was an inch and a half below the clavicle; I was the first who discovered the posterior wound.

The Doctor brought in a half-skeleton, by which he illustrated the character of the wound.

The subclavian vein is below the artery; seemed to be a simple flesh-wound, and, from the blood, it was very evident that the artery had escaped; united in the dressing of the wound; objected to the sponge when it was introduced; the sponge was of the size of a turkey's egg; it had to be stuffed into the wound; assisted in tying the bandage on; thought its introduction was improper; should have preferred lint; very many differences exist between myself and other medical gentlemen; I think I expressed a disapproval of the material introduced; the reaction of the next day was sufficient to warrant the expectation of recovery; was very intimate with King; not aware that he was laboring under a serious wound; personally know of the subsequent treatment.

[The Doctor here delivered a long anatomical lecture.]

A post-mortem examination affords the best evidence of the precise nature of the wound; was not present at Mr. King's post-mortem examination, on account of the special order of the attending physician; the application of the tourniquet was improper and injurious; Dr. Toland's reputation in the community is one thing — his reputation among the medical profession is another thing; I am nearly exclusively a surgeon; was in Jefferson Institute — as professor — for four years; have performed very many cases in San Francisco and elsewhere.

To the Judge—It was improper to put this tourniquet on the wound; I would have selected something besides a sponge to put in a wound; sponge came in contact with the vein and retained poisonous matter.

Only attended the case of King one or two days; suggested the removal of the sponge and tourniquet several times; there is no profession in which there is more rivalry than in the medical, unless it be the law; have lectured on the case; was not actuated by jealousy; my reason for lecturing on this case was to promote the right; withdrew from Mr. King's case on account of the discourtesy of the attending physicians; personal matters between us.

To Mr. Botts—Was excluded from the post-mortem examination; I am commissioned surgeon-general to the Vigilance Committee; I am the surgeon of the grand marshal's staff; have some seventy or eighty doctors under me.

The *Bulletin* article was admitted.

The court adjourned for an hour.

Here the testimony was closed, and the following speeches of counsel were made. The remarks of Mr. Coffroth and Heslep are omitted, as those of Gov. Foote and Mr. Botts embrace everything of interest in the case.

The following is the substance of the speech of Mr. Botts, who closed for the defense:—

Gentlemen of the Jury,—I was informed, during the progress of this trial, that it had pleased one of the gentlemen who represent the state to remark that he observed symptoms of anxiety and fear on the part of the counsel for the defense. The remark did honor to the sagacity of the acute observer.

When I consider, gentlemen, the large circle of friends drawn to the defendant by the attraction of a heart as warm as ever beat in the human breast, looking to us for the realization of their hope of his deliverance; when I remember that an ingenuous and affectionate youth has committed into our hands the life of his aged father, and that reputation which is now his only heritage,—I confess I am overwhelmed with embarrassment, and tremble in humble acknowledgment of my incompetency to do justice to this cause. To my mind, the thought of that mysterious and eternal sleep to which we are all doomed is so allied with awe, that it imparts a dignity and solemnity to the person of one who stands within the portals of the palace of death. And, gentlemen, do you not, too, recognize the solemnity of the duty you are called upon to perform? Do you not recognize the fact that it is no light and trivial thing even to put in jeopardy the life of a fellow-being? You do, gentlemen; I know you do. The day has passed,— the day has passed, thank God, when human blood flowed like water, and when gibbets and corpses were the proper ornaments of our refined and fashionable metropolis.

The time has come when a man accused of crime can find one spot, at least, in the state of California where he can have a fair trial, by a jury of his peers, in accordance with the time-honored usage of that noble race from which we are sprung. And, gentlemen, if there is a spark of sympathy in your breasts, it will lighten up at a recital of the wrongs and persecutions to which this man has been subjected. The defendant is an aged man. The frosts of nearly sixty winters have fallen upon his head. One night passed by Marie Antoinette in a prison of France was, by suffering and agony, prolonged into an age; and this man has learned, in the same way, to count weeks for months, and months for years. He has been driven from the bosom of society, compelled to flee as though a convicted felon, and seek an asylum in a distant province. But the bloodhounds were upon his track. They found him domiciled among the kind and hospitable people of Santa Bárbara. Expelled and driven thence, he was compelled to flee to the mountains. During the day he is skulking from rock to rock, and at night he goes down to the plains for a drop of water to cool his parched lips. In the mean time his substance is wasted or confiscated; and he comes to you now broken in spirit and ruined in fortune. And this has been done, not by a set of cannibals in the Fiji Islands, not in a savage province, but in a land where, from some mountain peak, the poor wanderer could still see the Stars and Stripes. But, alas! they no longer waved o'er the land of the free or the home of the brave.

Now, gentlemen, you will be told that this man fled from this indictment. It is not true; and the proof lies in this, that, as soon as it was safe for him to return,—aye, even sooner, perhaps, than prudence warranted,—he did return, and delivered himself into the hands of the law. Even then he was forced to seek his protection within the very verge of the Capitol. He was compelled to procure the passage of a law which would enable him to secure a change of *venue* without making his personal appearance in the city of San Francisco. This law was passed by the legislature of California with extraordinary unanimity. It was based upon the admission of the representatives of the Vigilance Committee, that it was true that this man could not go to San Francisco safely. And the act recites the fact that there is still a portion of this country where the majesty of the law is set at defiance,—where the government cannot protect her citizens. What a shame and what a reproach to that city! and what a blot upon your historical record! Never would I have voted for such a law. I would have said, "Perish fifty McGowans before I put upon record such an humiliating confession."

Can it, then, be pretended, gentlemen, for a moment that it was anything else than the lawless act of these lawless men that drove this man into exile? Why, and how, is he here now? Who brought him here? He never desired anything but a fair and impartial trial; *not the honorable trial of the Vigilance Committee*; not a trial from a body of men who, we have ascertained from one of their own number, look up testimony, and when they discover that it is *not exactly fit for the purpose*, disregard and ignore it, as old Curtis told you was the fact in his own case; not the honorable trial of the Vigilance Committee: but a fair and impartial trial by a jury of his peers.

But let us,—for our time is short, gentlemen,—let us proceed without further circumlocution to the consideration of the facts of this particular case. The defendant stands charged with the crime of murder. It is pretended that on the 14th day of May, 1856, he murdered one James King of Wm. Now, the evidence shows that upon the evening of that day a rencounter took place between James P. Casey and the deceased, in which King was wounded by a shot fired from a pistol in the hands of Casey. Three questions are presented by this state of facts. The first is, Did King die of the wound inflicted by Casey? Secondly, If King died from the wound, was that act murder, or manslaughter, or justifiable homicide? Thirdly, and chiefly, What was the complicity of the accused with that act?

Now as to the question whether King died of the wound inflicted by Casey,—because, certainly, if Casey did not kill King, or if King died in consequence of operations, or acts performed by others, whether they may have been committed, as we shall urge, by Doctor Toland, and those acting with him, on the one hand, or by Doctor Cole, as is contended by his associate, who represents the people, on the other hand, it is equally unimportant for us, for it is not contended that there was any complicity between us and either of these physicians. Now, gentlemen, I confess that this is a subject to which the gentleman who opened the case is much more equal than I am. Remember, the true rule of law is, and so His Honor will charge you, whatever may be the opinion to the contrary of the distinguished professor both of law and of physic,—who seems, by the way, to have obtained his views of the law rather from the Vigilance Committee than from any civilized system of jurisprudence,—the Court will charge you that it is the business of the commonwealth, before she can obtain a verdict, to satisfy you, beyond all reasonable doubt, that the act of murder was committed by the party charged with the deed. If there is reason to doubt that James King of Wm. died of the wound, and not of the treatment, there is an end of the prosecution. Well, now, let us look at Dr. Toland's testimony first, as it stood uncontradicted. Dr. Toland tells you that there were two or three causes operating, any one of which might have produced death. He does not pretend that any mortal part was wounded when the ball passed through the body of Mr. King. He says that King might have died of inflammation of the vein, and that inflammation of the vein we have shown, and he admitted it might have possibly been produced by the treatment. He tells you, again, that King lay all night upon a single mattress, upon a counter in the office of the Pacific Express Company; that the evening was raw and chilly, although he says that the room was warm; that many applications of cold water were made to his wound; and that King was, at the time, in delicate health. He tells you, that, upon an examination of King's body, immediately after his death, evidences were exhibited that justified the conclusion that he died of pleurisy, and that it was *possible* that, from the circumstances of the treatment alluded to, he might have caught a cold which terminated fatally. I do not pretend to tell you that Dr. Toland said that the probability was that King met his death from this source, but I call your attention to the fact that he admitted that such *possibly* was the case. Now, without going into the evidence on the other side, does Dr. Toland's testimony leave your minds without a doubt—*without a doubt*—that James King of Wm. died from the wound received from James P. Casey, and from nothing else? Can you, upon your oaths, say that that is the fact? Do you not perceive that if nothing else stood in the way of the conviction of Casey for this murder, if it were proven that McGowan started with Casey for the purpose and with the design of murdering, or, if you please, of assassinating, King, even then here would be a stumbling-block which the prosecution could never surmount. Why, there is not a man within the sound of my voice, who heard the testimony of Dr. Toland, who can say more than this: "*Probably*" James King of Wm. met his death from a pistol-shot; but it is impossible for human ingenuity, for human wit, to ascertain with certainty whether he died from cold or from the wound, and the defendant is entitled to the benefit of every doubt.

But, in addition to that, what do we have? We have the testimony of a physician, who, if I can be permitted to express an opinion at all upon such a subject, exhibited, under the most scientific cross-examination that I ever heard, the greatest intelligence and ability, to which the gentleman himself (Mr. Heslep) paid the highest compliment. Such a witness does not hesitate to say that the death of King was in consequence of the treatment, and not of the wound.

Now, then, gentlemen, how does the case stand? Here are two experts standing, at least, upon an equal footing; for, if we claim no superiority for our witness, the gentleman will, at least, admit his equality, when he remembers that he comes to us indorsed by the Vigilance Committee of San Francisco; that he is the great surgeon-general on the staff of the chief marshal of the executive committee of the Vigilance Committee. And, by the by, what will the Committee think when they hear that their attorney-general has been trying to deprecate his brother-in-arms, the great surgeon-general in the staff of the chief marshal? May it not be that they may expel the attorney-general for such disrespect to his superior officer?

Here, then, are two unimpeached witnesses, scientific men, between whose comparative merits you and I (who cannot understand the technical terms they use) cannot determine; the one thinking that in all probability Mr. King died of his wound, and the other well assured that the wound was not mortal, and that he was killed by his physicians. Does not this raise a doubt which must compel a verdict of not guilty?

But, if King died of the wound, what was the character of the offense committed by Casey?

I am going to speak of the deceased, and I will do it frankly and impartially. I knew him well; he was for many years my client; an intimate friend. He was honest, upright, and honorable. This was in the days of his prosperity. He met with sad reverses; he became poor; he returned from his daily labor to a famishing family; he drained the bitter cup of poverty to the very dregs. With some little pecuniary assistance afforded him, he resolved to start a newspaper in the city of San Francisco. At this point my opportunity for personal communication with him was lost. I knew him afterwards, through the columns of the *Bulletin*. All of good that I said concerning this man is based upon my intimate personal relations with him; all that was bad in his conduct was matter of public notoriety. He commenced a line of business that was already crowded to suffocation in the city of San Francisco. It was necessary to call attention to the new paper; it must be striking, else it would not pay; he resolves to cater to the public appetite for slander, but it was his poverty, not his will, consented. He takes the New York *Herald*, in its earlier days, for his model; he becomes a public libeler and a public nuisance. He is a public brawler too; he professes himself prepared and ready for such an encounter as he at last provoked. He stirs up heartburnings and strife, and expects to escape the effects of the angry passions he has aroused. As well might he who throws a brand into a powder-magazine hope to escape the explosion. He utters wholesale defamation, and dares his victim to the encounter. It is Selover to-day, Col. Baker to-morrow. At last he attacks the deceased Casey, alluding to his early aberrations and unfortunate career. Casey seeks an interview to beg him, it may be, to forbear; he pleads his repentance, his hope to bury the past in oblivion, and begs that he may be allowed the opportunity of reform. This ruthless censor of public morals denies the boon, drives him out with contempt and ignominy, and sends forth a number of his abusive sheet, in which he holds Casey up to public scorn, calls him a prison convict, a ballot-box stuffer, and declares that he deserves to be hung upon a gibbet.

Is it unreasonable to suppose that Casey, stung to madness by such conduct as this, sought King and shot him under the influence of irresistible passion? The fact that Casey had been, in reality, an inmate of Sing Sing does not weaken, but rather strengthens, this view of the case. The question is, not how justifiable King may have been, but what state of mind in Casey was this conduct calculated to produce. The law makes allowance for sudden heat and irresistible passion. Casey, says one of the people's witnesses, was a passionate man. Was not this provocation sufficient to sting him to madness, and reduce the killing from murder to manslaughter? Is it possible to confound this act with base assassination? What is it but that vulgar, blackguard, but very common thing, a street fight? This little fellow, Casey, whatever else he may have been,—and God knows he was bad enough,—was brave and magnanimous; and, according to the account of Gen. Estell, who had a better opportunity of hearing and seeing than anybody who describes it, it was a fair and equal combat. King, who is armed, is warned, and has full time to draw. He thrusts his hand into his bosom, where, it is afterwards discovered, he had a loaded pistol. Casey advanced fifty-five feet after he attracted King's attention, and warned him to defend himself before he fired. This is the testimony of Estell, and he is the only witness who, from his position, could have seen and heard what passed. Can this be called a cold-blooded murder? The Court will tell you that there can be no accessaries in manslaughter; and if you think Casey was only guilty of manslaughter, you must acquit the defendant.

But here the counsel for the state will talk largely of "the liberty of the press": he will tell you that it is the palladium of freedom, and that the deceased fell a martyr to this great principle. This is all gammon. When we speak of a free press, we mean freedom of speech, liberty to discuss political topics. But private character has always been held sacred by a right-thinking people. The world would become a bear-garden if every man was allowed to say even what he honestly thought of his neighbor: the freedom of speech must be kept in wholesome subjection. The press is a two-edged sword, and may be wielded for good or for evil. All liberty may degenerate into licentiousness; and where there is no restraint, there can be no freedom.

What would you call him that, daily, through your streets, should denounce his neighbors? Would not such a one be a common nuisance? and when he got his head broke, as he assuredly would, would not the community rejoice? If, instead of confining his pestilential breath to mere words, which die upon the air as they are spoken, he should print them in indelible characters, and scatter them to the four quarters of the globe, would the offense be less heinous? or would the stricken offender be more a subject of sympathy?

The law, it is said, affords a punishment for the libeler; but when, as in this case, the offender can beat you upon the execution, the law becomes impotent.

The power of the press is despotic. Some one has said that the best form of government is a despotism limited by the power of assassination. If we are to be subjected to the despotism of the press, let it, at least, be limited by the principle of personal responsibility.

But, granting that Casey murdered King, how is the defendant implicated in the act? This brings me to a review of the remaining testimony, which I will hasten over, because my time is limited. And to the hurried nature of this review I submit the more readily because, really, the testimony is of such a character as to make comment unnecessary. I assure you, that, when the state closed her evidence, I desired to submit this cause to you without argument and without testimony on the part of the defense; but on this I was overruled by my client, to whose wishes I was compelled to defer.

The first testimony at all relevant is that of Mr. Taylor, who testifies that McGowan had a revolver and a derringer loaded at his rooms on the morning of the fatal day. But he states that the practice of wearing arms is universal amongst the most respectable people of San Francisco; that he is called upon hourly by others, as he was by McGowan; that he had done the same thing for McGowan himself repeatedly before; and that Thomas King, the brother of the deceased, had been to his establishment on a similar errand.

Curtis—poor old Curtis—testified that he met McGowan and Whiteman, about half-past four, P. M., at Dan's Saloon, where a slim boy, not the boy Butts, came and got Whiteman's pistol for Casey. Over and above the prevarications and self-contradiction of this witness, he is flatly contradicted by Captain Dodge, whose testimony is confirmed by Mr. Grant. According to his own statements, Curtis must have met McGowan at fifteen minutes after four, at the latest; and by Dodge and Grant—making all possible estimate for erroneous estimate of time—we account for McGowan's whereabouts from four to half-past four.

But why should I trouble you with comments upon the testimony of this witness? The prosecution gives him up as a hopeless case. The most important, nay, the only, witness whose testimony has the slightest tendency to prove even a knowledge of Casey's intentions, upon the part of the accused, is entirely overlooked by the counsel who opened for the state. In a speech of two hours, the testimony of Curtis was never even alluded to. The fact is, the gentlemen from San Francisco came up provided with two strings to their bow. It is necessary that the defendant should be connected with Whiteman, and Whiteman with Casey. This is the theory of the indictment. The testimony to effect this object, the Vigilance Committee had ascertained, as we learn from Curtis, could be drawn from two sources: Curtis himself on the one hand, and the boy Butts on the other. But the two stories will not stand together, and, as we have seen, these *honorable* gentlemen, having, in their trial of McGowan, by chance gotten hold of Butts first, decline to examine Curtis when, as he says, one of their number could not persuade him to vary his story so as to confirm Butts's statement. What a *fair* and *honorable* trial is afforded an absent and unrepresented defendant by that *honorable* body, the Vigilance Committee!

But it so happens that Butts's reputation has been a little tarnished since he was the favorite witness of the Vigilance Committee rooms. Butts is a good boy, no doubt, but the community is prejudiced against Butts: the county jail and the chain-gang have detracted somewhat from Butts's respectability. On the other hand, Curtis is a gray-headed, decent-looking man. So the choice lies between Curtis's story of the slim boy and Dan's Saloon on the one hand, and the fat boy Butts and the Bank Exchange on the other. After some consideration, they determine in favor of Curtis, but they are both brought up for the trial, as a jockey brings two horses for a race. They will run Curtis unless an accident happens to him. Well, an accident did happen to poor Curtis: he broke down. So, reluctantly and unwillingly upon the part of the state, Butts's irons are knocked off, and he is transferred from his dungeon to the witness-stand; and Curtis is as completely forgotten by his old friends as if he had never lived.

(Here Mr. Heslep stated that he had left that part of the prosecution to his associate, Gov. Foote, who would take care of Curtis.)

Mr. Botts — That, then, is the game, is it? Then it stands thus: Heslep, Butts; Foote and Curtis. Why this division? Was it that Curtis was too heavy a load for the first gentleman, and that it needs all the strength of an ex-governor and an ex-senator to pack the old man through? Gentlemen, is a man to be tried for his life upon testimony such as this?

Taking now the testimony of Butts, and yielding to the tacit request of the opening counsel that we should forget that Curtis had ever been upon the stand, we trace McGowan every foot of the way and through every moment of time from four o'clock, when he first appears in the company of Captain Dodge, until we find him at the corner of Washington and Kearny streets, when the fatal shot is fired. Thus it is that not only has the counsel for the state failed to redeem his promise of showing McGowan at his station prepared to perform his rôle in the murder of King, but the defense, by the greatest good fortune, has been enabled to establish the negative of the proposition, thus bringing himself even within the new rule propounded by the representative of the Vigilance Committee, that a man must be held guilty unless he can prove his innocence. Not one tittle of evidence has been offered even tending to show a conspiracy between Casey, Whiteman, and McGowan to murder King. Not a particle of evidence to show that McGowan ever saw King, or entertained the slightest acrimony against him. The only attempt that has been made is to raise a suspicion that McGowan or Whiteman furnished the fatal weapon. You are left, I presume, under this new doctrine of the attorney-general of the Vigilance Committee to guess that the pistol, if furnished, was furnished for the purpose of aiding in murder; you must cleanse your heart of all charitable and Christian feelings, as if you were members of the Vigilance Committee. You must never draw an inference in favor of the prisoner. You must not suppose it possible that Casey told him he wanted the pistol for lawful purposes. From the mere fact of loaning a pistol you must infer a heart devoid of social virtue, and consign a human being to a felon's grave.

There was one phrase used by the opening counsel, against which I must enter my protest. He frequently called me his "friend Botts." Now, the present condition of my client admonishes that the friendship of one who comes under the ban of the Vigilance Committee is a dangerous thing. Many attempts, unsuccessful it is true, have been made to establish this relation between McGowan and Casey. Now, suppose it should please the Vigilance Committee to hang instead of expelling their attorney-general for his bad conduct to the surgeon-general, how then might it fare with me if they could prove that I had permitted him to call me his friend in this public manner, without contradiction? Under the circumstances, I prefer to imitate the sagacity and prudence of my experienced friend Governor Foote, and occupy the position of a neutral until further developments.

Yes, gentlemen, I was not less surprised than grieved to hear my respected friend the Governor—one of the first citizens in the commonwealth—declare, in the progress of this trial, that when the state was shaken to its center, when five thousand men in arms—a motley crew of foreigners and disaffected citizens—arrayed themselves against the laws of the land, at a time when all agreed that the state was in imminent danger,—that at such a time my friend remained neutral.

(Here Governor Foote interrupted Mr. Botts, and said he never used the term "neutral." Mr. Botts insisted that he had repeatedly used the term, in which he was supported by several of the bystanders, but suggested that the Governor had a right now to explain what he meant. The Governor then said, that all he intended to say was, that, during those exciting times, he was perfectly calm, and took part with neither side. Mr. Botts contended that the explanation was only a good definition of the word "neutral," and proceeded.)

But, gentlemen, it is neither the law nor the evidence that we have to fear upon this occasion; for there is no testimony in the case that any more tends to connect the defendant, than any of the witnesses who have appeared upon the stand, with this homicide. Indeed, whilst others seem to have been on the lookout for some violent result to this affair between Casey and King, he appears either ignorant of or indifferent to the approaching fight, and is found walking from the expected scene of action.

It is not, then, the testimony, but the influence of that once powerful organization known as the Vigilance Committee of San Francisco, that we have to dread. And, gentlemen, who and what are these men, that their behests are to be regarded by you? What are they but a band of traitors who have raised their sacrilegious hands against their country? What is there about them to make them respectable? Is it because they have degraded the character of our free institutions in the eyes of the civilized world? Is it because they have chilled the hopes of the philanthropist, and proved that the great problem of self-government remains still unsolved? Is it because they overawed our people with foreign mercenaries, snatched up our citizens into their infernal slaughter-house, and thrust their strangled bodies from the windows, or else, in mockery, threw us out the bloody corpse, saying, "See where he killed himself!"

But we are told that there are good men amongst them. O, yes! No doubt of it. There were good men, too, in the crowd that followed the Son of God up the Mount of Calvary. There were honest fanatics, no doubt, amongst the fiends that perpetrated the massacre of St. Bartholomew. What motives actuated these men can never be known certainly to any but the Great Searcher of all hearts, but, with our limited perceptions, we are compelled to derive motives from acts. And if the killing of King by Casey justifies us, as our opponents say it does, in concluding that Casey possessed a heart devoid of social virtue, why should the murder of Casey and Cora by the Vigilance Committee lead to the inference that its members are mild, gentle, and loving Christians?

Think not, whatever may be my detestation of their crimes, that I am animated by feelings of hostility towards these men. That feeling has been long since absorbed in pity. They have unlawfully taken the lives of their fellow-men. The Great Avenger is on their track. "Whoso sheddeth man's blood, by man shall his blood be shed." They have awakened from their bloody frenzy to find themselves surrounded by dangers. They are murderers in the eyes of the law, and in the eyes of all Christian communities. As has been well said of them, whilst they have banished their miserable victims from San Francisco, they have exiled themselves from the balance of the world. The circle is constantly narrowing around them, and the time will come when they cannot find a corner of the world in which to hide their heads.

But, gentlemen, I am admonished that my time is up, and I must conclude by thanking you for the profound attention with which you have listened to my remarks.

Closing Speech of Governor Foote.

Gov. Foote said, that, limited as he was for time, he should endeavor to compress as much as possible, and not pretend to give to the many topics which presented themselves the degree of attention their importance really demanded; and throughout the whole of his speech he evidently labored under the fear of exhausting the short time allowed him by the limit to the session of the court. He also spoke very rapidly, and the notes taken so hastily can only represent detached parts of his speech.

He said that he did not agree with the counsel for the defense in any of the legal propositions they had laid down. If he did not really believe that the prosecution had clearly made out a case, he trusted he should have had the honesty to have urged the entering of a *nolle prosequi*. They have misrepresented every feature of the evidence and every legal proposition arising in the case.

Notwithstanding all our protests, said he, both counsel insist on dragging the Vigilance Committee issue into this trial. Both have attacked the Committee, and coarsely assailed and vilified its members in a way never before suffered by any honorable body of men. He next passed a high eulogium upon the Committee and its acts, and said, that, although, being a lawyer, and residing across the bay from San Francisco, he could not, consistently with his ideas of propriety, unite with them, he approved and indorsed all their acts. He had only interfered to bring about peace, and for that purpose had seen the Governor, and spoke with authority when he now said, that, had Governor Johnson listened to him, within five days the Committee would have been disbanded entirely, and all the subsequent difficulties avoided. The Governor himself ordered the Sheriff to surrender the jail; and when the pilot and captain thus forsook the ship, the crew were forced to take charge. They did so, and have covered themselves with a glory, of which the gentlemen on the other side can never deprive them. Gibbets were erected, and blood did flow, but not freely, as was said by the defense; they spared many. Among them were Judge Terry, and McNab, one of their own witnesses. Governor Foote also spoke of his having urged Judge Terry to return to his place, as he might have to sit as judge on the very issues then raised in San Francisco; and he told him that Chief Justice Marshall would never have acted thus. But Terry rejected his advice, and thus got into difficulty. Mr. Botts, said Governor Foote, has lately been so successful in defending the worst criminals in the state, that his sense of moral rectitude has been considerably shaken, and he has been using the same kind of arguments in this case as in theirs. If he succeeds in having this and all his other clients set loose, he will make California such a hell upon earth as never existed since the days of Adam.

Mr. King has been disparagingly alluded to, and justice to the illustrious dead required that a reply should be given. Mr. Coffroth said he had known McGowan in the legislature of Pennsylvania. Satan was once in heaven, but he was ejected, and thrown over the battlements. He supposed the gentleman on the other side did not also sympathize with His Satanic Majesty, merely because he had fallen from his high estate, as McGowan did. They eulogize Casey, too, and Mr. Botts said he had known him. What does the paper that they have admitted in evidence show? That he was an unfortunate ballot-box stuffer. He came to California to reform, did he? I, too, have known Mr. King; and justice to the memory of the illustrious dead requires that I should speak of him. He then said he had known Mr. King's father, years ago, in Washington, and that his son had been educated and brought up properly. He passed a high eulogium upon the deceased as a man, a citizen, a husband and father, and in his latest position as an editor. An imperious necessity existed in San Francisco for just such a paper. He did his duty fully, fairly, and faithfully; and because he did so he was murdered. In the words of one of our domestic poets,—

"He died at his post doing duty!"

Here, in your presence, gentlemen of the jury, the ashes of the dead have been ruthlessly disturbed, and, to use one of Mr. Botts's own expressions, I expect that he will not be able to repose in quiet upon his pillow until he has made reparation and atonement to the memory of the illustrious dead. They eulogize Casey and Cora, and sympathize with the crew which the Vigilance Committee rose to drive out. Had the Vigilance Committee not been successful, and if that crew had continued uninterruptedly to rule over us, I would sooner take up my residence in the infernal regions than continue to live in this state. And so would every man who is the father of a family, and who has proper feelings and a proper sense of propriety. But, say they, Mr. King brought his death upon himself. They say that was a very abusive article. I deny it. It is a charitable, a liberal, and a just article. [Here he read the article.] If that is abusive and vile, how shall we characterize the language of those gentlemen here this evening? Why, I would not call it by its right name. Billingsgate is a term I never apply to remarks of gentlemen. Mr. King offered to rectify any wrong he had done, if the error was shown him. How many editors of the present day would do so? And the gentlemen say that such an article made Mr. King deserve the death he met! And they justify the act!

Mr. Botts — Governor, Governor! I did not. I said it was a provocation which reduced the criminality of the act from murder to manslaughter.

Gov. Foote — The gentleman said I would have done so.

Mr. Botts — I did not.

Gov. Foote — Well, no matter what his words were. He does say it was a manslaughter. I say it was not. It was a cold-blooded, premeditated, villainous *murder!* the most fiendish, cowardly, infernal outrage ever committed. [Here he again read from the article.] Mr. Botts thinks it very abusive for Mr. King to say that Casey ought to be hung. I say it, the man who would stuff a ballot-box ought to be hung; and if Mr. King, having a knowledge of the fact that Casey had done this act, had failed to publish it, he would have failed to do his duty as an editor, and would have been unworthy of his position.

Gov. Foote then spoke of the testimony of the physicians. Mr. Botts says the testimony of Dr. Cole raises a doubt in your minds, the benefit of which his client must have. But Dr. Cole may talk as he did forever, and may bring as many ugly, stinking corpses into court as he pleases, (and, in my opinion, that comes the nearest of anything in the world to humbug,) but he never could produce a doubt in my mind, or in any of your minds, that Mr. King did actually die from the effects of the wound inflicted upon him by Casey. Counsel next contrasted Dr. Cole with Dr. Toland, and his comparison was very unfavorable to the former. Mr. Botts, continued Gov. Foote, thought to compare me with Casey! and speaks of what I would probably do if an abusive newspaper article was written about me. He said he had been attacked by the press, and, he felt convinced, by hireling editors who were paid to injure him, but he defied the defense to point to an act of his which would justify them in attempting to draw such a parallel. It is not, either, true, in point of fact, said he, that I ever loaned my pistols to one man to shoot down his fellow-man, or to fight a duel with. But the gentleman himself, and all who are acquainted with me, know that I have always and many a time interfered to prevent bloodshed and infractions of the law.

Speaking of Gen. Estell's testimony, he said it was intended to suggest a doubt whether Mr. King drew his pistol. Understand me, I do not accuse him of perjury. But Estell is the only one who speaks to that point. Others were nearer than he was, and on the *qui vive*, and had their attention directed as much as his. They did not hear those words. I think he has slept and dreamt on it, and drawn on his imagination for his facts. He ought to have treated his memory with more consideration.

Gov. Foote said he should not attempt to defend San Francisco from the attacks of this young man (Coffroth). He is able, and will doubtless attain to eminence in his profession. But a man so young as he had no right to charge that the people of San Francisco labor under depraved tastes in any particular. Until he can give satisfactory evidence that his own tastes are refined in every particular, he ought not to set himself up as a judge in Israel! Mr. Coffroth speaks of his acquaintance with McGowan. He (Gov. Foote) did not know the prisoner at the bar, and God forbid that he should do him injustice. He knew nothing concerning his family in Philadelphia, and whether he was always a kind, affectionate husband and father, or whether he was neglectful, dissolute, and vicious. These facts not being in the record either way, the jury could pay no attention to them.

Gov. Foote then commenced to run rapidly over the evidence. This distinguished Pennsylvania legislator, it appears, early on the fatal morning, got a big navy revolver and a certain yellow-mounted derringer loaded. Not satisfied with such an armory, he gets also a knife. The wolf was early in his walk. What was the emergency that required this arming and extra-arming? Then, when he read the article in the paper, he made a threat, that "Casey would attend to that." And now Captain Dodge attempts to testify where McGowan was that day. Captain Dodge is a very fine young man, but *he drinks hard*. If there is anything that enfeebles the memory and confuses the faculties, it is strong drink. And he was as full as a tick that day, and, by his own testimony, drank four times in half an hour. Now he tries to remember where he was, and the time. Such testimony is not worthy of attention. My calculation of the time required to go where he said he went would just bring McGowan back onto Montgomery Street in time to be at the scene of the murder when it occurred. Mr. Botts may make his calculations, and you, gentlemen of the jury, must make your own. Then there is the boy Butts, who, in my opinion, has been lied on a great deal. Mr. Coffroth does not call his testimony in question. He told the truth. Just before the murder, McGowan and Whiteman were on the spot, at the Bank Exchange, and McGowan sent Whiteman out to see what Casey wanted. They were on the lookout! The defendant's counsel have called in question the truth of the testimony of our venerable witness, Curtis; yet never have I seen counsel so exercised and taken down as when he was delivering it. Why, Mr. Botts could not sit still in his seat, and was unable even civilly to receive suggestions from his associate counsel, such was his rage and anger as the evidence bore against them. Mr. Curtis was not examined by the Vigilance Committee concerning Casey's guilt. They did not need him. He was not an eye-witness of the transaction. Had they taken his testimony, they would have come to the same conclusion as every sensible man, that the boy who came to Whiteman in Dan's Saloon was not Butts, and that the two incidents spoken of by Butts and Curtis were separate and distinct.

Now, about the pistols. If not McGowan's,—particularly the gold hilted one,—whose do you suppose they were? Why did they not produce them here? Casey was led away—in triumph, armed *cap-à-pie*—by Whiteman, the friend of McGowan, and who had been his companion through all the day; and he received the pistol of Casey. Why was he not brought here, with the pistol, as a witness for his friend? He could have set the matter beyond all doubt, and cleared away all suspicions, perhaps.

Gov. Foote afterwards gave from the legal authorities the definition of an accessary. He is one who stands by,—which is, in sight, or near enough to conveniently render help if necessary to accomplish the crime. An accessary may also hire or employ others to commit the crime for him. If the jury believe that McGowan employed Whiteman to help Casey, they must bring in a verdict of guilty. He also, in a hurried manner, read from Russell on Crimes, concerning conspirators, and the part a person must take in the commission of an act to render him one.

As to the treatment of wounds, it is held that if a mortal disease grows out of a wound given by another, and the wounded man dies of the disease, nevertheless the wound itself must be regarded as the *causa causata,*—the true cause of the death,—for without it the man would never have had the disease. Speaking of the testimony of the physicians, Gov. Foote said Dr. Toland was evidently a man of greater acquirements and experience than Dr. Cole, and was not to be put down by him, even if their opinions did conflict. The five other physicians would weigh Dr. Cole's evidence down any hour. Concerning the testimony of Stillman, that Mr. King had a pistol on him, counsel said that, notwithstanding all Gen. Estell's testimony, that of the other witnesses made it clear that Mr. King only raised his hand after he was shot, to press it upon the wound. He was armed in accordance with that provision of the constitution which permits every citizen to bear arms in his own defense,—*in his own defense,*— NOT AS A MURDERER. When the defendant's counsel resorted to arguments with so little foundation as those they argued upon this point, it shows they are hard run for facts.

We do not, as the defendant's counsel said, intend to insist that McGowan fled from this indictment. He did undoubtedly fly through terror of the Vigilance Committee, for our courts he had defied before. But they tell us he has been persecuted. Persecuted! persecuted!! And by whom? Has any man before been indicted for murder and escaped even a governor's proclamation? Or had a special legislative act passed for his benefit? McGowan was in Sacramento,—in the same city with the Governor. Was he in jail? No;

he associated with *other gentlemen* on the public streets. And here, too, he was only committed to jail after the opening of the Court. It is unfair and ungenerous for the defense to make use of such word or argument in this case.

In a few words more, Gov. Foote then hastily closed his argument, and submitted the case. This was at half-past eleven o'clock.

Charge of Judge McKinstry.

Judge McKinstry, on the bench, then made a lengthy charge to the jury, which, owing to the short time allowed, was not put in writing. It occupied twenty minutes in its delivery. Judge McKinstry said he was glad the case had been so ably presented to the jury, as it rendered unnecessary many explanations of the law which otherwise it would have been his duty to make. It had been told to them that there was a period in the history of the state when the laws were subverted, and a certain organization usurped the power of the courts. With such matters of history they have nothing to do, and no examinations to make into them. Here no power but that of the laws operates; no other organization has a representation, and no notions of justice must be entertained, except that administered by established authority.

Every citizen has rights, which are not to be affected by popular clamor, or the demands, for or against him, of an ill-regulated press. The crime of which the prisoner stands charged is that of murder, and, by our statutes, all distinctions between the mode of proceeding against principals and accessaries are abolished. Hence, if you are satisfied that James King met his death under such circumstances as constituted the crime of murder, and that the defendant assisted in or counseled the act, then you are bound to find him guilty. If, however, you find that the crime committed was that of manslaughter, that crime implies no malice, but a sudden killing in the heat of passion, and there can be no accessary; therefore you would have to acquit the defendant. From the testimony offered by the two physicians, you have to determine whether Mr. King died from the effect of the wound itself or it was the result of malpractice. If from the wound, then the death was the result of the act itself; but if the result of the mode of treatment pursued by the physicians, then you have no further examination to make, and must acquit the defendant. If a person receive a wound, not in itself mortal, which superinduces a disease afterwards, causing death, this is murder; but if the treatment produce a new disease, which proves fatal, then the party inflicting the wound is not guilty of murder. I understood Doctor Toland to say that the wound caused lesion of the vein, and injury of the nerves in its vicinity, and, as another consequence, inflammation of the lining of the chest, which, with an inflammation of the vein itself, caused death. Doctor Cole says the wound itself was not mortal, but that death was caused by ill-treatment, and he proceeded to speak of the irritation caused by the use of the sponge and tourniquet, which, in his opinion, caused the fatal disease of phlebitis, or inflammation of the vein.

The question thus stands, and is one of fact for you to determine.

Pay, therefore, due attention to the statements of the physicians, and draw your own conclusions. If you believe Mr. King's death resulted from the shot itself, then the question is, What was the crime? If only manslaughter, then there can be no accessary, and no conviction of the defendant under this indictment. A newspaper article, however violent, unaccompanied by a personal assault, is not a sufficient provocation to reduce a killing from murder to manslaughter. If you are satisfied of the first point and not of the second, it will then be your duty to convict of murder in the second degree, if the defendant was present; but if not present, then he cannot be guilty. Murder in the second degree implies malice; express malice is to be evidenced by the case, as poisoning or lying in wait,—a deliberate intention must necessarily be proven. The presence of a party does not establish the fact that he aids or abets a crime. To convict, you must be convinced that there was some prior agreement or concert of action between them, or that he was at some convenient distance, ready to assist. If you believe the defendant did advise, counsel, and abet, at any previous time, this crime, you must convict, if you deem it murder in the first degree. You are to determine the credibility of witnesses by all the circumstances connected with their evidence, by the corroboration of other witnesses, or any other circumstances brought to light.

If you are satisfied a witness has made an intentional misstatement, you must reject all his testimony; but if mistaken on a single point, this need not invalidate his other testimony. If you find two witnesses conflicting, it is your duty to ascertain, if possible, which is correct, and if you cannot do this, to discard the evidence of both. If, after a fair examination of all the facts and testimony, you still have a reasonable doubt as to the guilt of the prisoner, you must acquit. The mere knowledge, on the part of a person, that a crime is to be committed, and his not making it known, does not constitute an offense. Neither does mere permission to commit a crime constitute an offense. If the jury are of the opinion that Casey committed a murder, and are not satisfied that the defendant aided and abetted the crime, they must acquit him. With these remarks, gentlemen of the jury, I leave the case in your hands.

VERDICT OF THE JURY—DISCHARGE OF MCGOWAN.

At ten minutes to 12 o'clock, the jury retired, under the charge of an officer, to make up their verdict. After an absence of about ten minutes, the jury returned. The foreman rendered the verdict of "Not Guilty," and each of the jurors separately agreed to it.

Mr. Coffroth asked if the prisoner was discharged. The Judge said, "No, not yet," as the verdict was not yet entered upon the minutes. The clerk made the entry, and read it aloud. Mr. Coffroth then formally moved for his discharge, which was done, and his friends surrounded him with the warmest congratulations.

THE ACQUITTAL.—The acquittal of McGowan, in the recent trial at Napa, can hardly have taken any one by surprise, who was at all conversant with the circumstances under which the indictment was found. In ordinary times, probably no such indictment would have been found by the Grand Jury. A charge of the character alleged in the indictment is difficult to sustain generally, and in this case became doubly difficult. Indeed, the prosecution did not and could not sustain the charge with proof which would justify a jury in finding a verdict of guilty. The trial, however, presents some very singular features, which we may examine hereafter at more length. The counsel for the defense managed so adroitly as to have every man who had ever expressed an opinion favoring the movement of the Vigilance Committee, excluded from the jury. Legally, the Vigilance question had nothing to do with the trial of McGowan, and we do not see how such a question could have been properly propounded to a man who had been summoned to serve as a juror. After having excluded from the jury all those who ever favored the Vigilance move, McGowan's counsel managed to try, to a limited extent, the Vigilance Committee with McGowan.—*Sacramento Union of June 2d.—Vigilance Press.*

ED. MCGOWAN'S TRIAL.—This famous trial closed at 12 o'clock on Monday night last. The prosecution made out no case against the defendant. Indeed, there was not evidence enough against him to hang a cat—and so thought the jury, for in just ten minutes from the time of their leaving the courtroom, they returned a verdict of Not Guilty. There was nothing whatever even tending to show any complicity in the death of Mr. King, or any connection, direct or indirect, with Casey in the transaction. And yet, had this man, now triumphantly acquitted after an impartial trial, fallen into the hands of the Vigilance Committee, he would have been hung, to a dead certainty. This case should teach the people of California the gross injustice, tyranny, and cruelty of which masses of men may become guilty when acting under excitement. A citizen, whom the laws of his country now declare innocent, has been hunted for months like a wild beast, driven from one hiding-place to another,—an exile even in his own country, with a reward on his head,—and exposed to all the perils and sufferings of a life of outlawry. The law gives him no redress. It merely declares that there is no stain of blood upon his hands. We are not the indorsers of Mr. McGowan, nor do we know whether he is a good or a bad man; but this we do know: that if extreme and long-continued suffering under a false accusation can entitle a man to popular sympathy, Ned should receive it. Communities should acknowledge and atone for their errors, no less than individuals.—*Napa Reporter.*

With feelings not easy to describe, I left the courtroom surrounded by swarms of congratulating friends.

Notwithstanding the ceaseless efforts of one Charles Hartsen (who disgraces the county bench of Napa County) to hunt up perjured testimony against me; notwithstanding the manifest perjury of the witness Curtis, who so miserably entangled himself in the mazes of falsehood,—I was declared acquitted and free! As for Judge Hartsen, and many others not now mentioned in connection with the bold attempt to rob me of my life by false swearing, I shall hereafter have more to say. As to the poor wretch Curtis, the mere report of whose testimony in the case must so surely consign him to infamy in the estimation of all just men who read it, I have nothing to say. If he can endure the consciousness of having attempted to rob a fellow-creature of his life, and at the same time damned his own soul, *for hire*, I can forget the temporary annoyance which his unspeakable villainy occasioned me.

In closing this history of my trial, I will call the reader's attention to the significant fact, that not one of the witnesses who testified at Napa as to my connection with the shooting of Mr. King, ever testified, either before the Grand Jury or Mr. J. Horace Kent, the coroner of San Francisco. The inquest-papers were furnished by Mr. Kent himself to my counsel, Mr. Coffroth, and a friend procured the record of the Grand Jury. Thus it will be seen that the evidence which was strong enough to procure my indictment was not considered by the prosecution sufficiently strong safely to go to trial upon; and, even after their utmost efforts to strengthen their case in every possible manner, the fact that I was triumphantly acquitted is a sufficient commentary on the unjust and cruel fanaticism which alone demanded and obtained my indictment.

CONCLUSION

"I said I was not what I seemed;
And now thou seest my words were true:
I have a tale thou hast not dreamed.
If sooth — its truth must others rue."
Bride of Abydos.

As I have now reached the end of my narrative, before bidding farewell to the reader I will dispose of some of the leading characters who figured in my adventures in the lower country. The woman whose house sheltered me while I was wrapped in the carpet at Santa Bárbara, I have never since seen. I learned, however, before I left that county, that her husband was in the state prison, where he had been sentenced for loaning his gun to another person, who killed a man with it. The poor fellow, who was thus implicated in the crime, was ignorant of the intention of the borrower. In gratitude for the good offices of his wife, when I was so sorely in need of a friend, I interested myself with some of my influential friends, at the capital and elsewhere, to have the case fully represented to the Governor, and not long since had the pleasure to see the executive clemency interposed, and the man restored to the arms of his good wife.

As to Jack Power, to whose courage and fidelity I unquestionably owe my life, words can never express the gratitude I feel for him. If, in the course of this story, I have alluded to transgressions with which he was *charged*, I have not done so from any belief of his guilt, but simply to show how unlikely it is that one who had acted so generously and honorably to a persecuted stranger should be guilty of such offenses as some of his enemies have hinted against him.

Pedro, who tried to sell me to my enemies when I was placing confidence in his promises of friendship, I forgive. I never desire, however, to see him, for I would fain spare him the mortification of looking upon my face. As to his brave and faithful wife, the *señora*, I live in the hope that some day it may be in my power to evince my gratitude to her and her children, and apologize for the hasty departure I took from her hospitable protection.

Good Doctor Den, and his family, I hope soon to take again by the hands and renew my thousand thanks for their generous friendship in my hour of peril.

And now, in bidding the reader farewell, let me say to him, that, if he has done me the honor to follow me through the preceding pages, I thank him for the compliment, and assure him that I attribute his patience more to the interest with which my story has invested a *principle*, than to any intrinsic merit which the book itself may possess. If, perchance, he has *honestly* differed with me in his opinions as to the "Vigilance Committee," so long as he has acted conscientiously, and been more the instrument than the director in the unhappy proceedings of that organization, I have in my heart no room for malice against him, but I sincerely hope that, in the future, the lesson of the last year will be to him something of a guide, should his strength of mind again be similarly tested. For him my story is told. But there are others, for whom I have not yet laid down my pen. A task less pleasing than that which I have just accomplished is now before me. If the simplicity and truthfulness with which I have sought to characterize this little story of my wrongs is any guaranty that what may come from me hereafter will be reliable, I have the satisfaction of knowing that I have perhaps prepared the public mind, calmly and dispassionately, to reason with me when I shall attempt the task of removing the specious tissue which veils the hideousness of *treason*, and temporarily prevents the putrescence of *hypocrisy* from offending the senses.

Unpleasant as is this task, I shall not shrink from it. In accordance with the views which first prompted me to intrude myself upon the notice of the public at all, I shall, in discharge of a duty which I still think may result usefully to my fellow-citizens, make it my special business to show the *honest* men, who have thoughtlessly embarked on the tide of conspiracy, how miserably they have taken the chances of moral and social wreck at the hands of the pilots to whom they have intrusted themselves.

With regard to the success of this volume, I can only await anxiously the verdict of the public. With all its imperfections,—its inaccuracies of expression, its manifold marks of haste, and sometimes, I fear, of carelessness,—it must go forth to the world, to sink or swim, upon its own merits. If the press of California but give this little waif upon the stream of literature a fair consideration, I am not without hope that, after every just censure shall have been passed upon its demerits, enough of approbation may be expressed to comfort its author with the reflection that his labor has not been all in vain.

There is, however, *one* press in this state, and *only* one, whose commendations would strike painfully upon my ear. Were any emanation from my pen to receive the encomiums of the San Francisco *Evening Bulletin*, I should feel that I had indeed most signally failed in the honest object of this book, and that it was justly a target for the most envenomed shafts of criticism.

The plaudits of one who has made personal infamy a stepping-stone to rebellion, who has thrown around craven cowardice a halo of glory, who has gilded slander with the sunbeams of justice, and invested hypocrisy with the attributes of religion, are not coveted by me. Let him rather open to their widest extent the sluice-gates of his filth, and vomit forth his disgusting spleen, lest with the retention of it he should not only damn this book, but, bursting himself, engender a moral pestilence in the land.

To the rest of the press of California I commend my book, trusting and believing that, if it is thought worthy of notice at all, it will receive *fair* consideration, and to the reader, who has honored me thus far, I repeat my thanks, and bid him an affectionate farewell.

FINIS

CPSIA information can be obtained
at www.ICGtesting.com
Printed in the USA
FSOW03n0725171116
27500FS